South Africa's
FLYING CHEETAHS IN KOREA

South Africa's
FLYING CHEETAHS IN KOREA

Dermot Moore
& Peter Bagshawe

ASHANTI PUBLISHING
(PTY) LIMITED
JOHANNESBURG

Published by Ashanti Publishing (Pty) Ltd
A Division of Ashanti International Films
P.O. Box 10021
Rivonia 2128

ISBN   1 874800 15 4 Standard Edition
       1 874800 24 3 Collector's Edition
       1 874800 25 1 Limited de Luxe Edition

© Dermot Moore
© Peter Bagshawe
© Richard Wood
First published 1991

Book Design: Dieter Mandlmeier
Typeset by Pointset, Randburg
Printed by CTP Book Printers, Cape Town

BK2376

*This book is dedicated to the 34 pilots
and two ground crew of 2 Squadron SAAF
who sacrificed their lives during
the Korean War, 1950 - 1953.*

Contents

Introduction

Air Vice-Marshal J E (Johnnie) Johnson CB, CBE, DSO**, DFC*

I like the story of the Flying Cheetah Squadron's arrival in Japan under Commandant SV Theron DSO, DFC, AFC, a very experienced leader who fought in the Desert and Italy and who had with him several hand-picked pilots with combat experience, many of them already decorated for gallantry. But on arrival in Japan the Americans treated them like novices until SV strapped a Mustang on his back and gave them an aerobatic show the likes of which the Americans had never seen before.

A few days later the Cheetahs were operating in Korea. At the time I was a few miles to the north at Taegu, a USAF reconnaissance fighter-bomber base. There being negligable air opposition, practically all our missions like those of the Cheetah Squadron were attacking enemy ground targets with guns, rockets, bombs and napalm. But there was a big difference between American and South African fighter-bombers. At Taegu we flew F-80Cs (Shooting Stars) whereas the South Africans operated in piston-engine Mustangs.

We preferred the jets for they did not have the Mustang's vunerable glycol cooling system and having few moving parts they could withstand more flak damage. Without a propeller they gave us a better view downwards and forwards and the cockpit of a Shooting Star was far quieter than that of the Mustang.

Mustang losses to ground fire were therefore greater than those of Shooting Stars and the book reveals that many South African pilots were brought down by flak including my old friend Denis Earp who after 65 missions was forced to bale out, was captured and spent 23 harrowing months as a prisoner of war. His son Michael, a helicopter pilot, was killed in the Border War.

For me the most moving story is the rescue of Vernon Kruger who when thanking Jan Blaauw for saving his life received the nonchalant reply: 'Forget it, we pilots must stand together.' This typifies the general high endeavour, leadership, fierce comradeship and sacrifice shown by the Cheetah Squadron throughout the Korean War. The book paints a vivid picture of what Shakespeare called 'We band of brothers' - a closely-knit team of pilots fighting so courageously halfway across the world from their homeland; a record which will live on in aviation history.

J E Johnson
Hargate Hall, Derbyshire 1991

Prologue

Major-General Dick Clifton SM

The appearance of this book at this particular time could not have been more opportune. It is being published at a time when, at long last, South Africa appears to be emerging from years of censure by the United Nations and disapproval bordering on ostracism by our erstwhile allies in two world wars and the conflict in Korea.

There is now a need for South Africans to regain the international respect they once commanded and the almost forgotten esteem of their brothers-in-arms in those former wars. I venture to suggest that this true story of a famous squadron of the South African Air Force fighting - rather ironically - for the United Nations in the Korean War goes a long way towards fulfilling that need.

Great credit is due to those responsible for producing this book. First we must applaud Al Venter, who recognised the need to tell the world and remind South Africans that WE WERE THERE and have done it in a way that will fire the reader's imagination. Then one thinks of Dermot Moore whose careful and thorough research for his doctoral thesis on 'The Role of the SAAF in Korea' marshalled the facts in easily accessible form for Peter Bagshawe, himself a Mustang pilot in the Second World War with the RAF, to undertake the formidable task of breathing life into those historical facts and bringing to life once more this vital phase in the annals of the South African Air Force.

It is interesting to speculate on the motivation behind the decision to send 2 Squadron to fight in Korea. Why did a Nationalist Party Government, whose members had so violently opposed participation in 'somebody else's war', while their party was in opposition during the Second World War, respond with such alacrity to the UN call for help? It is true that the South African Armed Forces had steadily run down in the four-and-a-half years since that war and there was an urgent need for their revitalisation and modernisation. I believe that the outbreak of the Korean War brought home to the South African Government the seriousness of international tension at that time and the necessity for

South Africa to be prepared for any eventuality. Korea provided a good opportunity to take part in the confrontation between East and West at negligible risk and minimum expense.

For South Africa, still a member of the Commonwealth, there was much to be gained by participating. It was a chance to confirm our continued reliability as an ally. Close co-operation with the USA and UK would pave the way to further military co-operation and the acquisition of modern armaments. Above all, it would rejuvenate the SADF by providing a clear operational objective and up-to-date experience of war in the air (and also to a more limited extent on the ground, for some SA Army officers were to be attached to the Commonwealth Division).

For the SAAF as a whole, the Korean experience was invaluable. For the individual volunteers who had the opportunity to serve with the squadron, it was an unforgettable experience. Travel to the Far East broadened their minds. They learned how the USAF operates. They rediscovered their aptitude for improvisation and their capacity for supreme effort under difficult conditions. Their morale soared when they discovered that they were every bit as good as their allies and infinitely better than their enemies. Above all, their national pride swelled when they found that the Americans admired and respected them. Individually and collectively they gained invaluable experience on the ground that stood the SAAF in good stead for years to come.

As regards the contribution of the SAAF to the total UN effort, it would be realistic to admit that the outcome of the Korean War would no doubt have been the same if the SAAF had not been there. Our contribution was nonetheless significant in sorties flown, damage inflicted on the enemy and the price paid. Thirty-four of the 209 pilots who flew there were killed in action or went missing, presumed dead - a casualty rate of over 16 percent, which meant that out of every six pilots who went to Korea, only five returned. Four others were seriously wounded, and of the eight prisoners of war who returned after hostilities ceased, two died not long afterwards as a result of their wounds or the shocking treatment they had to endure as captives.

There were others more fortunate who were rescued after being shot down behind enemy lines or in the sea. Some managed to fly their crippled aircraft back to friendly territory where they could bale out or crash-land, in some cases safely at base or on other airstrips, despite serious battle damage, so that they and their repaired aircraft could fly again. You will read of their exploits and marvel at their bravery and flying skill. Altogether 74 Mustangs and five Sabres were written off either by enemy action or in accidents, usually due to the hazards of flying in foul weather or operating from crude landing strips. For a single squadron this was indeed a high price to pay in a rather phoney war in a theatre so remote from our own fair land. Those who flew were well aware of the odds against them. They knew that the enemy had little mercy for its adversaries. They accepted the risks cheerfully with the same dauntless spirit that the SAAF has always displayed in action. The accuracy of their bombing, rocketing and strafing and the determination with which they pressed home their attacks, won the admiration of their allies and could not fail to win the respect of the enemy.

A squadron's achievements in combat must obviously be measured by the damage inflicted on the enemy. However, apart from not being entirely reliable - for only the enemy ever knows the whole truth - statistics tell only half the story. They give little indication of the professionalism and courage of those responsible or the *esprit de corps* of the unit which, although intangible, is the true barometer of that unit's success in combat. The gallantry of the pilots of the Cheetah Squadron and the tireless energy of those who supported them on the ground were rewarded by many decorations for individual achievements. The squadron as a whole was honoured by the award of a Distinguished Unit Citation by the President of the United States of America which recognised the contribution of all ranks. Perhaps the greatest honour conferred upon the squadron was the decision of the USAF 18 Fighter-Bomber Wing always to play the introductory bars of our National Anthem at their Retreat Ceremonies and to pay the same honours to this anthem as to their own.

In less serious vein, 2 Squadron's proud share in the Korean War is neatly depicted in the last verse of 'The Blues of Chinhae' - Theme Song of 18 Fighter-Bomber Wing - to the tune of 'Blues in the Night':

Now this ends my story,
Of Fame and of Glory;
Together we've known hectic days;
We've had many good laughs,
The 18th and South Afs,
For whom we have nothing but praise.
Oh I'm going to the ZI,*
To tell one and all
Of the deeds large and small,
Of the Group from Chinhae.

R Clifton
Knysna 1991

---

* Zone of the interior (American jargon for home)

Preface

Lieutenant-General Denis Earp SSA, SD, SM

When I came back to the Union of South Africa in September 1953, some two years and four months after I had left it on posting to 2 Squadron in Korea, I was mightily confused when I learned that it was the general belief of the South African public that the war in Korea had been a 'police action' and that, since we had not won it, we must have lost it.

That supposition was far from the truth. The term 'police action' had evidently misled the public into thinking that it must have been of limited scale, low intensity and little importance.

In fact, the Korean war was a particularly savage conflict of great historical significance. That is only now being appreciated, but until recently it has been entirely correct and appropriate to regard it as a *forgotten war.*

It was the first serious challenge that the communists had thrown down to the Western world. It was the first and, until Iraq, the only time that an army fought under United Nations auspices for purely military objectives. It is still the only war since 1945 in which two great powers have encountered one another on the field of battle. With the exception, perhaps, of the Cuban missile crisis, the United States came nearer to using nuclear weapons in 1950-1951 than at any other time since 1945.

Again, the statistics are appalling. The casualty figures alone speak for themselves.

The United Nations lost more than 142 000 men in Korea. The United States alone had 54 000 men killed in three years of fighting in Korea, compared with about 58 000 in the eleven years of the Vietnam war. The number of South Korean forces who were killed in that war is estimated at over a million.

The whole development of the Korean war was filled with events of great political and military moment: the sudden invasion without warning by communist North Korea; the rearguard action by the South Koreans and the Americans; the desperate defence of the Pusan perimeter; the daring amphibious landings at Inch'on; the advance to the Yalu River; the shock of the Chinese entry into the war in vast numbers and their advance to Seoul and, ultimately, the stabilization of the front line along the 38th parallel.

For the next two years there was hard and bitter fighting on that front. The very rugged terrain and the extremes of climate made the fighting all the more dangerous and unpleasant.

Then there was the enemy. The West learned with dismay the nature of their communist enemy, who captured civilians, including women and children, and put them to death as a matter of cold policy. The Geneva Convention on prisoners of war did not apply to prisoners of the communists, and such hostages were classed as war criminals if they refused to collaborate.

Captured pilots could be *brain-washed* to 'confess' publicly that they had 'used the germs of disease as weapons of war.'

After the Korean war it was learned with horror that forty-two per cent of prisoners taken by the Chinese and North Koreans had failed to survive. Torture, starvation and disease had taken their toll.

By comparison, the figure for non-Russian deaths among prisoners in Nazi Germany during the Hitler war was two per cent!

As for the question of not winning the war, the fact is that we stopped the North Korean attempt to take over, by force of arms, the Republic of Korea. Who can doubt that a relative degree of freedom is better than the absolute brutal tyranny of totalitarianism? South Korea, though authoritarian, is now one of the most dynamic industrial countries in the world. North Korea, its neighbour, is one of the most wretched, cruel and oppressive of all Stalinist societies. It is also one of the poorest.

So much for the 'police action' that we lost!

Through it all, the South Africans, all volunteers, fought with great courage and distinction, winning many decorations and awards, including Presidential Citations from both Korea and the United States. But they paid a high price. It cost the lives of thirty-six men and three squadrons' worth of aircraft.

Of all the many tributes paid to the South Africans in the Korean War, the one I like best is in the book *Truck-Busters* published by 18 Fighter-Bomber Wing, to which 2 Squadron SAAF was attached. It reads:

'Aye Ziga Zoomba' may be just a song, but it will live forever in the hearts of the 18th as one of the many contributions from the hardy air warriors from the Union of South Africa.

D J Earp
Pretoria 1991

Sources of Information

Chapters 1 to 17 of this work are based upon the academic thesis entitled 'The Role of the South African Air Force in the Korean War', which was submitted by Dermot Moore to the History Department of the University of South Africa for his Doctorate of Literature and Philosophy. Copies of the unabridged thesis may be consulted in the UNISA Library or at the SAAF Museum. They contain complete footnotes and a source list.

Various primary and secondary sources were used in the compilation of the original thesis. The general background material was gained from various published works and articles, of which the most significant were R E Appleman's *United States Army in the Korean War; South to the Naktong; North to the Yalu* (Washington, 1961); J F Schnabel's *United States Army in the Korean War: Policy and Direction - The First Year* (Washington, 1972), and R F Futrell et al: *The United States Air Force in Korea, 1950-1953* (New York, 1961).

The main repository of primary material used in this project is the Military Information Bureau of the SADF. Here the Korean documents are to be found in five main collections, as yet largely unsorted. They give the channels of command and administration from DHG in Pretoria to 2 Squadron in Korea, via the Office of the Senior Liaison Officer in Tokyo.

The original documents written in Korea provided the most important information. The two collections that were originally accumulated in squadron headquarters (War Diaries and Missions, and 2 Squadron Korea) were used far more extensively than those of the Senior Air Liaison Officer, the Director-General of the Air Force and the Adjutant-General. The first two collections, and to a lesser extent the other three, contain a mass of material consisting of letters, reports, operations orders, frag orders, the war diaries, mission debriefs, mission returns, aircraft accident investigations, signals and numerous other documents of an operational and administrative nature produced during nearly three years of operations.

Authors of works of contemporary history enjoy the bonus of being able to interview people who lived through the events in question. Those Korean veterans who contributed to the original study were selected mainly on the basis of their availability at the time and their access to significant information during the campaign.

Interviews were preceded by a study of the documentary evidence. Although the veterans were free to mention anything they considered important, particular questions were asked to clarify or amplify the written sources. A tape recorder was used to ensure that the oral evidence was processed with due regard to accuracy and detail. Because of the ever-changing set of circumstances under which the squadron operated in Korea, every member of each group of replacements had a unique experience of the campaign. Their accounts, often supported by entries in flying logbooks, were different, but complementary rather than contradictory. Chapter 18 concentrates on the personal reminiscences of Korean veterans and consists almost entirely of material generously provided by members of this select group of South African airmen.

Acknowledgements

The popularisation of academic history is always a problem to historians. The Flying Cheetahs in Korea is an attempt to deal with this problem in a positive manner.

The experience of working with a journalist is one that gives a historian new insights into his own craft. I am indebted to the publishers and my fellow author, Peter Bagshawe, for this opportunity to be a member of a team that has compiled a work that we hope will be of enduring value to all those who are interested in South African military history. Peter's professionalism has been an example and an inspiration to me. I should also like to acknowledge the contribution of the promoter of the original thesis, the late Professor Maurice Boucher of UNISA.

By blending the professional skills of journalist and historian we have attempted to produce a book accurate in both its broad analysis and in detail, while at the same time being readable. If we have suceeded it is largely due to the help and advice of a number of veterans of the Korean War to whom we owe much gratitude.

Dermot Moore
Johannesburg 1991

I acknowledge the magnificent task carried out by my fellow author, Dr Dermot Moore, in writing his thesis 'The Role of the South African Air Force in the Korean War 1950-1953'. It was completed in June 1982 after four and a half years of exceptionally hard work that earned him his Doctorate of Literature and Philosophy at the University of South Africa. One has only to examine the thesis to discover the extent of Dermot's research and the thorough way in which every aspect has been tackled, including interviews with those who served in Korea.

My part as co-author has been to convert the thesis into a more personal story without losing authority and authenticity. Battle situations have been summarised, a measure of statistical information has been eliminated and ranks replaced by first names wherever possible, but the data derived from 2 Squadron's War Diary has been fully utilised.

We thank that legendary personality and top scoring World War II fighter ace, Johnnie Johnson, for his introduction. Johnnie served in Korea with the USAF, and he is well known and respected throughout South Africa.

We are also grateful to Dick Clifton, who was asked to write the prologue, not only for his able pen, but because he was one of the well-proved commanding officers of 2 Squadron during the Korean War. It was during his term as Commanding Officer that the squadron was awarded the Distinguished Unit Citation by the President of the USA. Dick was awarded the American DFC and the Korean Order of Military Merit Chungmu with Gold Star during his tour of operations.

Denis Earp's preface has added some historical facts to the book that are greatly appreciated. Not only did Denis distinguish himself on operations in Korea with 2 squadron but, after being shot down, he set a courageous example to fellow prisoners of war. From 1984 to 1988 he reached the pinnacle of his career as Chief of the South African Air Force.

Finally our sincere thanks to all contributors to *The Cheetah Squadron Remembers*. Their memories are a fitting finale to this book about a South African squadron equal to the best.

Peter Bagshawe
Durban 1991

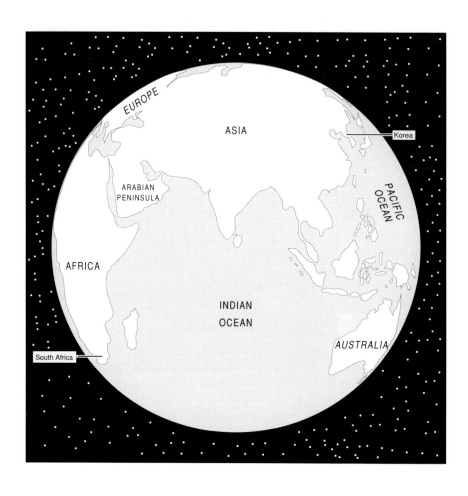

The First Volunteers

'Four silver streaks dived from the skies with guns blazing. It was a wondrous sight, and momentarily we forgot where we were and stood up in our foxholes, cheering as four Mustangs barely cleared the treetops while putting the enemy to rout.'

These lines were included in a letter to the Flying Cheetahs from an American infantryman on 23 June 1951 in appreciation of what he described as the most spectacular feat he had ever witnessed. His unit had launched an attack against the enemy and had reached the ridge-line of its objective when there was an overwhelming counter-attack that showed no sign of abating until the timely arrival of the Mustangs.

Every member of the United States 1st Marine division who witnessed what appeared to be a miracle agreed that the Hall of Fame had no greater men than those South African pilots who flew for the United Nations on that occasion.

This was one of the numerous missions on which 2 Squadron SAAF was to operate during three years in Korea while fighting against a fanatical communist enemy. The South African Government announced on 4 August 1950 that a fighter squadron had been offered to the United Nations, and after a lapse of three weeks the Chief of the General Staff confirmed that the offer had been accepted and 2 Squadron had been chosen for this formidable task. Just over 200 officers and men were needed to supplement the existing nucleus of the squadron, and when volunteers were called for, 332 officers and 1094 other ranks made themselves available. The 'Flying Cheetahs', as 2 Squadron came to be called as a result of its mascots, two cheetah cubs reared during the Abyssinian Campaign, had developed from 1 Squadron SAAF during September 1940 and already had a distinguished record in combat. By the end of the Second World War the squadron had shot down 102 enemy aircraft over East Africa, the Middle East and Italy.

On 27 August 1950, the names of the officers and other ranks chosen for service in Korea were announced. Key posts were allotted to 18 officers plus an additional 32 pilots and 157 other ranks. The key appointments were:

Commanding Officer:	Commandant S van Breda Theron DSO,DFC,AFC
Deputy Commanding Officer:	Major J P D Blaauw DFC
Flight Commanders:	Captain J F D Davis DFC and one bar
	Captain G B Lipawsky DFC and one bar
	Captain H O M Odendaal DFC and one bar
	Captain W J J Badenhorst AFC
Adjutant:	Captain P A le Grange
Paymaster:	Captain L von Caues
Equipment Officer:	Captain M Strydom
Engineering Officers:	Captain S N Brace MBE
	Lieutenant V T Kilburn MBE
Medical Officers:	Major H C Enslin
	Lieutenant M J Mentz
Operations Officer:	Captain M J Uys AFC
Intelligence Officer:	Lieutenant S J W Inglesby
Signals Officer:	Captain W D S Marais
Technical Weapons Officer:	Lieutenant M Brady
Chaplain:	Captain M E V Cloete MC

The officers were experienced in their own special fields and the combat leaders were pilots who had distinguished themselves during the Second World War. The contingent consisted of two components, SAAF Liaison HQ and 2 Squadron. The main tasks of the former included liaison with the United Nations forces and providing an administrative link between General HQ Pretoria and the SAAF contingent.

The Liaison HQ was to wield administrative control over 2 Squadron, but flying operations would be controlled by the USAF fighter-bomber wing with which the Cheetahs flew. Bearing in mind that the squadron would be working in close co-operation with the USAF, the American standard fighter unit's complement of aircraft and pilots was adopted. Flights were therefore increased to four, each consisting of a flight commander and eight pilots which together with the commanding officer and his deputy, totalled 38 pilots. Ground staff comprised the 12 officers and 157 other ranks already mentioned.

Commandant J D Pretorius and Major D Swanepoel of Air Liaison HQ left for Japan by flying-boat on 10 September to set up the necessary administration. As soon as the preliminaries had been completed, all personnel earmarked for Korea, with the exception of the squadron CO and a skeleton HQ staff, were sent on six days' embarkation leave.

The Korean contingent boarded the Royal Interocean Lines vessel *Tjisadane* on 26 September, and they were delighted to discover that their voyage was not to follow the familiar troopship pattern and that they would be treated as civilian passengers. In the afternoon the

Tjisadane steamed out of Durban harbour, a nostalgic moment for well-wishers who had witnessed the same scene during the Second World War, when so many South Africans had embarked, never to return.

Taking a last look at Durban

On 29 September, in one of the news bulletins that the ship's radio officer had arranged to broadcast daily, it was learnt that General MacArthur, the Commander of the United Nations forces, and Dr Syngman Rhee, the President of South Korea, had held a celebration to mark the liberation of the South Korean capital, Seoul. This created the impression that the war would be over before the Cheetahs arrived in Korea, when no doubt they would be recalled to South Africa. However, that did not happen and the *Tjisadane* continued at what seemed like a turtle's pace. The monotony of the long sea voyage was relieved by various means such as physical training lectures on topics relevant to the operations that lay ahead, and lighter diversions. On Sundays the chaplain conducted well-attended services in the officers' lounge, and on 5 October the war was forgotten for a while as everyone enjoyed the traditional 'Crossing the Line' ceremony.

The most welcome diversions of the long voyage were provided by the Royal Air Force after the *Tjisadane* anchored in Singapore harbour and later during a stop in Hong Kong. Our men found the hospitality of the RAF overwhelming. They were told that it was a small attempt to return the legendary hospitality that British soldiers, sailors and airmen had received in South Africa during the Second World War. In Singapore and Hong Kong, the news in the local press once again raised the possibility that the war might end before the squadron commenced operations. The expectation of such an anti-climax was well-founded, for on 24 October the American Eighth Army had set up its Advanced Headquarters at P'yongyang in the same building that until recently had housed the HQ of the North Korean Prime Minister and Commander-in-Chief of the North Korean forces, Kim Il Sung. At the same time the United Nations was preparing detailed plans for the occupation and military government of North Korea.

During the last stage of the voyage, the skipper of the *Tjisadane,* Captain Walter, gave a farewell dinner to his passengers and commended the good behaviour of 2 Squadron. When arriving in Kobe harbour, Japan, on 1 November, the men of the squadron were happy to know that after 35 days at sea it now appeared that the possibility of being recalled had diminished because Red Chinese 'volunteers' had been identified on the war front. A short leg to Yokkoidu harbour followed, and then final disembarkation at Yokahama on 4 November, when all ranks were paraded for inspection and welcoming addresses by General Sir Horace Robertson, Commander-in-Chief of the British Commonwealth forces, and General O S Pitcher of the USAF. One surprise was the arrival of an all-black brass band laid on by the Americans as a special gesture towards a South African contingent that they supposed would be black!

At Johnson Air Base the first working day revealed that although aircraft and equipment were ready for handing over by the USAF, there were various problems that led to the delay of the flying training programme until 8 November, testing the patience of our pilots who were already bored to death by the long sea voyage. The difficulties were inherent in a situation in which an entire fighter squadron was to be

Disembarking at the end of a long voyage

equipped with everything from aircraft to winter flying kit when so far away from the main source of supply. Two different accounting procedures had to be reconciled, tool kits made up, worn-out personal issues exchanged, and the USAF Mustangs to be taken over by the squadron, had to be brought up to standard after deterioration in storage.

In such circumstances it was inevitable that relations between the SAAF and the USAF should get off to an uncertain start, but differences were soon ironed out and smooth working relations established. Although flying training was delayed, ground training began immediately. This was thorough and included all the essentials our pilots should know about American airfield regulations, operational tactics, radio procedures, ditching and survival, escape and evasion and so on.

Within four days most problems had been sufficiently solved to enable seven pilots led by John Davis to become airborne in Mustangs bearing SAAF markings and the distinctive Flying Cheetah emblem, both to be so proudly carried for nearly three years. When flying training began our pilots were perturbed to find themselves treated as novices by the Americans, although they soon demonstrated their skill by achieving results on the weapons range that astonished their instructors who did not appear to be aware of their pupils' abilities. After a while it was decided that American instructors should be informed that most of the South African pilots had flown Mustangs in combat, that they were picked men, and that many of them had been decorated for gallantry or services as flying instructors during the Second World War.

The Commanding Officer, S van Breda Theron (SV to his friends), who was the most highly decorated fighter pilot in the SAAF, decided

Cmdt. S van Breda Theron DSO, DFC, AFC, the first 2 Squadron OC in Korea

that action speaks louder than words. He climbed into the cockpit of a Mustang and after acquiring flying clearance he carried out a series of skilled flying and aerobatic manoeuvres the like of which the Americans had never seen before. On landing he found himself the centre of an admiring circle, and a senior officer shook him by the hand: 'Commandant, we can't teach you anything about flying.' 'That's right,' said SV; 'and every pilot in my squadron is as good as I am, so give us the aircraft and we'll get on with the war.'

The day after the first training flights at Johnson Base an urgent signal was received calling for 2 Squadron to become operational with the least possible delay even if it meant sending only one flight. SV replied by assuring the Americans that nine experienced pilots would be ready for combat duties within a week, and at the same time he stressed the desirability of SAAF groundcrews accompanying the aircraft to service them. On 15 November, 13 officers, 21 other ranks and the necessary equipment were flown in two Dakotas from Johnson Air Base to Pusan East airfield (K-9) in Korea.

SV had decided that he and his flight commanders would be the first pilots of 2 Squadron to fly on operations. He wanted them to be in a position to lead future missions with confidence, and therefore they had to gain experience in good time. He and the four flight commanders, John Davis, Tank Odendaal, Lippy Lipawsky and Badie Badenhorst, took off in their Mustangs late in the day and arrived at K-9 airfield about the same time as the Dakotas.

And so, 104 days after the South African government had announced its decision to contribute a fighter squadron to the United Nations war effort, the Flying Cheetahs arrived in the combat zone.

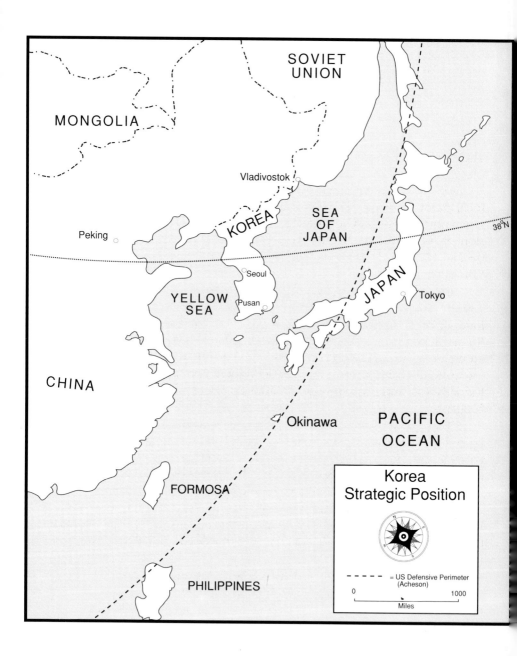

SOVIET
UNION

MONGOLIA

Vladivostok

Peking

KOREA

SEA
OF
JAPAN

38°N

Seoul

YELLOW
SEA

Pusan

JAPAN

Tokyo

CHINA

Okinawa

PACIFIC
OCEAN

FORMOSA

Korea
Strategic Position

PHILIPPINES

- - - - = US Defensive Perimeter
(Acheson)

0   1000

Miles

8

2

Seeds of War

The Korean Peninsula lies in the middle of a triangle between Russia, China and Japan, which explains why this rugged, mountainous country, 925km in length and averaging 240km in breadth, has been a focal point of rivalry between these three Eastern powers, especially Japan and China. They regarded Korea as a stepping stone to the invasion of their countries. In the second half of the 19th century Russia became the third dimension to the traditional rivalry between the Chinese and the Japanese over the peninsula.

After a war fought between China and Japan on Korean soil from 1894 to 1895, the influence of China was neutralised when the total independence of Korea was recognised. Ten years later, after defeating Russia, Japan proclaimed Korea a protectorate and placed its government under the supervision of a Resident-General. In 1907, the King was forced to abdicate in favour of his delinquent son, and in 1910, Japan formally annexed Korea thus terminating its brief independence and the 500-year-old Yi dynasty.

From that year onward until 1945, Koreans were totally subjugated by the Japanese who forced them to contribute towards Japan's agricultural and industrial requirements. By the mid-thirties, 8 per cent of the total Japanese food consumption came from Korea, and although industrial output increased almost 15-fold between 1932 and 1945, the main function of Korea was to supply light, secondary industries for Japan. Roads and railways were built to suit Japanese needs and military ambitions, and by 1940, 6 600km of railway and 5 300km of roads had been built.

Cheap labour was exploited and all key posts in the service administrations and business were monopolised, the Japanese denying all opportunity and benefits to Koreans. The plan was ultimately to integrate Korea as a province of Japan with its people loyal subjects of the Emperor. As a result of draconian suppression of nationalism, a number of loyal Koreans presented a Proclamation of Independence to the Japanese Governor-General, and at once the door to any future internal expression of nationalism was firmly closed. Schools were forbidden to teach the Korean language, all Koreans were ordered to adopt Japanese names, and even the Japanese Shinto religion was forced upon them.

Such tyrannical measures stirred Korean exiles to make known the plight of their country to the world, and a number of leaders gained a sympathetic hearing including Dr Syngman Rhee in Hawaii, Kim Il Sung in Manchuria and Kim Koo in Chungking. At the Cairo Conference in 1943, Allied leaders agreed that after a period of Trusteeship Korea would become a free independent nation. In May 1945 Russia announced its concurrence with this decision, and on 8 August declared war on Japan. Two days later the atomic bombs were dropped on Hiroshima and Nagasaki, and Japan was forced to sue for peace on 10 August. Consequently the agreement reached at the Cairo Conference became a non-starter.

President Truman was aware that although the Russian dictator, Joseph Stalin, had agreed to a Trusteeship before Korean independence, it would not prevent Russia from occupying as much of Korea as possible before the formal signing of the surrender; in fact Russian troops had already crossed the northern border into Korea two days after the Japanese had sued for peace. There was a shortage of American troops in the Far East at the time, so this move could not be countered by an immediate American landing in South Korea. Accordingly, President Truman proposed that for the sole purpose of facilitating the surrender, Korea should be split into two parts with the 38th parallel as the dividing line; a proposal to which Stalin did not object.

The formal surrender of Japan took place on 2 September, and General MacArthur, the Supreme Commander of the Allied Forces in the Far East, ordered that all Japanese forces north of the 38th parallel should surrender to the Russians and those south of it to the Americans. It was not until 8 September that the newly appointed American Commander, General Hodges, landed at Inch'on and accepted the surrender of the Japanese Governor-General at Seoul next day.

The 38th parallel was soon to become the Korean Iron Curtain and certainly not the line of convenience created for purposes of the surrender. It became a rigid boundary with no topographic or economic basis, cutting through provinces and towns; a wall between the mainly agricultural south and the industrial north, and ultimately a *casus belli*.

Although Korea had been divided politically for many years, unity of north and south was necessary to create a prosperous economy. The most influential figure in the south was Dr Syngman Rhee and in the north Kim Il Sung. Attempts to bring about the unification of Korea made no headway. In May 1947, the Americans proposed free elections throughout the country, but that was vetoed by the Russians, who then countered with a proposal that an Assembly comprising equal representation of north and south should be formed. This time it was the Americans who vetoed the proposal, and no compromise could be found.

Koreans had been yearning for national unity and independence after years of suffering under Japanese despotism. Many thought that their dream would become a reality when the Japanese were defeated; but the occupation of their country by two trustees frustrated their aspirations. The South needed the industrial production of the North and the North needed the agricultural production of the South, and partition made no sense to either side. Chong-Kyong-Mo put the people's feelings in a nutshell:

> Koreans shared with other people in Asia and in Europe who had been released from Japanese and German control a joyous anticipation of a new age, a new destiny, for we were suddenly free from hated alien rule ... to be released from these hardships, to see Koreans walk proud and tall again, to have the jail doors swung open and our patriots come out in the sun, to speak our own language, to plan and hope for a new Korea. These were the ecstatic aspirations of our freedom on 15 August 1945 - but Korea was not freed from foreign control and liberation was an illusion sanctified with a myth.

On 14 December 1947, the United Nations appointed a commission to consult the representatives of the Korean people for the purpose of finding a means of achieving independence for the entire country. The commission failed; the North Koreans would not even allow it to cross the 38th parallel. On 10 May 1948, elections were held in the south under United Nations supervision, and on 12 June the newly-elected National Assembly informed the North Koreans that 100 seats had been reserved for them. The gesture was ignored, and on 15 August the Republic of Korea was formally declared with Dr Syngman Rhee as President. The North Korean reply came on 9 September, when the Korean People's Democratic Republic was proclaimed with Kim Il Sung as Premier.

The United Nations then had no alternative but to declare that the government of the South Korean Republic was the only government based on the free will of the electorate. However, when the Republic applied for membership of the United Nations in 1948 the Russians vetoed the proposal, and so with two régimes based on totally different ideologies facing each other across the 38th parallel, war seemed inevitable; and to make the situation worse, Mao-Tse-Tung had taken over in China and did not relish a hostile régime on his borders.

A resolution ensued at the UN General Assembly calling for the

Kim Il Sung - Premier of the Korean People's Democratic Republic

total withdrawal of the occupying forces from Korea within 90 days of the establishment of a National Government. The Russians declared that all their troops would be out of North Korea by the end of the year. The Americans were delighted, and they let it be known that their troops could be better used elsewhere; but they did not withdraw entirely until 29 June 1949.

When the Russians withdrew from Korea they left behind 3 000 instructors and supervisors to train the North Korean army, whereas the Americans left only a token indigenous force of 482 poorly-equipped men to train an army that they considered necessary only for internal security. Furthermore, the American Secretary of State had made it clear that Korea lay outside the American defence perimeter in the Far East so supporting forces were unnecessary in that region.

The Russians were no doubt well aware that there was little chance of acquiring South Korea peacefully and they decided to take it by force by means of their Communist puppet in the north. Nor is there any doubt that when Mao-Tse-Tung spent ten weeks in Moscow between January and March 1950, he helped Stalin plan the invasion of South Korea. They had probably come to the conclusion that the plum was ripe for the picking, with the country in a state of political and financial turmoil; with a weak, ill-trained army and little support from an America tired of war and desirous only of peace and stability.

Before the invasion the communists launched an intensive propaganda campaign over P'yongyang Radio, and frequent incursions were made across the 38th parallel. By May the situation was tense. Between 15 and 24 June 1950, the North Koreans had moved all their army divisions to the vicinity of the 38th parallel and deployed them ready for an attack on South Korea. By this time the Korean People's army had grown into a formidable force of 135 000 men, and by 24 June 90 000 troops had been placed undetected behind the 38th parallel. There were seven infantry divisions, a tank brigade, an independent infantry regiment, a Border Constabulary Brigade and a motor-cycle regiment; without any doubt a well-trained and well-equipped army.

At 04h00 on Sunday 25 June 1950, just five years after the end of the Second World War, those 90 000 men poured across the 38th parallel confident in their military superiority and egged on by their Russian and Chinese backers, they swept all opposition before them making one mistake in their calculations. They did not believe that America would intervene, and they did not appreciate the significance of the fact that the Republic of Korea had been created under the auspices of the United Nations which would lose face if action was not taken to repel such blatant aggression. If it had not been for these obstacles, the North Koreans would have won an early victory and a different chapter in history may have been written. The United Nations responded without delay by calling upon the North Koreans to cease hostilities and withdraw behind the 38th parallel. The response of the North Koreans was to send fighter aircraft to strafe the Kimpo and Seoul airfields. On 26 June, 682 American women and children were transported from Seoul to Inch'on harbour, where they were evacuated in the Reinholt, a Norwegian cargo ship, escorted by fighters of the Fifth Air Force. On 27 June 748 people were evacuated by air, covered by USAF fighter aircraft, and during the day seven enemy aircraft were shot down by American F-80s.

The situation deteriorated rapidly. Seoul fell to the North Koreans, and the South Koreans retreated in disorder over the Han River, demolishing the bridges behind them. By this time the Americans had been authorised by President Truman to help the hard-pressed South Koreans, and F-80s, B-26 light bombers and B-29 Superfortresses flew from Japan to attack the advancing communist forces between the Han River and the 38th parallel. These operations caused havoc on roads crammed with enemy soldiers and equipment, and not only was the pace of the advance hampered, but also repairs to the Han River bridges. No less important was the fact that time was created to allow the South Koreans to reorganise themselves and for the Americans to rally and deploy their own forces on Korean soil.

The American Supreme Commander was then authorised to use air

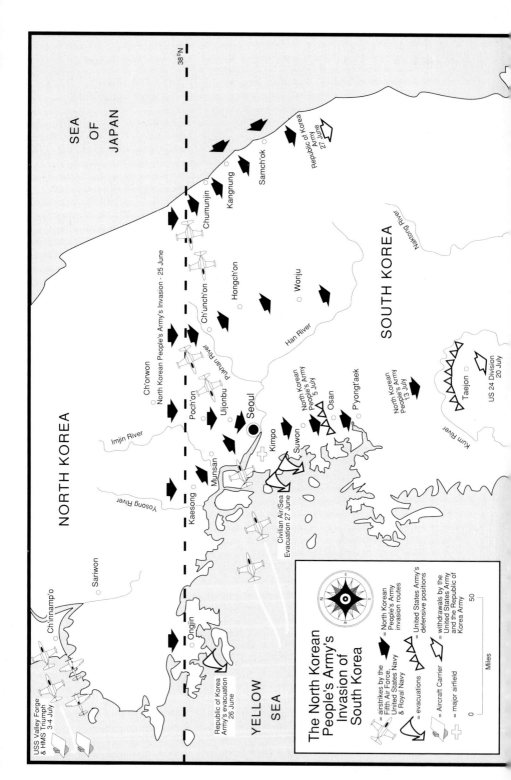

SEA
OF
JAPAN

38°N

NORTH KOREA

SOUTH KOREA

YELLOW
SEA

Chinnampo
Sariwon
Ongjin
Kaesong
Munsan
Ch'orwon
Poch'on
Uijonbu
Seoul
Kimpo
Suwon
Osan
Pyongt'aek
Ch'unch'on
Hongch'on
Wonju
Chumunjin
Kangnung
Samch'ok
Taejon

Yosong River
Imjin River
Pukhan River
Han River
Kum River
Naktong River

North Korean People's Army's Invasion - 25 June

Republic of Korea
Army 27 June

Republic of Korea
Army's evacuation
26 June

Civilian Air/Sea
Evacuation 27 June

North Korean
People's Army
5 July

North Korean
People's Army
13 July

US 24 Division
20 July

USS Valley Forge
& HMS Triumph
3-4 July

The North Korean
People's Army's
Invasion of
South Korea

= airstrikes by the
Fifth Air Force,
United States Navy
& Royal Navy

= evacuations

= Aircraft Carrier

= major airfield

= North Korean
People's Army
invasion routes

= United States Army's
defensive positions

= withdrawals by the
United States Army
and the Republic of
Korea Army

0   50

Miles

14

power north of the 38th parallel against targets within the borders of North Korea. On 3 July, American aircraft attacked North Korean airfields, and by the end of the month all enemy aircraft with the exception of 12 had been destroyed or put out of action.

The first American troops, after receiving authority on 30 June, landed on Korean soil on 1 July, and a period of intense fighting followed during the defence of the Pusan Peninsula. The war was now being fought under the banner of the United Nations, and it is necessary to explain how this organisation exercised its command. On 7 July 1950, a resolution was adopted in the UN General Assembly which established a Command under the President of the USA, who was authorised to make strategic decisions without reference to the UN. He was also authorised to appoint a commander-in-chief of the UN forces, and on 8 July, President Truman appointed General MacArthur, who was also the Commander of the United States Far Eastern Command. The units of all other nations volunteering to fight for the United Nations, including South Africa, thus fell under the operational control of the Commander-in-Chief of the United Nations Command and became part of the American military system.

The United States continued to pour troops and equipment into Korea. Dr Syngman Rhee's army was placed under General MacArthur's control, and by September not only did the UN forces outnumber the communists but they had a superior supply of equipment. It was air power, however, that won the day during a period of bitter fighting, and in fact it was air power that remained the key to success throughout the war. General MacArthur decided that the most effective way of ending the hard battle for the Pusan Peninsula was by launching an amphibious landing behind the communist lines at Inch'on on the west coast and cutting their communications and supplies. Despite opposition the landing was made, and it was a brilliant success turning the tables on the North Korean forces. Seoul was a difficult nut to crack, but after a week of fighting the UN recaptured the capital.

The American Eighth Army now broke out of the Pusan Perimeter, with intensive air support, and a planned northern route was followed. The communists were subjected to intense ground and air attacks, and after a week of such treatment they became demoralised and decided, on 22 September, to withdraw. As they retreated, UN aircraft kept up a relentless attack killing 7 500 troops, who were easy targets on the narrow twisting roads. With the enemy on the run, MacArthur's objective was the destruction of the North Korean forces followed by the unification of Korea. He was authorised to cross the 38th parallel, if necessary, but with victory in sight he was given various guide-lines to follow. Strategic targets in North Korea were not to be attacked, but only those tactical targets relevant to the operations of the day.

The United Nations made numerous plans to be followed as soon as peace was a reality, to bring about the unification and rehabilitation of Korea. A resolution in the General Assembly called for the establishment of a commission, similar to that introduced in 1948, which would carry on from where the original commission had left off. There was great pomp and ceremony in Seoul when a victory parade attended by Dr Syngman Rhee and General MacArthur celebrated the re- establishment of the Republic of Korea. Although victory appeared to be at hand, the North Koreans would not concede defeat or lay down their arms when called upon to do so by the United Nations; in fact they made it clear that their retreat had been planned and that they intended to advance south again in the near future.

Under these circumstances there was no alternative for the United Nations' forces but to move forward across the 38th parallel. The operations that followed were highly successful.

General Walker's Eighth Army, supported by the Fifth Air Force, advanced along the Kaesong-Sariwon axis with P'yongyang as its objective, while General Almond's X Corps embarked at Inch'on and Pusan with a view to making an amphibious landing at Wonsan on the east coast, supported by the American First Marine Air Wing. Then X Corps would join the Eighth Army and establish a general defensive line across the peninsula, and the North Korean forces would be encircled and destroyed.

The advance on both fronts moved faster than was expected. The Wonsan landing had been scheduled for 20 October, when 50 000 troops of X Corps arrived in an armada of 250 ships; but the South Korean forces had already reached the area and occupied it. A trouble-free landing was made on 26 October, with VII Division going ashore to the north at Iwon to alleviate congestion, and the advance continued. Meanwhile the Eighth Army had made good headway in the central area. P'yongyang was captured on 19 October and over the next two days, parachute troops and 4 000 tons of equipment and supplies were dropped north of the capital at Sukch'on and Sunch'on, which straddled the two main routes, in an attempt to cut off the fleeing North Korean forces, leaders and officials. The result was nearly 3 000 enemy troops killed, the same number captured and vast quantities of supplies taken, and as the Eighth Army advanced on a 50-mile front on 24 November, General Almond named 27 November as X Corp D-Day to deliver the *coup de grâce* to the North Korean forces.

United Nations intelligence had estimated that the enemy forces numbered between 123 734 and 170 935 communist troops of whom between 40 000 and 70 000 were Chinese, but General MacArthur was confident that China would not commit itself to a full-scale military invasion. He was sadly mistaken, for on 25 October, four Chinese armies

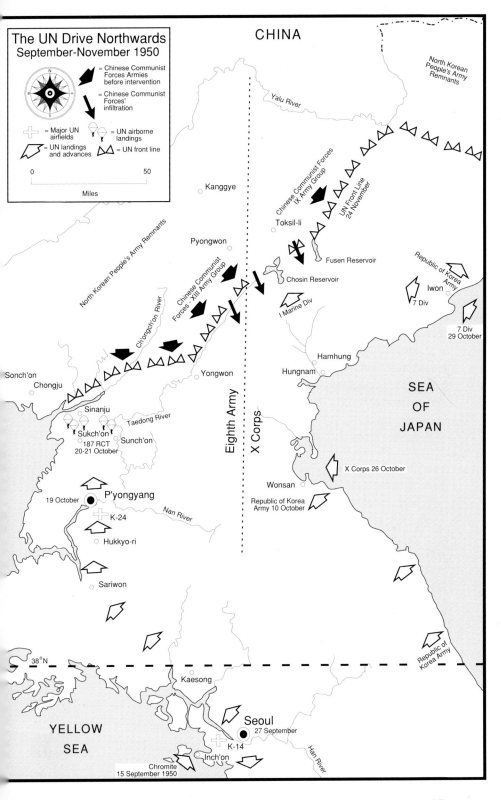

The UN Drive Northwards
September-November 1950

= Chinese Communist Forces Armies before intervention

= Chinese Communist Forces' infiltration

= Major UN airfields

= UN airborne landings

= UN landings and advances

= UN front line

0   50
Miles

CHINA

Yalu River

North Korean People's Army Remnants

Kanggye

North Korean People's Army Remnants

Chinese Communist Forces IX Army Group

Toksil-li

UN Front Line 24 November

Pyongwon

Fusen Reservoir

Chinese Communist Forces XIII Army Group

Chosin Reservoir

Republic of Korea Army

Iwon

Ch'ongch'on River

I Marine Div

7 Div

7 Div 29 October

Sonch'on

Chongju

Yongwon

Hamhung

Hungnam

SEA
OF
JAPAN

Sinanju

Taedong River

Sukch'on

Sunch'on

187 RCT
20-21 October

Eighth Army

X Corps

X Corps 26 October

Wonsan

19 October

P'yongyang

Nan River

Republic of Korea Army 10 October

K-24

Hukkyo-ri

Sariwon

38°N

YELLOW
SEA

Kaesong

Seoul
27 September

K-14

Inch'on

Chromite
15 September 1950

Han River

Republic of Korea Army

crossed the Manchurian border into Korea undetected in the densely wooded mountains. By the end of the month, two more armies had crossed over, and by the middle of November 300 000 Chinese troops were deployed at five points along the border ready to launch an offensive against the United Nations forces; and when they swarmed forward on the night of 24-25 November, not only were the United Nations forces in their path but also the newly operational detachment of the Flying Cheetahs.

The swift and unexpected Chinese invasion changed the course of the war entirely. On the night of 24 November, the UN forces were deployed along a front facing the Manchurian border between Hyesanjin to the east and the Ch'ongch'on River mouth to the west, and it seemed only a matter of days before victory would be theirs; yet the very next day they were in full retreat.

CHAPTER

3

Initiation

On arriving at K-9 airfield, Pusan East, on 16 November 1950, the Flying Cheetahs' advance detachment discovered that all units were in the process of moving to airfields nearer the front line. The detachment was to be based at K-24, P'yongyang East, recently captured from the communists. When the main body arrived from Japan, 2 Squadron would act as an additional unit directly under a provisional 6002 Wing USAF, commanded by Colonel C R Low, and controlling 18 Fighter-Bomber Group consisting of 12 and 67 squadrons. In the interim, the detachment of 2 Squadron would operate in this group along with the two USAF squadrons also based at K-24 making it possible for the Cheetah pilots to learn from their American comrades and familiarise themselves with the type of flying operations peculiar to Korea.

While the move was taking place, SV and his flight commanders benefited from some ground training with the emphasis on escape, invasion, rescue, and types and methods of attack.

At last the great day for the first operation arrived. While the ground staff prepared the Mustangs for action, representatives of the three squadrons attended an early-morning conference in the base commander's office where it was learnt that their squadrons were to be given priority during the move to K-24. The Cheetah Squadron's operational responsibilities were to consist of general reconnaissance, fighter escorts to bomber groups and close-support missions to ground troops. All aircraft taking off from K-9 on operational sorties were to land back at K-24. At the time, only four of the squadron's five Mustangs were serviceable, one of them needing an engine change. Tank Odendaal was ordered to ferry this aircraft over to K-24.

On 19 November, in clear weather and excellent visibility, SV Theron and Lippy Lipawsky took off at 07h00 on a close-support mission. Their Mustangs carried the standard armament for this type of operation which, besides six fixed machine guns, included two napalm bombs and six rockets. It was a mission in X Corps sector where the front line crossed the Ch'onch'on River, and with the assistance of an airborne Mosquito controller, good results were achieved including the

19

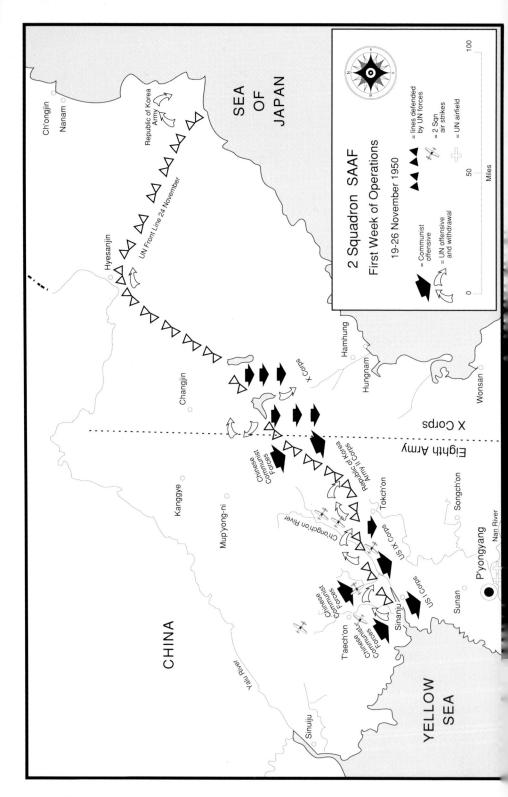

destruction of 13 camouflaged objects and five vehicles. Although this was the first official sortie in the Korean war, it was not the first over enemy territory by a SAAF pilot. On 8 October while on a familiarisation trip to Korea the senior Air Liaison officer, Jan Pretorius, had landed at K-9 and escorted a B-26 bomber to attack a target near the Manchurian border.

At 09h00 John Davis and Badie Badenhorst took off on the second mission, and in the afternoon they were directed against enemy positions facing the American 1 Corps near the town of T'each'on. One vehicle was destroyed and a number of camouflaged supply dumps set

A Mustang loaded and ready to go (note napalm tanks and rockets)

on fire. Tank Odendaal flew his first sortie the next day with Lippy Lipawsky, and they successfully attacked a train in a tunnel near Huich'on. Towards the end of November the Commanding General of the Far East Air Forces acknowledged the first ten Cheetah Squadron sorties with a letter to Commandant Theron congratulating him on the expeditious manner in which the squadron had become operational on 19 November.

A last minute change of weapons (note bombs on ground)

Although living conditions at P'yongyang East were not so pleasant as Pusan East, the distance to targets was greatly shortened and the duration of operational flights reduced. From K-9 a flight had taken as long as five hours, and the Cheetah pilots considered themselves lucky to have begun operations from the new airfield for this allowed them to spend more time over the target area. The duration of their first ten sorties was between one hour 40 minutes and three hours 40 minutes.

There were drawbacks at the P'yongyang airfields. They were too far from Operations Control at Seoul, radio communications were unreliable, and although the airfields were connected by land line, intelligence reports were sparse and often too late. Another problem was the reality of communist guerrillas operating behind the UN lines who inflicted casualties from time to time in and about P'yongyang, the result being that local labourers and inhabitants were denied access to the airfields.

A serious threat developed on 22 November, when 5 000 guerrillas were reported to be approaching P'yongyang from the north. SV was summoned by the base commander and informed of the situation. All officers and other ranks were alerted which seemed a futile exercise, for not one of the other ranks had been issued with rifles, in spite of frequent requests for them. Much to the relief of everybody, parachute troops were sent from P'yongyang and the guerrillas were chased into the hills after a brief skirmish.

The UN personnel at P'yongyang East were threatened from the air on this same eventful day. The air-raid alert was sounded, but no enemy aircraft were heard and no bombs were dropped, and the 'all clear' was sounded within an hour. For four days in a row two enemy aircraft approached K-24 and three 12 Squadron Mustangs were scrambled. No contact was made with the hostile aircraft which disappeared westwards. 8 Fighter-Bomber Wing at K-24 was less fortunate, especially at night. This was ascribed to the relative ease the hard-topped runway could be seen from the air unlike the dirt runway at K-24. The aircraft that made nightly attacks on K-23 were probably PO-2 biplanes used in a similar operation later in the war.

Although the forward airfields captured from the communists were well-established air bases, they had suffered at the hands of the UN bombing attacks and from their own demolition squads, with the result that the existing hangars and barracks had been badly damaged. The detachment personnel were obliged to pitch tents as living and office accommodation. Two tents were allocated for administrative purposes, one as an operations room and the other as a crew tent, while an old hangar of the North Korean Air Force served as a mess-hall for all ranks. It had been built of clay plastered over a wooden frame, and the wind blew incessantly through many gaping holes. The dirt floor was damp and cold. 'It was,' said one pilot, 'like a South African cowshed.' As the move to K-24 had been made during midwinter, while the monsoon was blowing in Siberia, the cold was extreme and the crude shelter was little

Snow hampered flying

help against the biting wind. Everything containing water, such as watercarts, jerry cans and bottles, froze solid, and food served hot became cold within a minute. It was like living in a blast freezer. The discomfort was slightly relieved when the domestic area was provided with tent stoves. No vehicles were available and all equipment had to be manhandled.

The weather, lack of equipment and the intensity of operations made severe demands on the ground crews. As the days were short, with first light at 06h45 and last light at 17h15, maximum use had to be made of the daylight hours for flying. That obliged the ground crews to get up at 05h00 to warm up the engines. The extreme cold made arming and refuelling the aircraft difficult, and the lack of transport and mechanical refuellers meant that the Americans had to be relied upon to a certain extent, and they too were battling with antiquated and frozen equipment. This situation was improved later when a weapons carrier was issued.

The sorties flown during the week of 21 to 26 November from K-24 were typical of the operations that were 2 Squadron's lot for the greater part of the Korean campaign, with interdiction and close-

Ground crew scrape snow off a Mustang's flying surfaces

support missions predominating. Combinations of either two SAAF and two USAF, or three SAAF and one USAF aircraft were flown, the Cheetah Squadron's Mustangs ranging over Western Korea in support of the Eighth Army while confined to a fairly narrow strip between the UN front line and the Manchurian border. The shortened communist lines of communication, at this time, hampered any opportunity for effective interdiction, but nevertheless the fighter-bombers were ordered to reduce the flow of enemy supplies and re-inforcements by carrying out armed reconnaissance missions throughout the area.

The seven sorties flown by the Cheetah pilots on 21 and 22 November enabled them to become familiar with the procedures of patrolling the communication routes to the north of the front line while looking for targets of opportunity and for information about enemy movements, dispositions and supply dumps; missions were relatively short, lasting from one-and-a-half to two hours each. On one of these missions, while attacking a North Korean village, John Davis and Badie Badenhorst were surprised to see palls of black and yellow smoke rising from some large buildings hit by napalm bombs and rockets. They were ostensibly used as warehouses. Even a school building exploded, revealing the true use to which it was put.

In co-ordination with the Eighth Army offensive of 24 November, the American Fifth Air Force fighter-bomber squadrons were switched to ground-support missions. During the early days of the offensive, three squadrons flew 345 close-support operations, the Flying Cheetahs contributing their fair share. When this news reached the main body of the squadron at Johnson Air Base, everyone became restless and vexed by the continued delays in departure. The pilots and ground crews at K-24 also resented this situation because it meant that more work fell on their shoulders.

The Eighth Army offensive began at 08h00 on 24 November. Half an hour later, Lippy Lipawsky and Dizzy Deans took off on the first close-support mission of the day. They were directed by a Mosquito controller on several attacks against a small hill held by the army. These attacks were well co-ordinated, and the results were good. Claims amounted to two mortar positions destroyed and about 50 enemy troops killed. In spite of the call for close-support, this was to be only one of two such missions flown by the squadron on that day.

In the afternoon John Davis and Elmer Wilson undertook another successful close-support mission resulting in claims for the destruction of one self-propelled gun, two vehicles and a supply dump. Another unusual mission was flown by Badie Badenhorst and Tinky Jones when they protected a USN minesweeper off the west coast near Ch'o-do Island. This op went off without mishap until Badie's Mustang developed engine trouble and the pair returned to base.

Soon after the Chinese had launched their huge offensive, six close-support sorties were flown by three aircraft in the morning and afternoon. The same routine was adopted next day, and during the afternoon Lippy Lipawsky, Tank Odendaal and Frank Richter attacked a village reported to be a troop concentration point. It was confirmed later that 300 enemy troops were killed in the attack.

Over these first ten days of operations, although there was little ground fire, flying was not without its risks. The single dirt runway at K-24 was either dusty or muddy, depending on the weather. Moreover, the already poor condition of the runway was not improved by the continual coming and going of heavy transport aircraft delivering supplies to the base.

Flying over Korean terrain was always dangerous, as SV Theron and John Davis had discovered during a close-support mission on 23

Frank Richter (left) and S. van Breda Theron

November. They had difficulty in making runs against communist troops dug-in on a hill where their approach was hampered by a power line running along the top of the ridge. At this point in the war, enemy aircraft were also a danger, and pilots were warned to keep on the alert against possible attack. Sightings of enemy aircraft were reported over a specially reserved radio channel listened to by a member of each flight.

Meanwhile the ebb and flow of the war during the last two weeks of November further delayed the main body of 2 Squadron at Johnson

Air Base. Before the Chinese offensive it seemed as though the stranded main party would reach Korea only after hostilities had ended, and they became increasingly frustrated as orders for the move were repeatedly issued and cancelled. On the morning of 19 November the long-awaited instruction was finally received; the flight to Korea was to be made at the first opportunity. Great activity ensued as preparations were hastily made, but on the same day the instruction was once more cancelled and 27 November given as the new date of departure.

SV Theron flew back to Japan to make the final arrangements at Johnson Air Base for the move, and in his absence John Davis was appointed acting CO. SV informed all ranks at Johnson Air Base about the situation in Korea and the operations that had been flown so far. Two more pilots, Pottie Potgieter and Jerks Maclean, flew their Mustangs to Korea to join the advance detachment, but the other members of the squadron were destined to be frustrated once again because of the sudden turn of events in Korea.

From 27 November until leaving K-24 on 2 December, the Cheetah Squadron pilots flew 43 sorties in close-support of the Eighth Army. Most of the targets were along the main communications route near Kunu-ri and Tokch'on. The flights comprised one USAF and three SAAF aircraft, and the armament for all missions consisted of two napalm bombs and six rockets. Aircraft remained on standby for immediate scramble. During operations they were directed by airborne Mosquito controllers who played a decisive part in the success of close-support operations during this period, and indeed throughout the war. The T-6 aircraft flown by the pilots were known in the SAAF as Harvard Trainers.

On several occasions, the Cheetahs were called on to rescue troops ambushed by Chinese who had infiltrated the retreating UN forces and thrown roadblocks across the escape routes. The narrow defiles were difficult for the UN troops to attack without help, and pilots had to use all their nerve and skill to root out an enemy entrenched in the rugged terrain. Mission 02-Charlie was a typical ambush-busting sortie, when four Mustangs (3 SAAF and 1 USAF) took off, led by John Davis, with Badie Badenhorst and Pottie Potgieter as the other two Cheetah pilots. Once airborne, John reported to Tactical Air Control, and was directed to a target just south of the important road and rail junction of Kunu-ri, where the Chinese, using two roadblocks, had ambushed south-moving UN troops.

The target was indicated as buildings held by the enemy parallel to the railway line and near to a road and rail bridge. Before the attack John's radio became unserviceable, so Badie took over the lead. Both bridges were effectively bombed and rocketed and the buildings were destroyed. At the time the ambushed troops and their vehicles were only a short distance from one of the bridges, but the attack was so well co-ordinated that they were unharmed. Many of the Chinese troops were killed, and the only flak encountered was from small-arms fire. On their return to base, Badie and John received a congratulatory message from the commander of the rescued troops.

The failure of the communist ground forces to conceal themselves during the first week of their advance gave the Cheetah pilots the opportunity to attack large numbers of exposed troops during a notable day when they flew on three successive missions along the southern bank of the Ch'ong-ch'on River. On all three occasions the Chinese troops were crammed together on the congested roads presenting easy targets and they were knocked down like skittles in a bowling alley. The returning pilots gave vivid accounts of soldiers falling as they were machine-gunned or as they fled the fearsome napalm blazes with their clothing on fire.

The last mission flown from K-24 next day was a sad but necessary operation to destroy 280 vehicles that had been abandoned by the Eighth Army retreating along the road between Kun-ri and Yongwon-ni.

By 28 November, gunfire and exploding bombs could be heard in

A napalm explosion

the north from K-24, and there was increasing evidence of the reversal of UN fortunes as armoured units passed by on their way southwards; weary troops telling tales of ambushes along the route when the magnificent support given by the Air Force attacking the roadblocks had allowed them to continue on their way. That night two North Korean guerrillas infiltrated K-23 and came near to killing the commander of the airfield. It was only the arrival of two American sentries who happened to turn up at the right moment that thwarted the attempt. Personnel at both airfields were ordered to be prepared for an immediate move south, and news that communist guerrillas were operating to the south of P'yongyang was disconcerting for it gave the impression that the UN airfields were surrounded.

On 1 December, 8 Fighter-Bomber Wing was bombed and strafed on K-23 by three communist fighters, and several aircraft were damaged. By this time 18 Fighter-Bomber Group had begun to withdraw from K-24 to K-13 at Suwon. All bulky equipment was flown out in C-17, C-54 and C-119 transport aircraft, while heavy equipment was carried by road and rail. Much of it was lost on the journey.

Fighter-bomber units were instructed to remain on K-24 until the last moment, so that operations could continue as long as possible from a base near to the advancing Chinese. Only the operations tent and two billets were left standing; the rest of the tents were pulled down and packed ready to move. Next day, when it was reported that the Chinese had reached the outskirts of P'yongyang, the evacuation of K-24 was completed, a C-119 flying out the 26 personnel of 2 Squadron plus their equipment. When they arrived at K-13, the tents were pitched on snow-covered ground, much of which had been churned into mud.

Like the other squadrons, the Cheetahs did not lose a single day of operations during the withdrawal. The pilots' aggressiveness was matched and supported by the ground crews who coped magnificently while contending with an acute shortage of equipment and extremely bad weather blown in by a north wind They worked day and night to keep the seven Mustangs ready for action, and the two armourers had the enormous task of handling and loading napalm bombs, rockets and machine-guns in the open without specialised equipment. Even after all the extra work and excitement of the move to K-13, the ground crews had no chance to rest; they had to keep the aircraft flying.

Since they lacked support until their comrades arrived from Johnson Air Base, it was decided that missions should be limited to one per aircraft per day. Wing operations, however, wanted a daily minimum of two, and that was accepted on condition that the missions were scheduled to allow ground crews time to service the Mustangs. Unfortunately, because of inadequate staff, spares and equipment, the desired sortie rate could not be achieved. In their efforts to maintain

Twenty-four-hour maintenance

maximum readiness, armourers often worked into the night to make any last-minute changes in armament and bomb load. American help also enabled the ground crews to keep the aircraft flying, and despite the difficulties, not only were 2 Squadron's aircraft kept going but they inflicted heavy losses on the communists.

After the Eighth Army broke contact with the enemy during the first week of December, fighter-bombers of the Fifth Air Force turned their attention from the enemy troops to their lengthening supply lines, so that interdiction missions against rolling stock, vehicle convoys and reinforcement troops on their way to the front line became frequent. The target areas covered by 2 Squadron from K-13 during December included two branches of the main supply route running northwards from P'yongyang to the Ch'ongch'on River, the western branch crossing the river at Sinanju and the eastern branch at Kunu-ri. Armed reconnaissance missions were also flown along the main supply route between Haeju and P'yongyang. Targets included the marshalling-yards at Kun-ri, P'yongyang and Sinanju, where harbour installations and shipping came under fire. Weather permitting, two missions of four aircraft each were flown, one in the early morning and the other in the afternoon.

It was during the course of a railway interdiction mission that the first aircraft of 2 Squadron was lost. The pilot, John Davis, was rescued from behind enemy lines by two remarkably brave American officers. It happened on 5 December 1950, when four pilots were ordered to destroy ten UN railway trucks that had fallen into the hands of the communists on the main line north of Sunan. The mission was led by Lippy Lipawsky, with Frank Richter at No 2, John Davis at No 3 and an American at No 4. En route for the target, the American pilot's aircraft developed engine trouble and he returned to base escorted by Frank Richter. John Davis moved into No 2 position.

When John and Lippy reached the target area, Lippy provided top cover while John descended to tree-top level to search for the railway trucks which he could not find in the reported position. Meanwhile Lippy had spotted some large supply dumps at a railway siding, so these

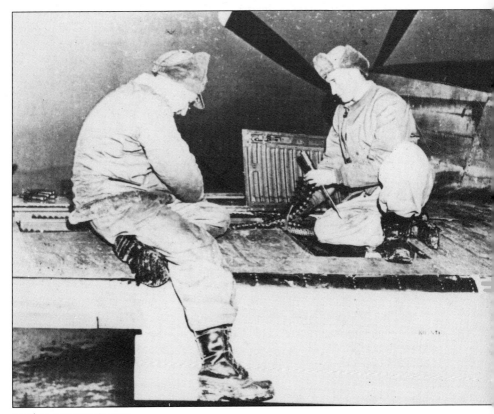

Loading a Mustang's guns

were attacked as an alternative. John made three strafing runs on the dumps at the southern end of the siding, but they failed to burn, and only when rockets were used did they burst into flames and billow white smoke. John's next two rocket attacks on a dump in the centre of the siding were wide, and when he attacked with his last rocket, the dump exploded with such force that Lippy, who was circling above, temporarily lost control of his aircraft. John, who had gone in very low to make sure that his last rocket hit the target, was knocked unconscious.

31

Lippy Lipawsky

By a remarkable chance his aircraft, which had been trimmed tail-heavy, cleared some hills in its path.

When he came to his senses John found that the elevator and aileron controls did not work, and he used his elevator trim to climb away. A survey of the damage revealed that both ailerons had been blown off and both main planes were full of holes, some as big as soup plates. There was a gaping hole in the floor of the cockpit and the engine was vibrating violently and streaming glycol.

John told Lippy that his aircraft had been hit, and a Mayday call was transmitted on the emergency channel that was picked up by the controller. The engine of the stricken Mustang overheated and cut within sight of friendly territory. The height was too low for John to bale out by stepping over the side, and he could not use the alternative method of rolling the aircraft over on to its back and catapulting himself out of the cockpit, for there were no ailerons. The only alternative was to make a forced landing on a straight stretch of road, but when the airspeed fell rapidly he was forced to crash-land in a freshly ploughed paddy field, the Mustang's wings knocking down two small trees just before touchdown. Although the aircraft was a total wreck, the radio still worked, and after John had been advised by Lippy that a helicopter was not available, he suggested that the road was suitable for a liaison type aircraft to land. He then climbed out of the cockpit and sat on the crumpled wing to await developments.

A few minutes later he saw a number of men carrying rifles whom he assumed to be North Koreans, but Lippy kept them off with a couple of strafing runs and when he and two USAF pilots, who had arrived in their F-80s to offer help, were obliged to fly back to base due to diminishing fuel, the men advanced to within spitting distance of the aircraft and sat in a semi-circle with their rifles across their knees.

For ten minutes they remained motionless and John became increasingly convinced that he was about to be shot. At last, an old man arose, saluted and raised the South Korean flag. They were members of the Democratic Youth Party and the UN police operating behind the communist lines. They offered to guide John to safety, but before any further deliberations could be held a T-6 aircraft flew over and the pilot dropped a note instructing John to burn his aircraft and walk in a southerly direction towards friendly territory. Although he carried out the first order, his two companions dissuaded him against obeying the second, warning that there were enemy troops in the hills nearby. Instead, they led him north towards their village. The T-6 pilot dropped another note advising that he was walking in the wrong direction, so he returned to the burning Mustang.

It seemed as though John's luck had run out, but rescue was not far away for Lippy waylaid an American liaison aircraft flown by Captain Jim Lawrence with Captain Lewis Millet as his observer and he led them to the crashed Mustang where Jim made a skilful landing on a straight, narrow road adjacent to it. Lewis climbed out of the cockpit and although he knew that the enemy was closing in, he insisted that John, who was in a state of shock, should take his seat.

Jim Lawrence flew John back to K-13 returning before dusk to find his observer under fire in an area infested by the enemy. He landed once more on the same stretch of road, picked up Lewis and took off again without damage to his aircraft. It is said that Lewis received the Congregational Medal of Honour for his brave action, but the truth is, and this comes from Lewis himself, that he and Jim were each given a bottle of whisky for their bravery. On another operation later in the war, Lewis did win the coveted medal.

4

United at Last

Three days after the Chinese offensive, General MacArthur summoned his generals and the decision was made to withdraw. This was the only realistic measure if the Chinese tidal wave was to be prevented from outflanking the Eighth Army and inflicting severe casualties. Unfortunately a line of defence to hold up the Chinese advance could not be found, for the high central Taebaek range of mountains was a barrier between X Corps and the Eighth Army across which communication was almost impossible.

General Almond was ordered to withdraw and evacuate X Corps via Hungnam to Pusan, an operation successfully completed by 24 December when the rearguard of the Corps withdrew under an umbrella of naval guns and carrier-based aircraft. Ninety-three ships evacuated 105 000 troops, 98 000 Korean civilians, 17 500 vehicles and 356 600 tons of cargo.

General Walker's Eighth Army withdrew to the south of P'yongyang on 5 December, and in contrast to the heavy fighting on the eastern flank, the communists did not follow, probably because their lines of communication would have been over extended and UN aircraft would have inflicted severe losses on their men and supplies. By mid-December, the Eighth Army had withdrawn to a line south of the Imjin River running through Yongp'yong, Hwach'on and Inje to Yangyang on the east coast.

On 23 December, General Walker was killed in a vehicle accident and General Ridgeway replaced him. Ridgeway took over at a time when the American troops had been in battle for a long period without a break and after a withdrawal in the face of numerically superior forces.

Their morale was at its lowest ebb and the will to fight was lacking. General Ridgeway set about rectifying the situation by personally visiting the units under his command, and after this demonstration of leadership he wrote a letter which was circularised to each man in the Eighth Army explaining why they were in Korea and what they were fighting for. In the latter half of December the rest of 2 Squadron arrived at Chinhae Air Base (K-10) on the south coast. Earlier, on 9 December a

General Ridgeway (left) and General van Fleet

small party had been sent to K-13 to reinforce the advance detachment.
This party included the Medical, Engineering and Armament Officers,
five pilots and their Mustangs and 18 other ranks. The pilots were
Ainsley Cooke, Steve Armstrong, Koos van Heerden, KB McDonald and
Tinky Jones who was returning from a brief visit to Japan. The new-
comers were warmly welcomed and put to work immediately. From
then on the squadron was to operate under 18 Fighter-Bomber Wing,
not 18 Fighter-Bomber Group. Up to this time the wing had consisted
of 12 and 67 squadrons USAF, but with the addition of the Cheetahs followed by 39 Squadron USAF soon afterwards, its strength was increased
to four squadrons. Eventually, after overcoming a number of transport
difficulties, all ground personnel arrived at K-10 at irregular intervals.
The airlift began on 17 December, and the remaining seven Mustangs
left Johnson Air Base in two flights, one led by Piet Swemmer and the
other by A B de Wet. Bad weather forced them to land at Itazuke, where
they spent the night and in the morning they flew on to K-10, where de
Wet crashed while landing because his boot jammed on the starboard
brake pedal causing the Mustang to tip over on its nose.

    The CO of 18 Fighter Bomber Wing, Colonel C R Low, presented

Commandant S V Theron with a formal letter confirming the appointment of 2 Squadron as a unit of his wing and setting out its responsibilities: the destruction of enemy airpower, the close-support of UN

South African and American flags fly side by side

ground forces, maximum-range reconnaissance and offensive strikes, interdiction of enemy ground lines and communications including attacks along the avenues of escape of enemy forces, escort or cover for UN air, sea and land forces, and the defence of military installations.

These were to be carried out subject to restrictions forbidding any target to be attacked beyond those explicit boundaries established by the current operations directives of 18 Fighter-Bomber Wing HQ. Attacks on hydro-electric plants or associated equipment in Korea, or surface vessels, or small craft in Korean coastal waters, were also forbidden except on the special authority of the Commanding General of the Fifth Air Force.

Another instruction followed specifying that K-13 was to be used as a staging-post for operations and that a small team would remain there for the purpose of re-fuelling and re-arming the aircraft of 2 Squadron. Furthermore, from 23 December a system was to be adopted whereby the three squadrons would provide flights on rotation. An example was given:

	12 USAF Squadron	67 USAF Squadron	2 SAAF Squadron
23 June	8 A/C	4 A/C	4 A/C
24 June	4 A/C	8 A/C	4 A/C
25 June	4 A/C	4 A/C	8 A/C

The squadron providing two flights was to remain at K-13 overnight.

Washday at K-10

Chinhae (K-10) Air Base

The newly-arrived personnel of 2 Squadron spent their first day at K-10 pitching tents for their own accommodation, administration and stores. Nissen huts were provided, but there was only enough room in them for 25 officers and 60 other ranks. Although ablution facilities were poor at first, they were soon improved with the luxury of hot showers.

Another early difficulty was that all meals had to be eaten standing up, for at that time no seating was provided in the communal mess-hall. Joe Joubert recorded that some careful planning was needed at meal-times to get greens for the pet black rabbit brought back from K-13 by Dizzy Deans. Wangling condensed milk for a 'cuppa', not normally provided between meals or after hours, was also a tricky business.

On Christmas Day 1950, there was a good dinner for everyone including the service detachment at K-13. Some of the fare resulted from the generosity of the Commercial Exchange of Southern Africa. All personnel were presented with gift parcels by their American Allies with whom Christmas was to herald increasing harmony.

In Chapter 2 the reasons for the war and the early battle situation are sketched because they were part of the scene into which 2 Squadron fitted as a component of the United Nations forces. Likewise the terrain and the weather were important factors in the war and readers should know not only about the vagaries of the weather but also about the often near impossible conditions that the Cheetah pilots flew in and the rugged ground they fought over. A brief description of how the pilots of the squadron were controlled on operations and what comprised close-support missions, will also demonstrate the variety of operations.

Weather and terrain have always influenced the success or failure of nations who have fought in Korea from time immemorial, and that was certainly true during the war from 1950 to 1953. The terrain comprises a multitude of treacherous mountain ranges throughout the length and breadth of the country, with heights from 200m in the south to 3 000m in the north; precipitous slopes, deep valleys and ravines overlooked by jagged peaks and sharp ridges; mountains often cutting across one another making identification difficult or impossible. In these

Living quarters showing oil drums coupled to the tent heaters

circumstances, the roads and railways follow the course of rivers and are punctuated with tunnels.

Peter Kotze, who flew with 2 Squadron, gives his impressions from an operational point of view:

'Air operations were both helped and hindered by this type of terrain. Movement by road was confined to narrow winding tracks in the mountainous areas, while in the low-lying areas vehicles moved along

Doempie Cloete hands out Christmas presents

The officers enjoy Christmas dinner

road beds built up above the rice paddies. Movement of large concentrations of troops and road traffic was therefore restricted, and it was almost impossible to avoid attack from the air when caught out in the open.

In the mountains, however, troops on foot could easily melt into the surrounding valleys and forests. The mountainous terrain presented other problems to airmen. From the air the numerous valleys and ridges looked alike making target identification extremely difficult. Over and above this, the narrow ravines did not allow a pilot much room to manoeuvre, and to pull away after an attack when trying to escape from the inevitable flak often aimed from slopes overlooking the valleys, was a hazardous undertaking.

A railway line target built up through rice paddy fields

As far as the weather was concerned, Korea is a country of extremes. It is affected by two monsoons annually, the winter monsoon blowing from Siberia between October and November and the summer monsoon from the tropical seas between June and July. The winter in the north is more severe than in the south, the average temperature in the mountains falling to a minimum of minus 17 degrees C when they became blanketed with snow.

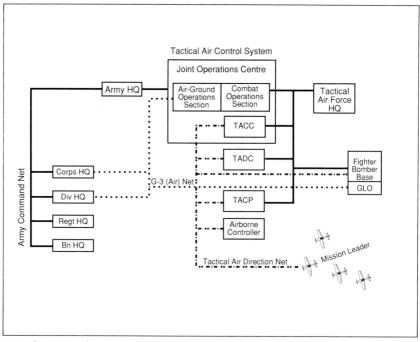

Tactical Air Control System

In summer the temperature can rise to 40 degrees C in both the north and south of the country. The summer monsoon is at its height in July bringing heavy rains, and from time to time a thick fog can result from the marriage of sea winds with humid inland air. Another hazard can prevail during September when typhoons sweep across the country from the south. Accurate forecasting was difficult under the general circumstances, which was another hazard that the Flying Cheetahs faced throughout the war.

An important necessity of modern war is an efficient tactical control system between the army and the air force. As soon as 2 Squadron began to operate in Korea it came under the American Tactical Air Control System consisting of a number of communication networks established by both the air force and the army.

The tasking and control procedures adopted were as follows: Every day at about 15h00 the operations officer of each tactical wing would get in touch with the Air Force HQ, when he would be told the type and numbers of sorties that his unit was expected to fly the following day. Soon afterwards a Fifth Air Force Frag Order was transmitted to the Wings by teletype giving details of the planned missions and the number of aircraft allocated to air alert and ground alert. About midnight confirmation was received when a courier delivered two copies of the Frag order to each base. If sudden changes in the ground situation warranted alterations to the Frag Order, the matter was handled by the Air Force duty officer in the Joint Operations Centre and by the Operations Officers of the various tactical wings.

The Frag Order specified take-off times and co-ordination of the air effort, requiring strict adherence at all times. Once airborne, the leader of the mission called the Tactical Air Control Centre giving the number and details of his mission. He was then instructed either to proceed as ordered or divert to a new mission. If he was on close-support the leader reported to a particular Mosquito airborne controller who marked the target area with smoke rockets as a reference point to guide the leader and his flight to the target. When the strike was over, the controller would give a summary of results, which were passed on to the Tactical Air Control Centre by the mission leader on his way back to base.

The two main types of operation in Korea were interdiction and close-support. The former needs little explanation, for these missions

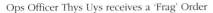

Ops Officer Thys Uys receives a 'Frag' Order

were mainly directed at enemy lines of communication and supplies and concentrations of troops.

There were four types of close-support missions:

Air Alert Strikes – Attacks made by aircraft already orbiting in the region of the ground forces they were supporting. Help was called for by the forward air controller at the request of the local ground commander. The lapse of time between request and strike was a matter of minutes.

Column Cover – Aircraft flew above rapidly advancing columns ready to give immediate close-support when needed.

Call Missions – Ground alerted flights were pre-briefed on the ground and aircraft were loaded with specialised weapons. The delay when such weapons were needed was two to four hours between request and strike.

Reconnaissance Missions – A visual or photographic reconnaissance flown to help the close-support effort by the accurate location of targets and the evaluation of strikes.

CHAPTER

5

Stemming the Chinese Hordes

From mid-December 1950 the UN Air Forces were given 11 interdiction areas along the main supply routes north of the 37th parallel, that Superfortresses bombed by night and fighter-bombers attacked by day. During the month, intelligence estimated that UN aircraft had been responsible for killing and wounding about 40 000 of the enemy.

From 23 December until the communist offensive at the New Year the aircraft of 2 Squadron were kept fully occupied in attacking a variety of targets including troops and stockpiles. With the entire squadron operational, the sortie rate rose to 16 a day, sometimes more, and on 27 and 29 December, 20 and 23 sorties were flown. Flights of four aircraft usually attacked concentrations of Chinese troops in occupied villages, while flights of two aircraft made armed reconnaissances along the main supply routes seeking targets of opportunity. Because of the staging from K-10 through K-13, these missions were of about two-and-a-half hours duration.

There was ample evidence of the effectiveness of the missions flown by the squadron. On Christmas day Tinky Jones led four aircraft on close-support against Chinese troops dug in along a ridge. The attack was so successful that, besides being congratulated by the forward controller, Tinky had the satisfaction of hearing him give the ground commander clearance for an attack. The squadron also ferretted out communist troops sheltering in the villages, occasionally seeing them flee with their clothes on fire from napalmed houses. On 28 December, during an attack led by SV Theron against three communist-occupied houses, Elmer Wilson claimed about 40 soldiers killed by a single rocket attack.

On 29 December the chief of the UN Air Forces, General Stratemeyer, and the chief of the Fifth Air Force, General Partridge, visited the squadron at K-10 to express their appreciation to the operations room staff for the way in which they were controlling 2 Squadron's operations. This visit was followed on 23 January 1951 by a visit from General Partridge, who presented SV Theron with a flag of the Union of South Africa.

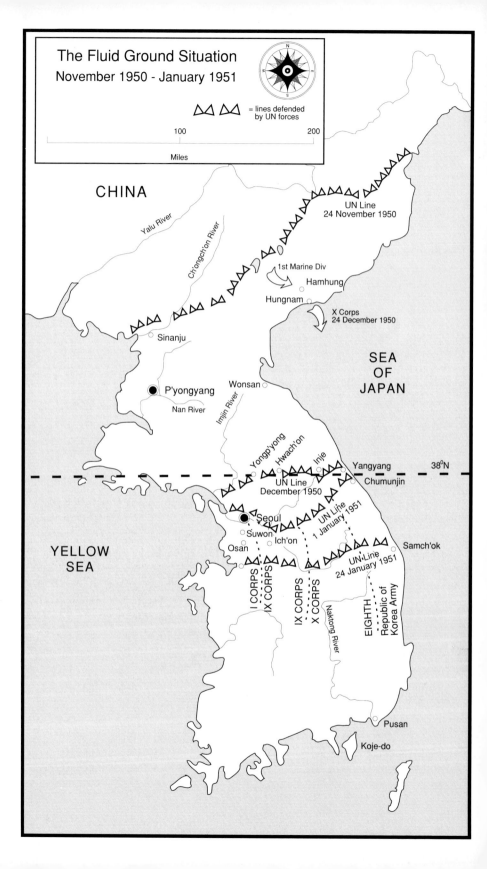

The Fluid Ground Situation
November 1950 - January 1951

△△ △△ = lines defended by UN forces

100   200
Miles

CHINA

Yalu River

Ch'ongch'on River

UN Line
24 November 1950

1st Marine Div

Hamhung

Hungnam

Sinanju

X Corps
24 December 1950

SEA
OF
JAPAN

P'yongyang

Wonsan

Nan River

Imjin River

Yongp'yong

Hwach'on

Inje

Yangyang

38°N

UN Line
December 1950

Chumunjin

UN Line
1 January 1951

Seoul

Suwon

Ich'on

Osan

Samch'ok

YELLOW
SEA

UN Line
24 January 1951

I CORPS

IX CORPS

IX CORPS

X CORPS

EIGHTH

Republic of
Korea Army

Naktong River

Pusan

Koje-do

Tinky Jones is decorated

At daybreak on 1 January 1951 the communists launched another big offensive, mainly along the west coast and the middle of the country, directed at Inch'on and Seoul. The United Nations forces withdrew on two occasions to different lines of defence, General Ridgeway's policy being not only to save UN lives but to extend the communist lines of communication so that the Air Force could inflict severe damage on both men and supplies.

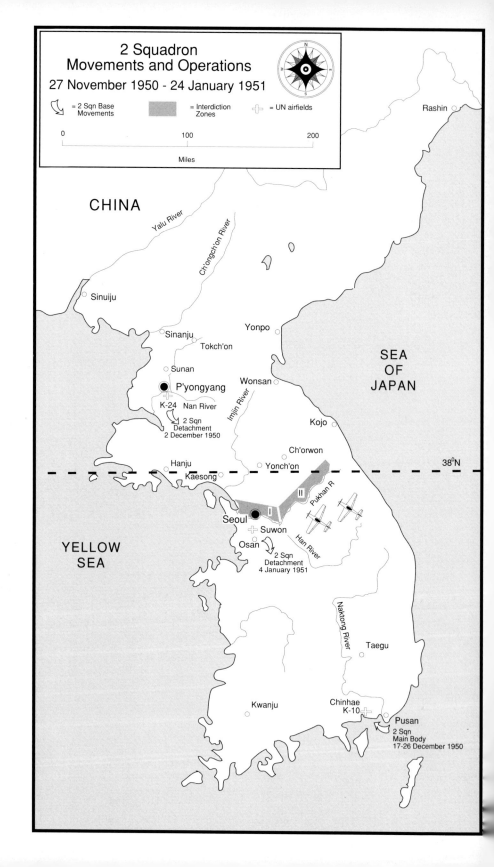

2 Squadron
Movements and Operations
27 November 1950 - 24 January 1951

= 2 Sqn Base Movements

= Interdiction Zones

= UN airfields

0   100   200

Miles

N
W   E
S

CHINA

Yalu River

Ch'ongch'on River

Sinuiju

Sinanju

Tokch'on

Yonpo

Sunan

P'yongyang

K-24   Nan River

2 Sqn
Detachment
2 December 1950

Wonsan

Imjin River

SEA
OF
JAPAN

Kojo

Ch'orwon

Hanju

Yonch'on

Kaesong

38°N

II   Pukhan R

Seoul   I

Suwon   Han River

Osan

2 Sqn
Detachment
4 January 1951

YELLOW
SEA

Naktong River

Taegu

Kwanju

Chinhae
K-10

Pusan

2 Sqn
Main Body
17-26 December 1950

Rashin

Snow between the flight lines

Snow on the flight lines

The New Year brought clear weather enabling UN aircraft to harass the advancing Communist forces continually as they moved southwards, and a maximum effort was made. From 1-5 January 1951 it was the overwhelming fighter-bomber support that time and again curbed the vast Communist armies threatening to win by sheer weight of numbers. The Eighth Army HQ estimated that the Air Force inflicted 38 000 casualties over 26 days during January 1951, and a Chinese Army Commander proclaimed that if it had not been for UN Air Power his forces, through the preponderance of their numbers, would have driven their adversaries into the sea. It had also to be borne in mind that the communist's main problem was acquiring supplies with minimum delay when their lines of communication were extended, and because of the topography all supply columns were easy targets for UN aircraft.

Before mid-January the enemy had run out of steam and their morale was low after suffering extremely heavy losses in their advance. The time was ripe for the UN forces to switch over to the offensive once more, and on 14 January an attack and withdrawal operation named *Wolfhound* was launched ascertaining that the bulk of Communist forces had withdrawn, so on 25 January X Corps was on the offensive once more in *Operation Thunderbolt*.

During this period General Stratemeyer warned all squadrons under his command that intelligence reports had indicated that the Chinese Air Force comprised 650 combat aircraft including 250 piston machines and MiG-15 jet fighters. These could threaten UN air superiority, although the Chinese pilots were young and inexperienced and no match for American and South African pilots, especially when flying Sabre jets.

A maximum air force effort was called for to oppose the communist offensive at the New Year, and the sortie rate of 2 Squadron rose to 24 a day. On 4 January the communist advance forced the evacuation of K-13 and all missions from then on were flown from K-10. On the same day Lippy Lipawsky returned from a mission and reported that the ground situation near the front line was confused and that it was difficult to identify close-support targets without the help of the UN Tactical Air Control teams, which were on the move and thus unable to co-operate.

Next day Piet Swemmer's Mustang developed engine trouble during a sortie and he was obliged to land at K-13. Fortunately for him the airfield was still in friendly hands, and when SV Theron and four ground crew arrived in a C-47 to repair the aircraft, enemy troops were only a short distance away. SV flew the Mustang back to K-10.

The high sortie rate during the first week of January taxed the ground crews to the limit. Various ailments resulting from working long hours out of doors in the extreme cold began to take their toll, particularly among the armourers, and as replacements for such casualties

Mission briefing - (L/R) Guy Paterson, Thys Uys, Porkey Kruger, Pottie Potgieter

John Davis briefs his pilots - (L/R) Derek Doveton, Pottie Potgieter, John Davis, Lippy Lipawsky

were not readily available a re-organisation of personnel was carried out to keep the aircraft operational.

Instead of the usual division into flights, the armourers were re-organised into crews, each under a senior NCO. Men whose task it was to load machine guns and who had to sit on cold mainplanes suffered from piles. This was remedied by giving each armourer a small canvas cushion!

After the abandonment of Seoul by the UN on 4 January and the subsequent breaking of contact with the communist ground forces, the emphasis was once more placed on interdiction missions. These usually took the form of armed reconnaissances by two or three aircraft. The Fifth Air Force divided the country west of the eastern mountain range into interdiction zones. River Area 1 comprised a strip to the north of the Han River from its mouth to its junction with the Pukham River. River Area 11 was a similar strip north-west of the Pukham River from its confluence with the Han River to the town of Hwach'on. Armed reconnaissance missions were sent to particular river areas where they were instructed to destroy troops, equipment and supplies, and to prevent them from crossing the river.

Other armed reconnaissance missions patrolled the two branches of the main supply routes from Seoul to Sarawon and from Seoul to Ch'orwon. When they found no worthwhile targets in these areas, pilots were instructed to attack airfields that had fallen into communist hands.

These orders established the pattern of operations until the last week in January, when *Operation Thunderbolt* got under way. The sortie rate then fell from over 20 a day to less than 16 a day enabling the ground crews to recover from the pressure under which they had been working. Before long 23 of the squadron's 24 aircraft were serviceable. Missions flown were generally of two-and-a-half hours duration. The pilots patrolling the main supply routes and river areas often found difficulty in spotting targets in the open, for the only movement in daylight was the pitiful lines of refugees trudging southwards. They were nearly all clad in white, the Korean colour of mourning. The numerous vehicle tracks in the snow indicated a high level of night activity, and when these tracks led into the villages they were bombed with good effect. Many houses exploded or burned fiercely indicating the presence of ammunition or fuel.

At times there were some variations from the general pattern of armed reconnaissance missions. One of these was designed to prevent the communists from repairing and using airfields that had recently been abandoned by the Fifth Air Force. These missions were timed to take place before last light, using 500lb general purpose bombs fitted with varied delay fuses and intended to hamper the Chinese crews repairing the runways under cover of darkness.

A special mission was carried out on 20 January, when a Chinese major-general was reputed to be active in the mountains south of the town of Kwanju in south-west Korea.

Dressed in civilian clothes and supported by an estimated force of 5-7000 guerrillas, he was engaged in turning the local population against the UN forces and the South Korean government. His methods were those of terror. Some weeks before he had captured three black American convoy drivers, who were then subjected to the humiliation of being led through the village streets by bull-rings inserted through their noses and carrying 'honey buckets'. Then, to drive the lesson home, they were decapitated at weekly intervals and their heads were displayed on stakes.

By 20 January XI Rok Division (Republic of Korea Division) and their advisers had isolated the communist guerrillas in an area containing 27 small villages. Air support was requested, and early in the morning three flights of four aircraft, one from each squadron at K-10, were ordered to attack the villages, five of which were destroyed, five others damaged and 511 guerrillas were killed. Ground troops then moved in and accounted for another 167 guerrillas.

A week later two letters were received, one from Shim Heng Tek,

Pre-mission wait (L/R) Piet Cilliers, Guy Paterson, KB Mcdonald, Jerks Maclean, Dougie Leah

A lecture on local combat conditions (L/R) SV Theron, Jan Willers, Bill Sykes, Pat Clulow, Piet Strydom, Martin Mentz, Hector Macdonald, Ray Armstrong

Chief of the Cholla Namdo Provincial Police and the other from Park Chul Soo, Governor of Cholla Namdo, praising the attacks on the guerrillas. The Governor expressed his gratitude for the heroic accomplishments of 18 Fighter-Bomber Wing while fighting for peace, a free world and the independence of Korea.

During the month the communists' retaliation to air attacks with small-arms and light anti-aircraft fire was intensified. On 3 January Dizzy Deans, leading two reconnaissance missions from K-13, observed a large building near Kujo on the east coast, well behind the communist lines. Painted on the roof were the words 'YMCA Korean Police – Please help'. He made a low pass but observed nothing further. Later evidence confirmed that this was a flak trap. Dizzy had another narrow escape while leading four aircraft against an enemy-occupied village. He encountered intense small-arms fire, and soon after the attack his engine began to vibrate. He managed to reach K-2, where he made a safe emergency landing.

Later in the month Syd de la Harpe's Mustang was hit in the wing by AA fragments and the day after, Koos van Heerden flew into a high tension wire. His aircraft suffered only a dented spinner; but sadly, during the months ahead, the squadron's luck began to run out when various operational hazards claimed their first victims.

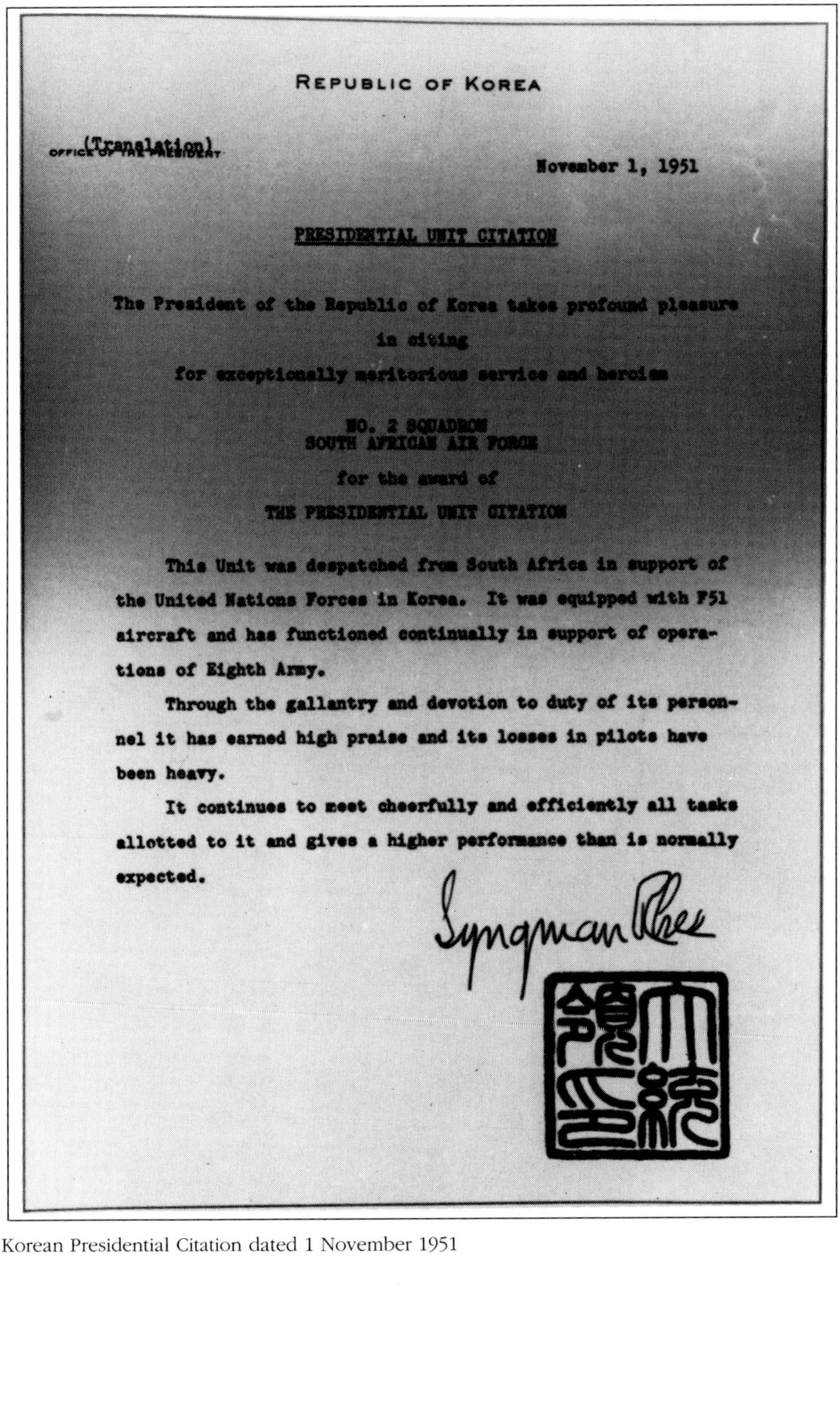

REPUBLIC OF KOREA

(Translation)
OFFICE OF THE PRESIDENT

November 1, 1951

PRESIDENTIAL UNIT CITATION

The President of the Republic of Korea takes profound pleasure
in citing
for exceptionally meritorious service and heroism

NO. 2 SQUADRON
SOUTH AFRICAN AIR FORCE
for the award of
THE PRESIDENTIAL UNIT CITATION

This Unit was despatched from South Africa in support of
the United Nations Forces in Korea. It was equipped with F51
aircraft and has functioned continually in support of operations of Eighth Army.

Through the gallantry and devotion to duty of its personnel it has earned high praise and its losses in pilots have
been heavy.

It continues to meet cheerfully and efficiently all tasks
allotted to it and gives a higher performance than is normally
expected.

Syngman Rhee

Korean Presidential Citation dated 1 November 1951

55

CHAPTER

6

The Pace Hots Up

The next 10 months, from 25 January to 12 November 1951, saw some of the heaviest fighting of the war both on the ground and in the air. An analysis of the Flying Cheetahs' mission returns shows that these months comprised a period of intense activity; in fact 32 per cent of the squadron's operational days in the Korean war fell between these dates when 41 per cent of its sorties were flown, and of the 96 Mustangs lost during the entire war, 59 per cent were during these torrid months.

Operation Thunderbolt was successful. By 9 February, communist resistance had crumbled and the UN forces had advanced on Seoul, recapturing Inch'on and Kimpo airfield. *Operation Roundup* followed, and although it came up against strong resistance, including a Chinese counter-attack that nearly penetrated the UN lines, the position was stabilised, and on 21 February the UN forces were on the move again under the code name of *Operation Killer*.

After two weeks of slow progress in the mud and spring thaw the UN attained its objective, a line through Yangp'yong on the Han River extending east to north of Chipjong-ni to the sea of Japan. Along the route they had witnessed the heavy losses inflicted on the communist troops and their equipment.

Meanwhile the Chinese had realised that their ground forces needed air support if they were to have any chance of defeating the UN. They decided to try to rectify the deficiency by training more pilots, introducing more MiG-15s, building new airstrips and repairing those that had been damaged. By the end of January 1951 Chinese MiG-15s were in total control of the Korean north-western airspace, and the area between the Yalu and Ch'ongch'on Rivers became known to UN pilots as MiG alley.

The communist plans to oppose general superiority of the UN in the air made little headway. Their supplies and personnel replacements had to be transported a considerable distance south to their front-line troops, and UN bombers and fighter-bombers continued to seek them out and destroy them wherever they might be. All that they could do was to devise a more effective logistical system, improve their defence,

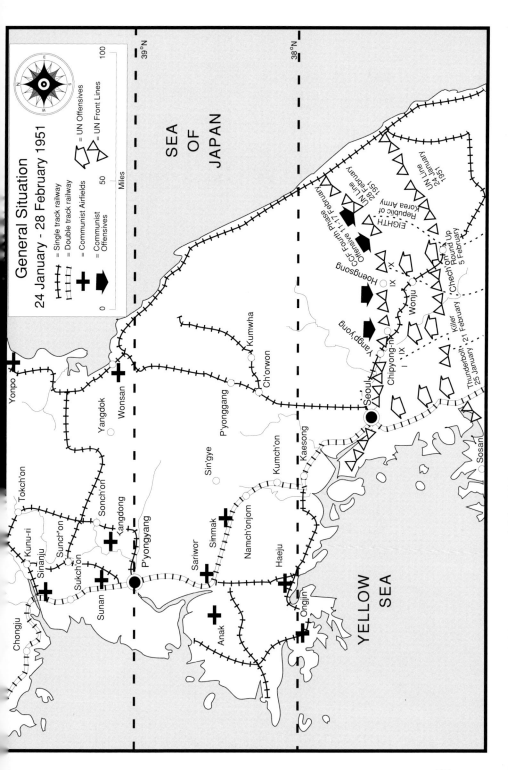

General Situation
24 January - 28 February 1951

Legend:
- = Single track railway
- = Double track railway
- = Communist Airfields
- ✚ = Communist Offensives
- ⬦ = UN Offensives
- △ = UN Front Lines

Miles
0   50   100

SEA OF JAPAN

YELLOW SEA

39°N
38°N

Yonpo
Tokch'on
Kunu-ri
Sinanju
Chongju
Such'on
Sukch'on
Sunan
Kangdong
Sonch'on
Yangdok
Wonsan
P'yongyang
Sariwor
Anak
Sinmak
Sin'gye
P'yonggang
Kumwha
Ch'orwon
Namch'onjom
Haeju
Kumch'on
Kaesong
Ongjin
Sosan
Seoul
Wonju
Chipyong-ni
Yangp'yong
Hoengsong
Kumhwa

CCF Fourth phase Offensive 1-17 February

UN Line 28 February 1951
UN Line 21 January 1951

EIGHTH
Republic of Korea Army

Killer 21 February
Thunderbolt 25 January
Chech'on Round Up 5 February

X
XI

57

and increase the pace and efficiency of repairs to roads and railways. The Cheetah pilots found ample evidence of all three attempts in February 1951 and the months that followed.

In common with the other squadrons of 18 Fighter-Bomber Wing, 2 Squadron concentrated on armed reconnaissance operations from late January to the end of February 1951. Occasionally these missions were diverted to give close-support while others were briefed in advance for close-support or interdiction targets when intelligence managed to locate concentrations of troops or supplies. An important part of the communist supply system was the double-track railway line and road running from Seoul through Kaesong, Sariwon, P'yongyang and Sinanju, to Sinuyu and Manchuria.

There were numerous sidelines and roads that served as alternatives if the main route became unusable. The other main north-south route was the road and railway line running the entire length of the peninsula along the east coast. These two routes were connected by lateral railway lines and roads from P'yongyang to Wonsan, and from Seoul to Wonsan. Roads linking the smaller towns to the main routes and to each other completed the network. The aircraft of 18 Fighter-Bomber Wing found targets along this entire system, but 2 Squadron paid particular attention to the routes between Seoul and Sariwon, Wonsan and the Chosin Reservoir, and Wonsan and P'yongyang.

The armed reconnaissance missions were made by flights of two aircraft, occasionally four, with as many as seven to eight missions flown

A napalm tank is fitted under a Mustang's wing

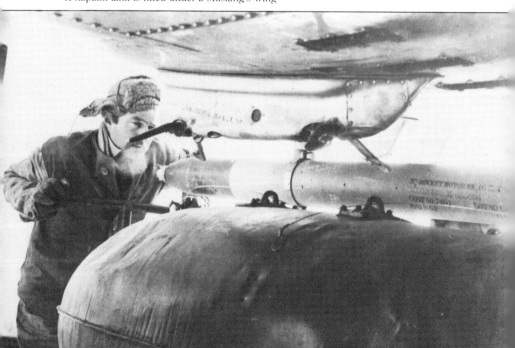

Improvised fuses for makeshift napalm bombs

by Cheetah pilots on a single day. The standard armament, apart from machine guns, consisted of napalm and rockets, but missions of long duration (3-4 hours) were made by flights of four aircraft armed only with rockets.

A day of operational flying that was a good example of 2 Squadron's activities during the month, was 4 February, when four armed reconnaissance missions of four aircraft were flown along the supply routes. Each mission was between three and four hours' duration, and the claims for the day totalled 19 vehicles destroyed and three damaged, one fuel dump and seven buildings destroyed, and one bridge and two tanks damaged. The most successful mission of the day was led by SV Theron who with four aircraft patrolled the Sin'gye-Yangdok road. A stationary convoy of well-camouflaged vehicles was rocketed and strafed, and 13 of the 20 vehicles were set on fire. The remaining seven were left undamaged after all ammunition had been expended.

Reports had been received that a number of tunnels on the northern railway lines were being used as daytime shelters for trains travelling along the supply routes. B-26 night-intruder crews had spotted the trains moving from one tunnel to the other under the cover of darkness and pilots on first-light reconnaissance

An armourer sets the fuses in the rockets

patrols had seen smoke emerging from them. Jan Blaauw was instructed to lead eight Mustangs to bomb a tunnel near Ch'ongjin. Each carried a single 500lb high-explosive bomb fitted with a 15-second delay fuse. One aircraft was forced to return to base with a fuel-flow problem.

When they reached the target the remaining seven aircraft found it was in a position that made a glide approach too dangerous, so the less accurate technique of dive-bombing was used. Of the seven bombs dropped, two cut the tracks at the east and west ends of the tunnel and another exploded inside, throwing débris out at both ends. This operation must have caused the Chinese some multiple headaches and added another hazard to their supply problems.

The communists also restricted road movement to the hours of darkness in an attempt to evade armed reconnaissance aircraft. Several ruses were used to conceal large convoys from detection from the air. Special camouflaged shelters were built along the main roads to allow trucks to pull off and hide in safety during the hours of daylight. Wooded country, orchards and hedgerows gave cover for convoys. Trucks were even disguised as' small houses enabling a 'village' to be formed at short notice.

Project Tack was conceived as an attempt to outwit the drivers of the convoys. Early in February Dakotas flew low above four selected roads south of P'yongyang and dropped more than eight tons of roofing nails. Fighter-bombers were ordered to reconnoitre these routes at first light and destroy the many vehicles expected to be immobilised with punctured tyres. Pilots of the Cheetah Squadron flew two missions without finding any crippled vehicle; and in fact only 28 stationary vehicles were found by the entire Fifth Air Force! During the last two weeks of February, the interdiction effort was intensified, and each squadron was made responsible for a particular area, one mission relieving another before returning to base. No 2 Squadron was assigned an area north-west of Seoul.

On 19 February, Colonel C R Low handed over the command of 18 Fighter-Bomber Wing to Colonel T C Rogers who radically changed the armed reconnaissance concept. He believed that the only way to detect camouflaged vehicles was by flying under 1 000ft and making a thorough search of the ground including every building, haystack, ravine, wooded area and roadside. Flights were therefore briefed to approach their reconnaissance routes at the lowest practicable altitude and to conduct a methodical search over their assigned routes. From the onset of *Operation Thunderbolt* until the end of February only a few missions by 2 Squadron consisted of close-support operations. When the ground situation demanded it, however, armed reconnaissance missions already airborne were diverted to help the hard-pressed infantry. During this period 21,6 per cent of combat sorties by 2 Squadron were flown on close-support missions, with 78 per cent on interdiction and 0,4 per cent on rescue patrols. One of these close-support operations was led by John Davis during *Operation Thunderbolt*. He gave a vivid description of what he called his first real close-support show in Korea: 'UN troops were situated exceptionally close to the target area. I could see them standing on top of their tanks and vehicles enjoying a grandstand view of the attack as we dealt death and destruction to the enemy entrenched in a village.' During the month, two reconnaissance missions on which the squadron aircraft were carrying drop-tanks were diverted to help ground troops in the American IX Corps sector. The targets were communist-occupied houses and a command post. In both cases the drop-tanks were used as incendiary bombs with great success. On three occasions the squadron was called upon to help the UN defenders of Chipyong-ni. All strikes were directed against troops occupying trenches along mountain ridges, and they demonstrated how effective napalm was against entrenched infantry.

February was a month of varied operations. Two missions illustrated both the difficulties and the successes of this intensive operational period. Towards the end of the month Badie Badenhorst led a four-aircraft flight scrambled on a close-support mission. On reaching the target he found that it was not easy to identify, and because of the danger of

KB Mcdonald - thirsty after a mission

mistaking friendly troops for enemy he refused to attack. Tank Odendaal and his flight had a different experience when they were scrambled later in the day. Their target was a concentration of about 700 troops sheltering in a valley east of Hoengsong where the hilltops were covered by cloud. Tank led his pilots to the target flying along narrow valleys, and although the weather and terrain did not allow them to see the results of the attack, the controller reported later that they were excellent.

KB McDonald tells how the commander of 18 Fighter-Bomber Wing, Colonel Rogers, who had struck up good relations with the 'South Afs' as he called the Cheetah pilots, was chatting with SV Theron who mentioned a bridge south of P'yongyang that no American fighter-bomber or heavy-bomber squadrons had been able to destroy. 'Give the Cheetahs a chance,' said SV. 'We'll knock it down for you.' KB remembers that mission so well because all the bombs fell slap on target and demolished the bridge. Denis Featherstone had been briefed to use his gun-camera to photograph the result, and when he returned to base and the negative was developed, SV personally delivered a print to the Colonel who was highly delighted with the result.

The communists were not slow to exploit the vulnerability of the Mustang to ground fire. In most other respects this aircraft was a good carrier of ground-attack weapons, and its superior performance had also been proved in air combat in the Second World War. Besides its manoeuvrability, the Mustang had first-rate endurance and excellent armament and load-carrying capabilities. Its main weakness was the cooling system which was extremely vulnerable. All the vital parts were exposed to ground fire including the radiator, the air outlet door and the pipes conveying the glycol coolant to the engine. If a bullet of even the smallest calibre hit any of these parts, there would be a rapid loss of cooling fluid, and the pilot would have only minutes before the engine either seized or caught fire.

The enemy often made extensive use of flak traps. These consisted of a bait, usually damaged or dummy vehicles overlooked by well-concealed surrounding anti-aircraft positions on the slopes adjoining a valley. The gun crews would wait for an aircraft to enter their trap like a spider waiting for a fly to settle on its web. Another trap was set by stringing a strong well-camouflaged cable across a valley to destroy an aircraft making a low-level strafing attack.

Cheetah pilots encountered two such communist traps during this period. On one occasion, John Davis was leading a two aircraft armed reconnaissance patrol along the main supply route between Seoul and Kaesong. He spotted a battery of ten guns and ten trucks arranged in a half-moon. His experience aroused his suspicions and he decided that the guns were dummies placed in the open to draw the attention of patrolling pilots away from supply dumps in the vicinity. Acting upon

Bridges were frequent but difficult targets

this intuition, he ignored the possible flak trap and attacked the nearest village. The explosions that followed were big enough to prove the presence of an ammunition dump.

Then there was Jan Blaauw who was briefed to lead four Mustangs against enemy tanks reported to be near the road between Kumwaha and T'ongch'on. He found the tanks which turned out to be dummies and flak-trap bait. Jan's aircraft was hit five times by ground fire, but luckily the damage was slight.

Other pilots were not so fortunate. By 2 February the squadron had been operational in Korea for 54 days and had flown 899 combat sorties with the loss of only one aircraft. The 900th sortie saw the end of this remarkable record when Elmer Wilson became the first casualty. He took off in the early morning from K-10 leading four Mustangs on an armed reconnaissance of the Wonsan area. Soon after becoming airborne his No 4 developed engine trouble and returned to base leaving three aircraft to continue the mission.

When he reached the area Elmer went down in search of targets while Mike Frost and Ian Gow provided top cover. Just north-east of Wonsan the searching Mustang suddenly developed engine trouble, and although Mike and Ian did not observe any flak, a glycol leak indicated a hit in the cooling system. Elmer immediately climbed to gain altitude and baled out north of Wonsan. His parachute opened and he made a good descent into a cold and choppy sea. Although Ian saw the parachute sink almost immediately, he and Mike descended to sea level to search for their missing leader.

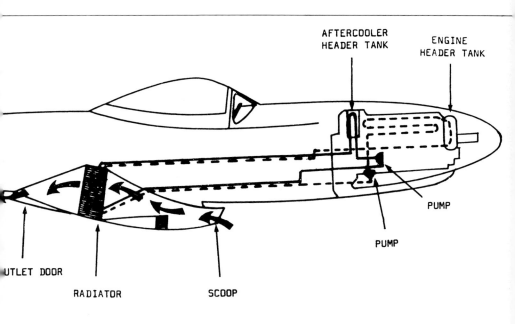

AFTERCOOLER
HEADER TANK

ENGINE
HEADER TANK

PUMP

PUMP

UTLET DOOR

RADIATOR

SCOOP

AIRFLOW

ENGINE COOLANT LINES

AFTERCOOLER COOLANT LINES

The cooling system of a F-51 D Mustang

Mustangs are re-armed at a forward airfield

They were soon joined by US Navy Corsairs, Shooting Stars and an amphibious SA-16 rescue aircraft. The crew spotted Elmer and landed nearby. They caught a glimpse of his Mae West in the high swells and although they battled to reach the bobbing pilot for 35 minutes, the attempt was abandoned when the Mae West disappeared from sight. In his official report the pilot of the SA-16 stated that he presumed the pilot had succumbed to the icy water.

An amphibious rescue aircraft

The squadron had hardly recovered from the shock of this first loss when SV Theron returned from a mission along the Wonsan-Hamhung road with the sad news that Doug Leah was also missing in action. The flight had found three camouflaged vehicles on the road just north of Yonghong. As they had previously attacked a supply dump, their only remaining weapons were their machine-guns, and when Doug pulled out right from a second strafing run his starboard wing hit the ground, the aircraft cartwheeled and burst into flames, and its wreckage was spread over a wide area. There was no sign of enemy flak; perhaps the wing hit a flak-trap cable?

General Partridge pins the DFC on Tank Odendaal

There is an old belief among soldiers and airmen that casualties occur in threes. The events in February seemed to verify this notion, for in mid-month Derek Doveton was flying on an armed reconnaissance of the Kaesong-Haeju-Sariwon route, with Doug McKellar as his wingman, when they found a camouflaged vehicle near Kaesong which they attacked repeatedly. After the fourth pass the vehicle caught fire and Derek told Doug to continue the reconnaissance while he went in for a last run. As Doug carried out these instructions he saw Derek's Mustang bounce off a hillside in a cloud of smoke. It somersaulted, hit the ground and burst into flames.

By this time the Flying Cheetahs had begun to make their mark in Korea, and by the end of February they had already flown 1 217 combat sorties (407 missions). The Fifth Air Force formally recognised the accomplishments of the squadron by awarding 38 air medals, 19 First Oak Leaf Clusters, two Second Oak Leaf Clusters and three Third Oak Leaf Clusters. SV Theron, John Davis, Tank Odendaal, Lippy Lipawsky and Badie Badenhorst received the DFC.

Although American pilots flew operational tours of 100 sorties, the South African maximum under normal circumstances was 75, a total that was decided upon for very good reasons. Apart from the stresses of operational flying, there was the unpredictable Korean weather, the vulnerability of Mustangs to flak, and the threat offered by the superior MiG-15s. There was also the knowledge that a pilot's chance of escape or even survival after being shot down and captured by the enemy was a doubtful quantity. The Chinese and North Koreans were not bound by the Geneva Convention and it was presumed that they followed their own codes of justice. In view of the extensive use of napalm fire-bombs and the enormous destruction wrought by UN aircraft it was naturally assumed that the communists were unlikely to be sympathetic towards their prisoners.

The first draft of replacement pilots arrived at K-10 on 24 February 1951. Among them was Commandant Ray Armstrong who had been nominated to take over from SV Theron when his tour was complete. They flew from South Africa and no time was lost in issuing them with kit and devising a training programme under Badie Badenhorst.

Jubilant ground crew celebrate a postal delivery

A recording of voices from home

The new arrivals found the quality of life at K-10 superior to that experienced by those who had arrived at Chinhae a month before. There were stocks of commodities that had been imported direct from the USA, two laundries, a barber's shop, a post exchange and a branch of the American Special Services, making it possible to send recorded messages home. There were also off-duty facilities for hunting, hiking, sailing and fishing. South African ingenuity even produced a serviceable boat made from two long-range fuel tanks bolted together. This improvised vessel was equipped with a mast, a sail and paddles, and it proved not only seaworthy but easy to handle in Chinhae Bay.

Most of the circumstances that previously kindled a negative influence on morale had been eliminated. Letters, newspapers and parcels were arriving from home regularly as well as a very welcome free issue of brandy and cigarettes. Morale improved noticeably together with a growing sense of comradeship with the Americans. This spirit of goodwill was expressed by Colonel C R Low at a party given by the pilots of 2 Squadron to mark the end of his term in command of 18

Fighter-Bomber Wing. In his farewell speech he spoke of the immense satisfaction that he had derived from his association with the Flying Cheetahs.

There was a gratifying development when airmen showed a keen interest in helping the pitiful lot of the innumerable homeless Korean orphans. The sight of these cold, hungry children raking through rubbish-bins in search of food made a deep impression on everyone, and when the Squadron's chaplain, 'Doempie' Cloete, made an appeal for donations towards an orphanage that had been established in Chinhae, not only was 191 dollars collected, but items from food parcels were also contributed. Assistance to the orphanage was to become a regular feature of squadron life at K-10.

A sailboat improvised from drop tanks

CHAPTER

7

Two Steps Forward - One Step Back

By the end of February 1951 *Operation Killer* had attained its objectives, and General Ridgeway was planning another offensive, *Operation Ripper,* calculated to take Seoul. It was launched on 7 March, when the Fifth Air Force flew 575 sorties, of which 200 were in close-support. Seoul fell on 14 March, and it was ascertained that of the former population of 1 500 000 only 200 000 were still living there.

Operation Ripper did not achieve the results expected. A higher kill had been hoped for, and although it appeared that the communists were preparing for a spring offensive, General Ridgeway wanted to advance as far as possible and keep the Chinese on the run. *Operation Rugged* was therefore launched on 5 April when the Kansan line was reached, and then it was forward towards the Utah line. The communist 'Iron Triangle', an area of communications and supply including Ch'orwon, Kumwha and P'yongyang, was the next objective.

It was while this advance was taking place that President Truman relieved General MacArthur of his command and replaced him with General Ridgeway. For some time a difference of opinion on the future conduct of the war had been brewing between Truman and MacArthur, mainly because of MacArthur's insistence that the war should be extended over the Chinese border and Truman refused to risk the possibility of a global war.

General J A van Fleet was appointed the new commander of the Eighth Army and he took over in time to meet the pressure of the enemy's spring offensive that the Chinese hoped would lead to a decisive military defeat of the UN. General van Fleet decided to follow General Ridgeway's policy of withdrawing to a succession of defensive lines inflicting the maximum damage at the minimum cost in UN lives and calling upon the Fifth Air Force to hammer the advancing enemy.

Three Chinese armies, a total of 350 000 troops, attacked by the light of the full moon on 22 April. It was a typical Chinese attack using human wave tactics without air support against well organised UN forces backed by the full power of its Air Forces, which flew over 1 000 sorties a day and inflicted heavy casualties. The final tally when the fighting

A flight of Mustangs heads for the front line

died down was 70 000 Chinese and 11 000 UN casualties. The UN forces lost ground, but they held a line from north of Seoul through Sabangu to Taep'o-ri, north of the 38th parallel.

On the nights of 15 and 16 May, 21 Chinese and nine North Korean divisions made another offensive, but it fizzled out in four days. It was to be the last communist offensive until June 1953. These movements of the UN ground forces back-and-forth between 1 March and 19 May 1951 made great demands upon the supporting fighter-bombers.

During March the Cheetahs flew their greatest number of sorties in a single month of the Korean war; 633 combat sorties averaging 20,4 a day. The use of napalm bombs, rockets and machine-gun ammunition also reached its peak during the month. In this period, 2 Squadron flew 1 281 sorties, or 10 per cent of the total number of sorties flown during the entire war. These missions were made from four airfields, K-9, K-10, K-13 and K-16.

With the coming of the torrential summer rains it was feared that flying operations would be hampered if the earth runway at K-10 broke up under heavy traffic. The decision was therefore made that a runway of pierced steel planking (PSP) should be laid. During this period 2 Squadron moved to Pusan East (K-9) where it came under the control of 35 Interceptor Wing. The other squadrons operated from Pusan (K-1). The Cheetahs stayed at K-9 for a month, and on 23 April returned to K-10 where many more improvements had been made, besides those to the runway. Living and recreational facilities had been improved and the infrastructure of the base had been adapted to allow for operations

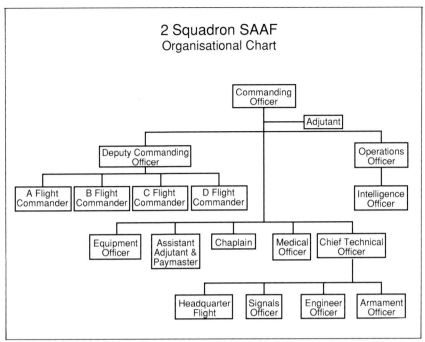

2 Squadron SAAF
Organisational Chart

- Commanding Officer
  - Adjutant
  - Deputy Commanding Officer
    - A Flight Commander
    - B Flight Commander
    - C Flight Commander
    - D Flight Commander
  - Operations Officer
    - Intelligence Officer
  - Equipment Officer
  - Assistant Adjutant & Paymaster
  - Chaplain
  - Medical Officer
  - Chief Technical Officer
    - Headquarter Flight
    - Signals Officer
    - Engineer Officer
    - Armament Officer

Squadron administration

in all kinds of weather; in fact, some pilots thought that the new facilities were equal to those of a permanent South African Air Force station. The squadrons of 18 Fighter-Bomber Wing once more began to stage through forward bases as the UN advances had made it possible for operations to be carried out from airfields situated between the 38th and 39th parallels. On 11 May a group of 20 groundcrew left for K-13 to establish a re-arming and refuelling detachment for the aircraft of 2 Squadron, and next day all squadrons followed suit.

Although the recommissioning of the forward bases brought the starting point of missions nearer the front line, the rotation procedure became somewhat tedious, for a flight of four aircraft had to fly on an operational mission from K-10 every day, land back at K-13 after the mission to refuel and re-arm, and then fly two more missions the same day. The flight spent the night at K-13 and flew another mission in the morning before returning to K-10. Some of the practical implications of this routine were not very pleasant for the pilots. Because of the limited storage space in a fighter aircraft, each pilot could only carry a small amount of baggage consisting of his toiletries and a change of underwear, and his other clothes had to be worn throughout all the missions.

In the spring of 1951 the Cheetahs concentrated on finding targets of opportunity along road and rail routes running north from Seoul to P'yongyang and those linking the latter with Wonsan and Hamhung. In early March armed reconnaissance missions were briefed to search particular stretches of the supply routes, but later, as the communists became more adept at avoiding the searching aircraft and began building up for their April offensive, interdiction missions were armed with bombs and rockets and were briefed to cut certain stretches of road and rail or to bomb selected bridges and tunnels.

In May the enemy greatly increased the anti-aircraft defences and also improved deception techniques and control of supply units under cover of darkness. In an attempt to defeat these improved tactics UN pilots became increasingly adept at detecting and destroying camouflaged vehicles in shelters and tunnels, while the movement of convoys at night was hampered by B-26 night intruder missions. At this point the Flying Cheetahs gained fresh laurels by effective truck-hunting.

On 1 March, 2 Squadron established a new record by flying 32 combat sorties in a single day consisting of eight patrol missions over roads north-east of Ch'orwon and eight close-support missions. One of the armed reconnaissance missions flown by Doug McKellar and Dizzy Deans was a notable success. They found seven trucks hidden in an area surrounded by high hills, which made these vehicles difficult to approach, but they solved the problem by dive-bombing with napalm, a procedure never before used in the squadron, and scored direct hits.

Tinky Jones also led a successful close-support mission that destroyed two tanks in the southern part of Seoul. Although the squadron did not take part in night raids, the pilots got a good taste of the radar bombing technique when Lippy Lipawsky led a four-aircraft flight that carried out an experimental radar directed drop through the overcast. The ground controller directed the flight on four different bombing runs at increasing altitudes before he finally gave the order to release bombs at 22 000ft.

Lippy's instructions were constantly interrupted by other controllers, and when they reached the most suitable position his pilots found little satisfaction in releasing their bombs blindly into the cloud. He reported that the entire procedure was inefficient and that a separate radio channel was necessary.

Apart from a number of ideas and innovations for finding and destroying enemy vehicles, the Cheetahs, now led by Commandant Ray Armstrong, who had taken over from SV, were convinced that there was no substitute for close systematic ground-searching for hidden vehicles.

Techniques developed by Badie Badenhorst and Porkey Kruger, and careful planning and co-ordination by Ray Armstrong, enabled 2 Squadron to excel in truck-hunting in late March and early April. Some of these techniques entailed flying across the patrol routes in overlapping circles with pilots returning to the same areas. Thus they were able to notice the slightest changes on the ground. Also, when a single

Ray Armstrong

vehicle was spotted, the flight leader waited until the whole convoy had been sighted before leading his pilots in to the attack.

On 24 March, Jan Blaauw and Pottie Potgieter found 12 camouflaged trucks drawn up alongside a road south of Sinmak. As was customary at the time, the Mustangs were carrying only rockets, but Jan and Pottie were able to use these so effectively that ten of the trucks were destroyed and one damaged. Further successes against camouflaged vehicles were scored by Tank Odendaal and Porkey Kruger, when they wrote off nine trucks south of T'osan. The squadron was congratulated by General Partridge and General Stratemeyer for its efficiency in seeking out and destroying so many camouflaged vehicles. Early in April the Cheetahs took part in an attempt to paralyse the North Korean supply system by cutting roads and railway lines and destroying bridges. In three days they dropped 132 bombs fitted with delay fuses to hamper the communist repair gangs.

Before the Chinese spring offensive there was no sign of the threatened challenge to UN air superiority, but as a precautionary measure all squadrons at K-9 were instructed to disperse their aircraft as widely as possible in the crowded dispersal area.

Ray Armstrong called his pilots together in the operations room to warn them of such an eventuality and remind them of the lessons learnt in the Second World War from enemy air attacks: A number of decisions were taken to tighten up existing procedures. As for attacks by enemy jets, Ray told his pilots that it had been proved in the Second World War that a jet fighter pilot was handicapped by speed and the inability to turn sharply in combat against a conventional aircraft. Therefore a MiG had to be spotted before an attack so that a turn towards it could be made at an appropriate juncture. Ray also warned that when attacked by enemy aircraft, a formation must stick together and fight as a team.

Armed reconnaissance missions met with increasing success as April progressed. Porkey Kruger and Syd de la Harpe set a new squadron record for the number of enemy vehicles destroyed during a single mission when they found a convoy of 19 vehicles at Songwol-li, a village on a side-road near Sinmak, and destroyed 18 of them. Porkey actually claimed 21 destroyed at de-briefing, and Ray Armstrong became somewhat sceptical about the authenticity of his claims, so he decided to fly as his wingman on the next armed reconnaissance.

They duly took off and patrolled the main supply route north-west of Kaesong. At first there was no joy, and they were about to return when Porkey spotted 30 trucks tucked away in a ravine. Despite the narrowness of the valley they attacked the trucks which burnt intensely. On returning to base Ray sent out another mission to finish off any of the vehicles that might have survived the first attack. His doubts about the younger pilot's spotting ability and claims were changed to admiration and he recommended Porkey for an American DFC, approved a month later.

On the same day Horse Sweeney also won a DFC when he added a tank to the squadron's tally of 32 vehicles destroyed. The citation for his award on 13 June tells the story:

> Leading a flight of two Mustangs near Kumch'on, and although the anti-aircraft fire was accurate throughout the period spent in the area, Captain J M Sweeney continued to fly at low level while investigating suspicious objects. His disregard for his personal safety and unremitting perseverance was rewarded when he sighted an enemy tank and a cleverly concealed anti-tank gun. He unhesitatingly attacked both targets with relentless accuracy and left the area only after the total destruction of both was assured. In the process, the aircraft which Captain Sweeney was flying was hit in the left gun bay by an explosive shell which burnt all the rocket and electrical wiring. Quite undeterred, Captain Sweeney continued on his mission and caused severe damage to an enemy village before returning to base.

Horse Sweeney

The intense pressure on both air and ground crews was relieved on 17 April when 18 Fighter-Bomber Wing told its squadrons that only 16 sorties a day would be flown in the immediate future. This temporary reduction was to allow the ground crews to improve the serviceability of the aircraft in preparation for an all-out effort against the expected communist offensive. This reduction did not diminish the squadron's zeal to stay on top in the competitive truck-busting campaign.

Effective truck hunting depended largely on a thorough co-ordinated search of clearly defended areas and the exploitation of the flexibility of airpower by the rapid dissemination of information once a convoy had been located. To achieve a co-ordinated search, Ray Armstrong subdivided the area assigned to the squadron and allocated a flight to each sub-area. In that way pilots became thoroughly acquainted with the terrain and its potential for concealment.

As for broadcasting the location of targets over the radio, every UN flight over Korea could hear this information and sometimes another squadron would home in for the kill. Although the Cheetahs were fully

77

aware of the need for close co-operation with their American comrades, they were determined, in a spirit of friendly rivalry, that the vehicles they found should be destroyed by their own pilots. They therefore ensured confidentiality by talking Afrikaans over the radio, until Ray Armstrong overheard a frustrated American pilot call 'foul', and he ordered his pilots to stick to English!

On 9 May, the squadron received a message from General Stratemeyer:

1. On 12 April 1951, just two months after flying its 1 000th sortie, No 2 Squadron, South African Air Force, completed 2 000 combat sorties in support of the United Nations forces in Korea. This continuing high sortie rate is most noteworthy.
2. I wish to express my sincere appreciation to the personnel of No 2 Squadron who have contributed to this commendable effort.
   Signed: George E Stratemeyer
   Lieutenant-General, USAF
   Commanding.

An endorsement by the Commanding General of the Fifth Air Force, General Partridge, accompanied General Stratemeyer's letter. It stressed that the enviable combat record of the squadron in the Korean campaign was a splendid tribute to the fighting spirit of the freedom-loving people of South Africa and reflected great credit upon the squadron and the United Nations.

During March most of the squadron's close-support missions were in support of *Operation Ripper* against targets between the Han and Pukham Rivers. Pressure by the UN forced the Chinese infantry to break cover, and large numbers were caught in the open by marauding fighter-bombers.

Lippy Lipawsky led a flight of four aircraft against a 300-strong communist infantry column moving up a narrow valley. In the de-briefing he gave a vivid account of how enemy troops died after the first napalm strike. Similar carnage occurred five days later when a Mosquito controller found 1 200 men fleeing along a road east of Hongch'on. He directed six air strikes against this group, two of which were carried out by Cheetah Squadron flights. The US 7th Division moving up the road shortly afterwards found 600 dead and 300 wounded. *Operation Tomahawk* gave the squadron experience of a particular type of close-support. Three flights of two aircraft apiece were successively briefed to provide continuous cover to the US 1 Corps armoured column, each flight, with its aircraft carrying two fragmentation bombs and six rockets, spent three hours over the column before being relieved. When the flights were not beating off threats to the column, they were ordered to attack close-support targets nearby.

Joe Joubert considers the problem of moving his Mustang through the slush

After 23 April the pressure of the communist offensive made it necessary to divert aircraft already airborne on interdiction missions to close-support targets. On one occasion two Cheetah armed reconnaissance missions were called upon to give close-support. They joined under the leadership of Porkey Kruger and were directed against Chinese infantry crossing the Imjin River. A large number of these troops were killed with rockets and strafing.

On 4 May a most remarkable close-support mission was led by Joe Joubert who had been sent on a road cutting mission and therefore his four aircraft were armed with bombs and rockets. The front line was crossed in rapidly deteriorating weather and visibility was worsened by a new communist strategem of using smoke generators to create a haze over the front.

Soon after crossing the line, the flight was diverted to help the ground forces south of Koksu-ri on the northern side of the Han River. When they reached the target the visibility was poor; clouds were covering the high ridges and the weather was deteriorating rapidly. Joe led several attacks on enemy positions below a ridgeline without harming adjacent friendly troops, and after this strike the UN ground forces were able to take the ridge with little difficulty. Joe was awarded the DFC for his outstanding leadership.

On 9 May a departure from close-support and interdiction missions occurred when the Cheetahs took part in *Operation Buster*, a raid by 312 aircraft from the Fifth Air Force and First Marine Air Wing, directed at Sinuiju airfield which was to become operational in support of the Chinese offensive. It was therefore necessary to neutralise it. On this occasion 2 Squadron acted as a rescue standby and orbited over the Yellow Sea west of Ch'o-do Island where pilots in distress had been briefed to make for.

As it happened there were no casualties during the attack on the airfield and the Cheetahs' part in the patrol passed without incident. The operation was a great success with 106 buildings, a large aviation fuel dump and 26 ammunition dumps destroyed. Several Chinese aircraft were also hit on the ground and heavy casualties were inflicted on enemy personnel.

Foxy Ruiter

On 2 March, the squadron lost two of its most experienced pilots of the Second World War, Foxy Ruiter and Badie Badenhorst. Foxy was leading a four-aircraft mission north of Wonson when his Mustang developed engine trouble. While flying to the west of the target he reported that his coolant temperature was fluctuating. His No 2, Micky Rorke, checked the outlet and reported that it was working normally, but Foxy decided to return to base and told Micky to escort him.

Badie Badenhorst

After a few minutes Micky saw white glycol smoke pouring from his leader's Mustang, and Foxy, realising that he had only a few minutes' grace, attempted to crash-land on the beach at Yo-do Island. He misjudged his approach and overshot, and while turning left a wing hit the sea. The aircraft sank almost immediately, and in spite of a search by the three remaining members of the flight, no trace of Foxy or his Mustang were found.

Badie was lost the same day. He was leading a long-range armed reconnaissance mission towards a section of the main supply route between Sinanju and Chonju. While crossing the Ch'ongch'on River at an altitude of 500ft, the flight suddenly drew heavy anti-aircraft fire. Badie's No 2 heard his leader say: 'Look out - there's bags of heavy flak.........' He stopped in mid-sentence and there was no further radio contact with him. His Mustang appeared to be out of control, and after climbing and diving steeply towards Sinanju it pitched over and crashed into the town in flames.

Piet Swemmer narrowly escaped becoming the third fatality within a week when his engine cut on take-off and he landed in a rice paddy at the end of the runway. He was unhurt, but his aircraft was a write-off.

On 10 March John Davis led a strike of four aircraft against communist infantry dug in along a ridge near Yandogwon-ni, between the Han and Pukham Rivers. The Mustangs drew intense small-arms fire from the target area, and as John turned into the attack, his aircraft went into a spin, failed to recover and hit the ground carrying a full load of napalm and rockets. It burnt fiercely while the rest of the flight pressed home the attack. The loss of another experienced flight commander of the Second World War was a tragic occasion.

Some of the other pilots were more fortunate. Three days after the loss of John Davis, Jan Blaauw had a narrow escape during a strike against some railway trucks. His Mustang was hit in the mainplane by an explosive shell, and he had great difficulty in bringing his aircraft back to base and making a safe landing.

Pottie Potgieter was the first Cheetah pilot in the Korean war to be wounded in action. During March, while patrolling the Imjin River with Joe Joubert, he noticed moderate but accurate anti-aircraft fire coming from both river-banks to the north of Munsan. Pottie's Mustang was hit in the starboard side of the cockpit by a shell that pierced the radio control box and struck Pottie in the chest causing a superficial wound. This did not deter him or Joe who only returned to base after rocketing and strafing targets in the Kaesong area.

Next day Steve Armstrong had the good fortune to land in friendly territory after he had baled out. He had been flying No 2 to his CO, Ray Armstrong, on the way to patrol the supply routes north-east of Kaesong, when his engine began to run roughly. After about ten

Piet Swemmer (left) and Pottie Potgieter

minutes the cockpit was filled with smoke, and flames appeared from under the top cowling in front of the windscreen. He applied the emergency drills and landed safely on a hillside behind the front line, southwest of Wonju. A number of friendly Koreans stayed with him until a helicopter arrived.

April nearly passed without the loss of any other aircraft, but on the last day of the month Piet Celliers was shot down behind enemy lines. As a leader of a four-aircraft mission he had been briefed to attack a railway tunnel on the main supply route east of Sinmak. His pilots released their bombs on the tunnel and then broke into two separate groups to find targets of opportunity for their rockets and machine-guns. Soon after leaving the primary target Piet's aircraft was hit by anti-aircraft fire and burst into flames. His wingman, Guy Paterson, saw him bale out successfully near Sinmak.

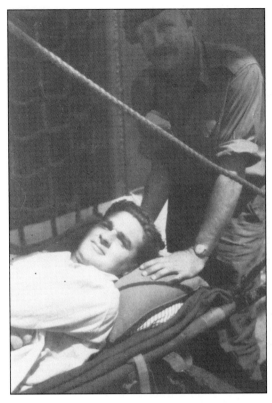

Piet Cilliers carried aboard a hospital ship

Guy reported this to the rescue service and then recalled the second element of the flight to help protect his leader. Another flight that was diverted after bombing a tunnel in the Sohong area relieved them, and soon afterwards the rescue helicopter retrieved Piet from hostile territory. He was grounded for three months with a lacerated wound in the right calf.

Horse Sweeney was also wounded three days later. He was flying No 3 in an interdiction mission against a railway tunnel between Kaesong and Namch'onjom. They attacked the primary target without mishap and the pilots were strafing some vehicles in the face of intense automatic fire when Horse's Mustang was hit in the trim-tab of the port aileron and in the starboard side of the cockpit. He suffered a lacerated wound in the right buttock and began to lose blood rapidly. Jan Blaauw coaxed the wounded pilot back to K-16, where he passed out on landing. He was evacuated by air to K-10 where the squadron medical officer declared him unfit to fly for six months.

By the middle of May, 11 of the original draft of 2 Squadron pilots had completed their tours and returned home. One who was almost due to go and nearly failed to make it was Vernon Kruger. The story of his rescue from behind the enemy lines on his 74th sortie has become one of the legends of South African military aviation.

Vernon Kruger

At 15h30 one afternoon towards the end of May, Jan Blaauw took off from K-16 with Vernon, Martin Mentz and Pat Clulow, and they bombed their primary target, a bridge near Ch'orwon. They then began a reconnaissance westward, and while they were flying over Taep'yong Vernon's Mustang was hit in the starboard mainplane and caught fire. Vernon baled out and in the process suffered burns to his hand and face and a dislocated right shoulder.

Jan told Pat to gain altitude and inform the rescue service while he and Martin kept a watch over the downed pilot. By 17h15, all three of them were running short of fuel with no sign of a rescue helicopter or a flight to relieve them, so Jan ordered Pat and Martin to return to base while he remained behind.

This decision was made by Jan in the knowledge that if he stayed he would not have enough fuel to return to base. He was also aware of the prevailing belief that the communists would shoot a captured pilot out of hand. After 15 minutes he was joined by two Corsairs, but at 18h45 his fuel ran out and he crash-landed beside Vernon bruising his face in the process. After spending another 30 minutes on the ground, both men were taken out by helicopter under enemy fire. On returning to the forward base, Jan telephoned his CO to report on the unusual manner in which he had lost his aircraft, and he was surprised to receive warm commendation for his action. Ray Armstrong was impressed by the courage of his second-in-command and the good effect that this action would have on the morale of the pilots which had been severely strained by the recent losses. Jan was awarded the American Silver Star for his gallantry on this occasion - the highest award made by the United States to members of foreign armed services. The full story of this celebrated action is told by Vernon Kruger in Chapter 18.

Jan Blaauw

8

Intransigence

During this difficult period in mid-1951 a high level of morale was maintained by the regular arrival of mail from home and such thoughtful gestures as individually addressed parcels from the Gift and Comforts Fund.

The losses and narrow escapes had placed the pilots of the Cheetah Squadron under considerable strain, and something extra was needed to relieve the tension. That something was the inspiration of a young officer from the Eastern Cape, Micky Rorke, who felt that although the American Officers' Club was comfortable and friendly, it lacked atmosphere, so, with the help of Flight Sergeant Bob Monroe, he decided to do something about it. In a borrowed jeep Mickey drove to Pusan and bought ten dollars' worth of drinks at a British NAAFI. On returning to Chinhae he built a bar next to his bed with ammunition boxes. He was now in business. His prices, with Scotch whisky at seven cents a tot, were much lower than those charged in the American Club. The venture was a great success.

Rorke's Inn was then established in a tent and later in a wood and iron building, and the pub became an institution of the Cheetah Squadron until the end of the war. It was a rendezvous where pilots could feel at home and let off steam, where tradition and esprit de corps were fostered and where pilots could sing away their anxieties and give expression to their exuberance after a successful action, or drown their sorrows after a comrade had been lost. Many of the songs that they sang were from previous wars, but some had a distinctive flavour of the Korean experience.

Charles Scott Shaw, 2 Squadron's chaplain for over a year after Doempie Cloete left, said of Rorke's Inn:

We had our own pilots' pub, a cosy little room started by one of our gallant pilots, Micky Rorke. There was a stormwater drain adjoining the pub, and to gain access one had to cross Rorke's Drift, as it was called, on a narrow plank. During winter nights Rorke's Inn, with its dartboard and good companionship, rang with music and laughter, but it was a sobering thought to remember that one had to walk back across the plank in the chilly night air after a few drinks! If you fell into the drift you landed in the ooze and slime. One or two fellows did fall in and were not given a chance to forget it. They were ostracised for a week afterwards!

A doctor, so the story goes, was thrown into Rorke's Drift. The pilots were feeling a little touchy and tender after returning from a particularly grim operation. The doctor, with complete lack of tact, had entered the pub and triumphantly announced that he'd acquired a canvas bag for the bits and pieces of the body of the next pilot to crash. The doctor and his canvas bag were thrown into the slime of Rorke's Drift!

Unfortunately this renowned pub outlived its founder. On 15 May 1951 Micky was taking off for a four-aircraft interdiction mission, his third mission of the day. His Mustang became airborne after hitting a bump, failed to climb and crashed near a damaged B-26 bomber parked off the end of the runway. The two napalm bombs Micky released before impact, exploded and turned both aircraft into an inferno.

Mickey Rorke is buried at Pusan - Doempie Cloete officiates

Bob Munroe - Proprietor of Rorke's Inn

In May, as pilots were approaching the maximum number of hours allowed for a tour of operations, it was feared that the remaining complement would be insufficient while the replacements were being trained before being sent on operations. It was therefore decided on 22 May to limit sorties to 16 a day and grant permission to some pilots to extend their tours from 75 to 100 sorties, which would help to maintain a hard core of experienced pilots on operations. This reduced rate was maintained until the end of June, when 12 pilots who had arrived at the end of May became operational. After that, batches of replacement pilots arrived regularly at six-week intervals.

The Chinese offensive was stopped in mid-May, and a limited UN

A novel international cricket match

Steel runway planking is put to a novel use

advance was launched by the Eighth Army along the entire front, the communists offering little resistance. Very soon all South Korea except the left flank was cleared of the enemy, and the Eighth Army consolidated its positions along the Kansas line. There were some communist strong-points near the Iron Triangle and its surrounding ridges, but by 11 June Ch'orwon and Kumwha had been taken.

Towards the end of May an intensive interdiction campaign was launched by the Fifth Air Force for the purpose of destroying communist transport between the 39th Parallel and the front line. The western sector was allotted to 18 Fighter-Bomber Wing, and aircraft bombed sections of the roads and railway lines in areas where repairs would be difficult to carry out. The programme comprised two to six interdiction missions a day for 2 Squadron. The targets bombed were mainly along the road and rail route between Kaesong and Sariwon, the alternative route between these two towns, and along the secondary north-to-south road network.

On the nights of 15 and 16 June, K-16 was attacked by PO-2 aircraft known as 'Bedcheck Charlies', fabric-covered bi-planes used purely as nuisance value. They flew over airfields at night when their pilots threw a grenade or two over the sides of the open cockpits.

As the first anniversary of the outbreak of the Korean war drew near, the Soviet Deputy Minister of Foreign Affairs, Jakob Malik, suggested over a UN radio programme that a peaceful settlement could be negotiated between the warring parties. No doubt Russia and its allies had begun to appreciate the seriousness of the enormous losses that the communist forces were suffering and realised that it was a war they could never win.

Four days later Andrei Gromyko told the US ambassador in Moscow that an armistice should be negotiated between the field commanders. General Ridgeway suggested that negotiations could be held aboard a hospital ship in Wonsan harbour, but eventually talks began at Kaesong on 10 July. With the possibility of an armistice, both sides decided to rest on their laurels for a while, and they dug in on their defensive lines when there was time to consider future activities.

The Chinese commanders realised that their lack of success against the UN forces had resulted from the failure of the promised air support. The Chinese Air Force was therefore urged to launch a big offensive but as it turned out, their plan differed very little from their previous efforts, except for an appeal for an international volunteer air force.

The retaliation by the UN was straightforward. A regular watch was kept on the 34 North Korean airfields, and as soon as repair work was almost finished, intensive bombing raids rendered them useless again. At first, as repairs became a reality, the Fifth Air Force fighter-bombers, covered by Sabre jets, carried out the bombing strikes, but when losses caused by the improved communist anti-aircraft defences became too costly, Superfortresses took over a share of the strikes on night operations.

As it happened, the wavering peace negotiations not only brought about a change of tactics on the ground but also a change in air strategy. The army took on a defensive role, while the Air Force was briefed to attack the enemy's means of making war, a pressure that had to be maintained until a cease-fire became a reality. After a few days of talks with the communists, General Ridgeway lost patience with their intransigence and ordered his new Chief of the Air Force, General Weyland, to intensify operations against selected targets. This order was later changed when it was decided that less severe pressure was preferable and only tactical targets should be attacked. However, the peace talks ceased abruptly when the communists made the excuse that UN bombs had been dropped in the Kaesong area.

During this period the shift in emphasis from ground offensives had a direct influence on the activities of 2 Squadron. Apart from the extensive airfield neutralisation programme, an interdiction campaign on the North Korean transport infrastructure was launched. It included bridges, tunnels, marshalling yards, roads and railway lines. The main weapon employed on these missions was the general purpose bomb instead of napalm.

Although there were heavy demands by the more systematic interdiction campaign, 2 Squadron continued to carry out its close-support

Doempie Cloete gives the 'thumbs-up'

operations. Throughout the period of 20 May to 31 August 1951, one or two sorties were flown every day in support of the Eighth Army. The missions in May and June were made during the advance to the forward positions north of the Kansas Line, while in July and August support was given to the limited ground operations to develop a new defence line.

Close-support missions were of a different kind on 26 and 27 June, when 2 Squadron provided column cover to 24 US Division task force as it thrust forward from the UN front line east of Kumwha. On the first day two Cheetah flights of four aircraft were instructed to remain on a 30-minute alert throughout the day when three missions were flown.

Next day continuous cover was given to the division by flights armed with napalm and rockets, flying over the advancing columns in relays. Seven missions, each lasting approximately two hours, were flown, when pilots kept dislodging communist troops from commanding ridges and silencing hostile artillery batteries. Twice during July the squadron committed its entire effort to close-support, and flew seven missions against Chinese troops hidden in bunkers on a series of hills on the south bank of the Imjin River.

The Flying Cheetahs experienced their first summer monsoon during June and July, when south-easterly winds blew in moist air, and even when rain was not falling, the overcast weather often made it difficult for leaders to locate their targets. On six days during these months the weather created impossible flying conditions. It also influenced the type of mission flown, and when low cloud over North Korea made interdiction targets inaccessible, fighter-bombers were directed to close-support targets identified by Mosquito controllers.

In July, Gus Marshall, accompanied by John Howe, Jessie Verster and Larry Eager, led an unusual mission. They took off from K-16 and set course for their interdiction sector north-east of Kaesong. While en route to the target area a Mosquito controller was heard making a desperate call for help with an urgent close-support task. Gus diverted his flight in response to the call and the controller guided him to a concentration of communist troops on the south bank of the Imjin River. The enemy was entrenched in difficult terrain and armed with numerous automatic weapons and anti-aircraft batteries.

Disregarding the danger, Gus led his flight in a series of skilfully co-ordinated attacks on the target. The flak was so intense that the controller expected aircraft casualties and instructed a USAF flight to stand by to cover a rescue operation. Both John Howe and Jessie Verster were surprised at their survival, and all four pilots were decorated, Gus Marshall with the DFC and the others with Air Medals.

Two notable 'Strangle' missions were flown in early June. Piet Strydom led four Mustangs against a section of secondary road cut into

Gus Marshall on completing 100 sorties

a hillside near Inch'on. Piet and his pilots effectively blocked a road in two places by causing a rockslide with their bombs. Then Syd de la Harpe led one of three interdiction missions against a road near Koksan with a river on one side and a steep mountain on the other. His flight cut the road in such a manner that it would have been impossible to make a by-pass.

Bob Rogers led an outstanding 'Strangle' mission. He was an experienced squadron commander in the Second World War. On 16 July, he was ordered to lead four aircraft on an interdiction mission to the

Bob Rogers (left) looks on while two American pilots make a pre-mission map check

Suan area. The target was covered with cloud on the hilltops, but undeterred, he found a gap over the main highway and with his wingman, Frank Montanari, he made a number of rocket and machine-gun attacks on a convoy of 11 vehicles. Although the narrow valley denied them room to manoeuvre, Bob and Frank destroyed eight and damaged three vehicles before climbing through the cloud to rejoin the other two members of the flight, Jack Haskins and Brian Martin. This episode had a sequel when on 17 August Bob was awarded the American DFC.*

The cumulative effect of the road interdiction programme was not satisfactory, and pilots reported that the communists were losing no time in repairing damaged roads; in fact, their ability to improvise with local materials and to muster virtually unlimited labour, both military and civilian, enabled them to repair roads and bridges in a remarkably short time. Those responsible for the communists' logistics were also helped by the lull in the fighting during July which greatly reduced the amount of supplies needed by the frontline troops.

---

* The above episode is illustrated by Ron Belling's jacket painting

A toast to a successful mission - Jack Haskins (left)

During the attacks on North Korean airfields the Fifth Air Force had to contend with an enlarged and more determined Chinese air force with better-trained pilots. Ray Armstrong had prepared to meet such a development, and this paid off on 8 July when he led eight Mustangs in a formation of 32 aircraft on a raid on Kandong airfield. It went off as planned, with two Cheetah flights going in last. The pilots dropped their bombs along the runway, most of them scoring direct hits, and as they were re-forming after the attack, Ray heard an American call 'MiGs' over the radio. He saw several enemy jets circling above the point where the Americans were busy reforming.

The MiG-15s did not appear to be interested in the Cheetah formation at first so Ray set course for the secondary target. However, while turning east, six MiGs dived towards the Cheetahs, adopting the pattern of attack that Ray had expected. Two came in on a quarter attack from the north, followed by two from the south, while the remaining pair provided top cover.

Ray used the defensive tactics that he had discussed with the squadron in April, and as the first two jets closed in he turned his flight towards them forcing the Chinese pilots to pull out of their dive without firing a shot. Further passes were thwarted as both flights turned about continually crossing over each other so that one of them was always in a position to meet an attack. As the Mustangs slowly lost height, the communist pilots made five or six more unsuccessful passes, some so near that the Cheetah pilots could see their faces. The MiGs then broke away northwards. The entire engagement had lasted five minutes.

On the same day Hardy Snyman led a successful strike against Ongjin airfield. His flight scored six hits on the runway. Another raid followed with two flights led by John Swanepoel in a formation of 32 aircraft against Sariwon airfield. This raid left communist repair crews

Emergency treatment practiced on Hardy Snyman

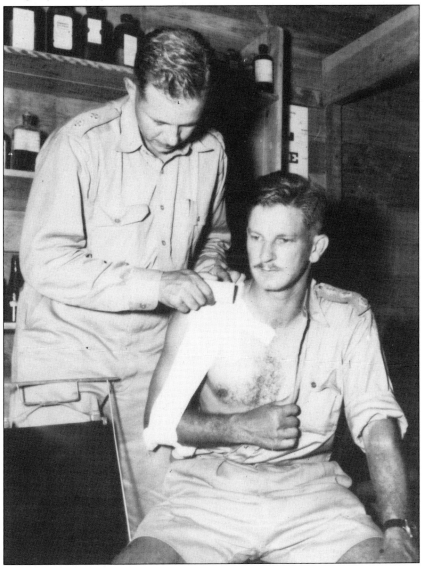

with a dangerous job for the night, for the bombs had been fitted with six-hour delay fuses. Under similar circumstances, all the available aircraft were committed to the airfield neutralisation programme for five days in late June and early July when the airfields at Sariwon, Anak, Haeju, Ongjin and Sinmak were the targets. The activities of the Flying Cheetahs undoubtedly helped to convince the communist planners that their airfield repair plan was a failure, and they abandoned it on 12 July.

The Cheetahs also took part in attacks on North Korean targets; deep penetration strikes designed to persuade the communist negotiators at Kaesong to be less intransigent. On the morning of 30 July, 91 Shooting Stars were briefed to suppress flak over P'yongyang in preparation for a raid by 354 Marine and Fifth Air Force fighter-bombers. A formation of 69 aircraft was dispatched by 18 Fighter-Bomber Wing on this raid including 12 Mustangs of 2 Squadron led by Bob Rogers. They napalmed and strafed an ammunition factory and were credited with 80 per cent cover of the target. In the afternoon three flights returned to P'yongyang on a similar mission but found the whole area covered with cloud, so they were diverted to a secondary target.

Two weeks later 18 Fighter-Bomber Wing again took part in mass raids on P'yongyang. However, because of the temporary abandonment of the partly flooded K-16, the raids had to be flown from K-10, which meant flying nearly twice the distance. They were described by pilots as real bum-busters! The long distance also entailed the swopping of one napalm bomb for a long-range tank, thus reducing load effectiveness.

Jan Blaauw, who had taken command of the squadron from Ray Armstrong on 26 July, led a morning raid with four flights of two aircraft plus two reserves on P'yongyang in a wing formation of 64 aircraft. When they reached the target area they dropped their napalm on a cluster of warehouses by the river bank and then strafed two anti-aircraft batteries. During the attack they came under intense anti-aircraft fire, and some of the pilots were somewhat apprehensive when they took off again later on a similar mission.

Jan Blaauw led the entire fighter-bomber wing of 64 Mustangs, including 17 from the Cheetah Squadron, on the afternoon raid. The target was a vehicle repair shop which was destroyed, and then they turned their guns on two river boats. This time the anti-aircraft guns offered only moderate opposition, but as Ian de Jongh was pulling out of his napalm run, he called up to say he had been hit, was heading for the coast and didn't think he'd make it.

Willem van den Bos, flying in the same flight, saw the stricken Mustang streaming glycol as it left the target area. Willem had been best man at the wedding of Ian's sister to Derek Doveton, whose sad death in action has been described earlier in these pages, and therefore he

Ian de Jongh

had a keen interest in Ian's welfare; but the napalm tank under the port wing of Willem's aircraft had hung up during the attack which prevented him from keeping up with Ian's aircraft. When Willem at last managed to jettison the tank it was too late, and his friend had disappeared westward into scattered cloud and was never seen or heard of again. Ian de Jongh was one of South Africa's most talented athletes. He held the national high-jump record and was undoubtedly a future Springbok rugby player.

Sadly, six Americans of 18 Fighter-Bomber Wing also lost their lives on this raid. The Cheetahs flew 35 sorties in a single day, a new record for the squadron in Korea.

The unsettled August weather caused operations from the forward base at K-16 to be suspended, for on 9 August the Han River, swollen by summer rains, threatened to flood runways and dispersal areas at Seoul. The re-arming and re-fuelling detachments were withdrawn until the river subsided nine days later. When the three officers and 54 other ranks returned to K-16 they were accompanied by all serviceable aircraft as the southern base was threatened by a typhoon.

During the last two weeks of August, 2 Squadron's targets were changed from roads to railway lines, because the Fifth Air Force had learnt that the bulk of communist supplies came from Manchuria by rail rather than by road since the former means of transport was far cheaper. It was therefore obvious that a better contribution to *Operation Strangle* would be made by cutting railway lines.

The main targets lay between Ch'ongju and Sariwon, Sinanju and Kunu-ri, Sunch'on and Sungch'on and Sariwon and Kaesong. The narrow railway lines were not easy targets, and even the multi-track sections were difficult to hit under certain conditions. On 22 August, for example, two Cheetah flights attacked a marshalling yard on the line between Kunu-ri and Sunch'on with an extraordinary lack of success when a high cross wind made accurate bombing impossible.

A number of rail-cutting strikes were successful during the last week in August. Raids were organised by 18 Fighter-Bomber Wing with two Cheetah flights flying as a part of a formation of up to 36 aircraft. Three formations covered by high-flying Sabres carried out two raids daily against the railway between Kaesong and the Ch'ongch'on River. As the communists defended their marshalling yards and bridges with improved anti-aircraft batteries, it became necessary to assign at least one flight per mission to the task of suppressing flak. By the end of August the communists were feeling the destruction of their railways and they were hard put to find ways of keeping the system working.

9

Luck Ran Out For Some

Between 20 May and 31 August 1951 a sad record was established with the loss of seven Cheetah pilots, either killed or missing in action, two more captured and 20 Mustangs crashed, some of them totally destroyed.

While flying on an armed reconnaissance mission early one morning at the beginning of June, Hector Macdonald became the first pilot to be captured by the communists. His flight napalmed a target at Ch'orwon and then flew northwards to look for targets of opportunity. Suddenly the leader, Albert Götze, heard a call over the radio: 'I'm baling out, I'm baling out!' But, as no call sign was given, he did not know who was baling out until he noticed that his No 2 was missing.

Searching for half an hour, Albie found wreckage strewn across the railway line near Ch'orwon, but he could not identify it. He had the impression that a high-speed landing had been attempted. Nothing more was heard of Hector, and it was assumed that he had been killed.

About six weeks later a 'Voice of India' radio broadcast was picked up in Usakos, South West Africa, which mentioned that a certain Lieutenant Macdonald was a prisoner of the communists. That was confirmed when Hector wrote to his brother four months later. The letter had been sent through the good offices of the 'Chinese People's Committee for World Peace against American Aggression.'

The next pilot was lost on 9 June, when Terry Liebenberg crashed on take-off. It was an accident similar to the one in which Micky Rorke was killed. Terry had experienced a lucky escape a week earlier, when his Mustang swung off the runway on landing. Nearly two weeks passed before the third disaster occurred, when Bob Frisby was leading an interdiction mission near Namch'anjom. His Mustang was hit by flak, and he called over the radio to say that he was baling out. Ray Armstrong, who was flying at No 3 position, saw the Mustang's canopy shoot off and a brown object fall from the crippled aircraft; but observed no parachute. Bob's aircraft crashed into a river-bed, and it was generally believed that he had baled out and that his parachute had failed to open.

Albie Götze

Within ten days of each other two more Cheetah pilots were lost. Jessie Verster was ferrying a Mustang from K-10 to K-16, where he failed to arrive. The wreckage of his aircraft and his body were found near the village of Sosan on the west coast. The engineering officer, Vic Kilburn, was sent to investigate the accident, and he found a hole in the ground made by the Mustang with the propeller buried below the surface. A Korean who had seen the crash told Vic that black smoke had been pouring from the aircraft, and while it was flying very low it had suddenly plunged straight into the ground, throwing the pilot clear just before the impact.

Vic found that the local Koreans had made a coffin for Jessie's body, which was placed on a makeshift altar with a cross flanked by two lighted candles and some flowers. Two school easels supported a number of wreaths, and the UN flag was displayed with inscriptions in Korean and English. Jessie was later buried in the UN cemetery at Tandok. The other casualty was an experienced pilot of the

Jessie Verster

Second World War, Bunny Pearce, who was killed under circumstances that will never be known. Bunny strayed from his flight while climbing through cloud above K-10 and failed to respond when the leader, Gus Marshall, called him on the radio. The wreckage of his Mustang was found near K-10 and it was evident that his aircraft, like that of Jessie Verster's, had hit the ground under power. He had left the Mustang before it crashed, and his body was found in a rice paddy nearby.

The Cheetahs suffered one of the severest blows of the entire campaign on 23 July when Freddy Bekker and Roy Du Plooy were killed and Mike Halley was captured. They had taken off from K-16, with Tony Green as the fourth member of the flight, to make a weather reconnaissance along the west coast. On completing their observations they bombed a bridge near Ch'orwon and then proceeded, at low altitude and in close formation, to look for other targets. While passing over a low hill they suddenly caught the full force of a salvo from a hidden communist anti-aircraft battery. Freddy's aircraft immediately caught fire and began to break up. He managed to jettison the canopy but he was enveloped in flames and crashed before he could bale out.

Mike's aircraft was hit as he went to investigate the wreckage of Freddy's Mustang, and he was forced to bale out; but he landed safely and waved to the circling pilots. Roy du Plooy then went down to protect Mike who was being threatened by the approach of communist troops camouflaged with branches of trees.

Meanwhile Tony Green raised the alarm on the emergency channel, and after about an hour a helicopter pilot announced his approach. Unfortunately Mike had already been captured. Before that Roy had continued to protect him until he ran out of ammunition, when he disappeared, and although the wreckage of his aircraft was found in the vicinity, his body was never found. In recognition of his gallantry in risking his own life to defend his wingman, Roy received the posthumous award of the American Silver Star.

These sad losses were partly balanced by some narrow escapes. On 22 July the cooling system of Bob Staat's Mustang was damaged by ground fire and he was obliged to abandon his aircraft over Wonsan harbour. He had the good fortune to be rescued from his inflated dinghy

Roy Duplooy's posthumous American Silver Star

by the crew of an American destroyer within 20 minutes. Unfortunately Bob was killed soon after returning for his second tour of operations.

Two days later Hardy Snyman's Mustang was hit over enemy territory. He managed to reach the east coast before the engine seized up forcing him to bale out into the sea. He was rescued by an SA-16 amphibian, and back at K-10 it was discovered that his right shoulder had been dislocated when his arm got tangled in his parachute harness. Another Mustang was lost during July, but the pilot, John Howe, was picked up by a helicopter in friendly territory after he had abandoned his aircraft when it developed a glycol leak.

A series of crash-landings occurred during August after a road bridge was attacked over the Imjin River near Ch'orwon. Mike Muller's Mustang was badly damaged by his own rocket blast, and with the hydraulic system out of action and the rudder cables severed, he made a flapless wheels-up landing at K-2. Mike had previously experienced a similar mishap during the same month when, due to hydraulic system failure, he landed without flaps at high speed.

Tony Green, who had been the only survivor of the fateful mission on the 23 July, nearly became a casualty himself at the end of August when his Mustang developed coolant failure on take-off from K-16. He jettisoned his bombs and crash-landed in a river-bed nearby. He emerged from the wreck shaken but unhurt.

The last landing mishap in August occurred while Jan Blaauw was returning from an interdiction mission on which his aircraft was seriously damaged. The rudder controls were shot away, and on landing his Mustang swung off the runway straight for a parked C-47. Jan avoided a collision by collapsing his undercarriage. When he inspected the aircraft, the engineering officer, Zulu van Rensburg, counted 12 hits on the wrecked aircraft.

Amidst all the stress created by casualties and accidents described in this chapter, the pilots and ground crews still found time for relaxation and recreation. Some resourceful handymen turned their attention to boat-building, while others used wood from ammunition boxes to make furniture. The summer also brought opportunities for games, and on 3 June a soccer team formed by the squadron played in the first match against a team from the Korean navy. The result was a 1-1 draw.

One of the most popular morale-building activities was the traditional braaivleis with a few extras for the benefit of American guests. At one such party which was a resounding success, the Cheetahs entertained 40 USAF personnel from 18 Fighter-Bomber Wing HQ and the other squadrons in the Wing. Meat and beer were available in abundance, but the highlight of the evening was the performance of a Zulu war dance by a SAAF impi ! The dancers' faces were blackened and they were dressed appropriately for the occasion. The stars of the show were the CO of the squadron, Ray Armstrong, and the Chaplain, Doempie Cloete.

Zulu War Dance

In August the first replacement of ground staff began to arrive in large numbers. Four officers and 66 other ranks landed at K-10, and within five days the change-over had been completed. The officer replacements were as follows:-

Adjutant: – Captain L P J Hechter for Captain P A le Grange.
Operations Officer: – Captain A Q de Wet for Captain M T Uys
Equipment Officer: – Captain D B Stofberg for Captain M Strydom.
Engineering Officer: – Lieutenant W J van Rensburg for Lieutenant V T Kilburn.

The ground personnel whose tour was over, consisting of six officers and 66 other ranks, left K-10 by air for Japan to embark on the MV Boissevain for the voyage home. The Korean war was over for them, but it would be more than two years before the last Cheetah Squadron personnel left the Far East.

A witchdoctor entertains the Americans

CHAPTER
10

Records Tumble

There was a limited offensive by the UN forces along the entire front during September and October 1951. The main plan was to improve defence positions and to maintain pressure on the communists. Of the small general advances, perhaps 'Operation Commando' was the most significant, when a new line was established to defend the Seoul-Ch'orwon railway line. There was also some heavy fighting in the mountainous terrain on the western side of the 'Punchbowl'.

On 25 October peace talks were once again convened at Panmunjom, and not only were limited offensives curtailed but on 12 November General van Fleet was told by General Ridgeway that a policy of active defence was to be adopted until further notice. He was also warned that the Eighth Army must be prepared to go on the offensive as soon as the opportunity arose to inflict substantial casualties.

At the beginning of September the Chinese Air Force made its appearance with new improvements, and UN intelligence announced that the complement of communist jets had been raised to 525 MiG-15s. The American Sabre jets were as good as the MiGs, but the Fifth Air Force had only two squadrons, based at Kimpo airfield (K-14). If more Sabres were to be introduced, then a number of airfields would have to be rebuilt and their runways extended. A start was made on Seoul airfield (K-16) and the re-armament and refuelling detachment of 2 Squadron was moved to Hoengsung airfield (K-44) from where the Cheetahs operated from 1 October.

Although the Sabres and Thunderjets provided a covering umbrella, UN fighter-bombers were frequently attacked by MiG-15s, and the Cheetahs witnessed incursions on several occasions. During September Barry Wiggett led two flights in a wing formation of 36 aircraft against rail and road bridges south of Kunu-ri. The last squadron over the target was 39 Squadron USAF which had joined 18 Fighter-Bomber Wing in May 1951 and as the 'Tail End Charlie' pulled out of the dive, three MiG's came in low and shot him down.

The screening of fighter-bombers by top cover was fairly effective, as Cheetah pilots confirmed during a railway interdiction mission north of P'yongyang. There was an aerial battle between F-86s and MiG-15s, and the enemy aircraft were kept at bay while the squadron attacked the target without interference.

A month later 2 Squadron had its second encounter with MiG-15s. On the morning of 2 November, eight Mustangs took off from K-46 on a group railway interdiction mission. Low cloud over the base caused confusion after take-off, with the result that two aircraft aborted and two returned early. The remaining four carried on to the target south of Sunan, where they found about 15 MiG-15s waiting for them. Two of the enemy aircraft broke away from the group and made a pass at the Mustangs. The leader, Amo Janse van Rensburg, followed the accepted procedure and turned his flight towards the attack, which caused the MiG-15s to break away. A third MiG then positioned itself high above the Cheetahs at 5 o'clock, but the attack was not pressed home, and as the Mustangs once more turned towards the enemy aircraft it broke away to the north.

Barry Wiggett (left) and Jan Blaauw plan a mission

Mustang with a full load climbs into the Korean sky

The efforts of the Chinese Air Force during this period met with little success, although they did hamper the activities of the fighter-bombers to a certain extent. The communists began to repair their existing airfields once more and to build new ones, and although heavy attacks were made by UN aircraft, which led to numerous air battles between MiG-15s and escorting UN Sabre jets, UN intelligence reported at the end of October that 90 enemy aircraft were on airfields south of the Yalu River.

During September and October fighter-bomber operations consisted mostly of interdiction missions to destroy railway lines. These comprised group formations of between 32 and 64 aircraft, usually one in the morning and another in the afternoon. Later, group formations were abandoned when the communist defences were greatly increased and suppression of flak became a necessary part of an operation. A squadron would take off, briefed to suppress flak in the target area, and the other squadrons would follow at five-minute intervals.

The railway interdiction missions flown by 2 Squadron during September were directed mainly against the section of double track between P'yongyang and Sinanju. Early in the month, before the threat of MiG-15s increased, sections of the main line between Sinanju and Sonch'on were attacked. Other lines that received the attention of the Cheetahs were the single tracks from P'yongyang to Kunu-ri, Sinanju to Kunu-ri, and Wonsan to Songch'on. On 1 September two flights took off as part of a wing formation from K-16. They were led by Larry Eagar and Willem van den Bos, and after cutting a section of the main railway

110

line in three places south-east of Sonch'on the two flights split up, with Larry and Willem looking for targets of opportunity along the main supply route. Willem found 300 railway wagons north of Sonch'on, which his flight attacked. They destroyed 15 and damaged 100. That afternoon the squadron returned to this very profitable target and Larry Eagar destroyed six more wagons and damaged 20.

Another flight flew with the wing on the same day, led by Mick Grinder. After making three cuts on the main line midway between Sunch'on and Sinanju, the flight proceeded on a routine reconnaissance of the main supply route. Throughout the mission they came under moderate but accurate AA fire. Towards the end of the reconnaissance Mick drew flak while investigating anti-aircraft positions in a wooded area south of Youn-dong. He called up on the radio to say that his aircraft had been hit, but he still proceeded to rocket and strafe the AA positions, followed by the rest of the flight. Six AA guns were destroyed. Sadly, Mick did not survive the attack. His No 2, Barry Wiggett, lost sight of him as he pulled up into the sun after a strafing run. Although Barry saw a canopy and some papers floating down at 1 500ft, there was no sign of a parachute. Later the wrecked aircraft was found, but there was no sign of life. From all accounts it appeared that Mick was emotionally upset when his close friend Ian de Jongh was shot down, and he started a personal vendetta against ack-ack gunners. He survived only two weeks after Ian's death before the guns got him.

On 19 September Bob Rogers led two flights on a wing raid on a railway bridge south of Sinanju. The attack went off as planned, and

Mike Grunder

Bob led his flights southwards to reconnoitre the main supply route. Farther south he found 150 railway wagons, which they attacked until they had used up all their ammunition. The claim amounted to a modest two wagons destroyed and 50 damaged.

We have already noted that the communists devised ingenious methods of deceiving pilots, and during October Cheetah flights came across several examples, such as a by-pass bridge at Sunch'on. Daylight photographs had indicated that there were two spans missing from the middle of the bridge, and it was assumed that it was unserviceable. However, photographs taken at night showed the two missing spans in place, which meant that the spans had been removed at dawn and replaced at dusk so that traffic could continue to use the bridge during the night without fear of attack. The combination of anti-aircraft defences, ingenious repair tactics and deception almost neutralised railway operations in November 1951.

Strangely enough, records show that as the intensity of the ground war decreased, so 2 Squadron's commitment to close-support increased. Between September and November 1951, when the Eighth Army was committed to limited offensives, 18 Fighter-Bomber Wing allocated close-support missions to a single squadron on daily rotation. That meant that the Cheetahs carried out such missions every fourth day.

The squadron also carried out occasional close-support missions on days when it was tasked primarily on interdiction duties. The targets lay along the Eighth Army front and they paid particular attention to the enemy resisting the gradual advance of IX Corps towards Kumsong and the attempts of X Corps to capture the key ridges to the west of the 'Punchbowl'.

One of the most important close-support efforts by 2 Squadron took place on 26 September 1951, the first anniversary of its departure from South Africa for the Far East. On that day the four squadrons of the Wing flew 122 combat sorties, and the Cheetahs improved their own record for the campaign by flying 40 sorties. These were flown during ten missions along the IX and X corps fronts, in which napalm, rockets and machine-guns were used against communist soldiers in well-established defensive positions. The claims for the day amounted to 13 buildings and two field guns destroyed, four buildings damaged, and an unknown number of enemy troops killed.

Most of the pilots on duty that day flew three missions, but one flight, consisting of Denis Earp, Chris Lombard, Daantjie Marchand and Horse Horsecroft, was credited with four missions. Their duration varied from 1hr 5mins to 1hr 35mins. Such a strenuous programme made great demands on both pilots and ground crews. The new record of 40 sorties in a single day did not stand for long, for on 4 October Cheetah oper-

Willem van den Bos

ations reached a peak when 48 combat sorties were flown in one day in support of IX and X Corps.

During the day Basil Wilson chalked up the squadron's total of 5 000 sorties for the campaign. The first mission took off at 05h45 and the last landed at 19h00. There were no aborts during more than 12 hours of continuous combat, a remarkable effort in view of the fact that the squadron possessed only 15 combat-ready aircraft, eight of which flew four consecutive missions. This achievement was almost equalled three weeks later when ten close-support missions and one air-rescue-patrol were flown. A faulty radio, detected during a pre-flight check, caused one pilot to abort while still on the ground, giving the squadron 43 combat sorties on 25 October. The same pattern of close-support missions continued into the next month, with 40 missions flown again on 8 November.

When a pilot was shot down it was the leader's responsibility to alert air-rescue, or if the leader himself went down then it was the responsibility of his deputy to make contact. An air-rescue patrol would also be provided to protect the downed pilot from enemy interference while he was awaiting rescue. It was the duty of the leader or second-in-command to guide in the rescue helicopter, and if necessary hand

113

Mike Muller

over the patrolling to a relieving flight. Detailed air rescue data, including radio frequencies and locations of air and sea rescue facilities, were given to all pilots during pre-flight briefings. The existence of the air-rescue system was good for the morale of the Cheetah pilots who believed that pilots landing in enemy territory would be shot on capture, especially if they fell into the hands of North Korean militia in an area where a strike had just been carried out.

Between 1 September and 12 November 1951 the pilots of 2 Squadron took part in several air rescue patrols. On 5 September, 12 out of a total of 24 rescue sorties were flown, and it was on that day that Willem van den Bos was shot down while engaged in the rescue of an American pilot. During the search behind enemy lines north-east of Sunch'on, Willem's Mustang was hit in the cooling system by small-arms fire, and his engine failed at 800ft. He decided to crash-land, and chose the bed of a shallow stream to land in. The aircraft caught fire while it was still airborne, but Willem made a successful landing, leapt from the cockpit and took cover in a nearby ditch.

Meanwhile two more Cheetah flights led by Don Parker and Flash Biden arrived on the scene to help, and about three-quarters of an hour

114

after being shot down Willem was rescued by helicopter and flown to a ship in Wonsan harbour. Unfortunately Flash Biden was lost a few hours later, when his Mustang failed to pull out of a shallow dive during a napalm attack against a communist artillery position in the 'Punchbowl' area.

Four days later the rescue helicopters were again alerted when Dormie Barlow was forced to bale out 20 minutes after take-off because of engine failure. The abandoned Mustang crashed just below Dormie, and the explosion of its bombs caused his parachute to collapse partially. He landed heavily and was knocked unconscious. When he came to he was alarmed to find a crowd of curious Koreans surrounding him. Fortunately this had taken place in friendly territory, and a helicopter came promptly to the rescue and flew Dormie to 121 Evacuation Hospital, where he was treated for an injured back.

On 3 October Mike Muller, who had survived a crash landing in August, had another unhappy experience. An hour after taking off from K-16 leading one of two Cheetah flights in a wing formation briefed for a raid against the Kunu-ri - Kanggye railway line, there were two loud explosions under his aircraft and glycol began spewing from the engine and streaming past the cockpit. Capped by his No 3, Amo Janse van

The standard survival kit

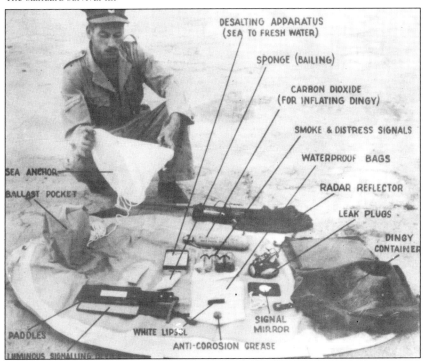

115

Rensburg and the other two members of the flight, Eric Keevy and Frank Grobler, Mike headed eastwards, but within minutes the engine temperature was off the clock and he had to bale out. Mike tells the story of the entire drama in Chapter 18.

Another Cheetah pilot was less fortunate. After he had completed 65 sorties Denis Earp became the victim of a set of circumstances in which the rescue drill failed. On 27 September he was forced to bale out behind the enemy's forward position north-east of Keasong, when his Mustang was damaged in the cooling system. During the descent he drew small-arms fire from the ground, but he escaped injury apart from twisting a knee on landing. His flight began to circle the area, and it was

Denis Earp is decorated

Chris Lombard

joined by a flight from 39 Squadron. But these aircraft could not see the communist soldiers closing in on Denis, who was very much aware of his predicament.

He was in the path of a Chinese search party spread out in three lines searching the undergrowth. They had camouflaged themselves with branches and they moved only when the aircraft were out of sight. Denis hid in a ditch and avoided discovery by all three lines of searchers as they passed nearby. He decided that his best course of action would be to follow the search party, and as he was on the point of leaving the shelter of the ditch to do so, a single soldier stumbled upon him. Denis and the startled Chinese infantryman stood facing each other, the former trying to free his revolver from its holster and the latter fumbling with the safety catch of his rifle. Before either could do anything, the alarm was given, and Denis began a term of 23 harrowing months as a prisoner of war.

The failure to rescue Chris Lombard when he baled out over enemy territory on 7 October gave rise to a mystery that was cleared up only

Ron Beamish

when he was released after the armistice. While on his way to attack the main railway line north of Sonch'on he was forced to abandon his aircraft because of the failure of the electrical system. He descended safely, and his flight saw him lay out his parachute and walk about.

The valley where he landed seemed to be deserted, and after 47 minutes the Cheetah aircraft, which were running low on fuel, were relieved by an American flight of F-80s. These pilots reported that they had seen Chris running up a river-bed accompanied by two figures, but when the rescue helicopter arrived he could not be found. There was at the time no means of knowing whether he had been helped by friendly guerrilla fighters or captured by the communists; but as we know now, it was the latter.

Besides Mick Grunder and Flash Biden, three more Cheetah pilots were lost in action during this period. Frank Montanari was leading a reconnaissance at first light near P'yongyang when they found the target area enveloped in heavy cloud. Frank saw some gaps and ordered his pilots to patrol the area while he went down low to reconnoitre a road.

Joe Meiring

His aircraft was hit by heavy flak and his No 2, Ron Beamish, saw the crippled Mustang streaming glycol as it pulled away from the road. Frank then attempted to crash-land in a river-bed, but the aircraft disintegrated on impact. Heavy flak prevented close investigation.

Within a week of each other, two young pilots, Critton Pappas and Theo Joyce, went missing under similar circumstances. On 29 October, while he was on a railway interdiction mission near Inch'on, Critton disappeared during the attack. A brilliant explosion on a hill south of the town suggested that he had crashed into the hillside on his bombing run. On 4 November Theo disappeared during an attack on a village north-east of Sibyon-ni. It was his first combat mission. Bats Maskell reported seeing a bright silvery flash as Theo's aircraft pulled out of the bombing dive. It appeared that his Mustang had exploded after being hit by anti-aircraft fire, although no flak had been seen in the vicinity. Sabotage at base could not be ruled out.

119

Joe Meiring was more fortunate. On 30 October he led a close-support mission against an enemy command post in the village of T'osan. The target was well defended by anti-aircraft guns, and as he was pulling out after dropping napalm, his Mustang was hit in the starboard wing, tailplane and fuselage. The front line was a short distance to the south, and he headed for an emergency landing-strip behind the UN positions. After touching down, the crippled aircraft bounced, hit the ground once more, ran out of airstrip, jumped a wide ditch and came to rest in a heap of sand. Joe's harness broke and he was thrown forward, hitting his head against the gunsight. Fortunately the hard helmet that he was wearing saved serious injury. The Cheetahs went in low over their targets but paid the price for the increased accuracy obtained. Horse Sivertsen, Jean de Wet and Ken Whitehead had unpleasant experiences when their Mustangs were damaged by flying debris over the target. On 20 September Horse was leading a glide bombing attack using general purpose bombs with eight-second delay fuses against a railway yard between Chonju and Sinanju. To make sure of hitting the target he delayed releasing his bombs and flew into a mass of black earth thrown up by the explosion of a bomb from another aircraft. The wheels, tailplane and canopy of his machine were badly damaged, and the engine began to run roughly. Horse was escorted back to K-16 by a USAF flight, and on arrival the airfield was cleared for an emergency landing. While turning on to finals he had difficulty in controlling the Mustang which suddenly lost power. It hit the ground at high speed before reaching the runway and although Horse's most serious injury was a lacerated forehead, the aircraft was a write-off.

Five days later AB de Wet's face was cut when his canopy was smashed by the debris thrown up by an ox-cart that exploded violently when strafed! Ken Whitehead's aircraft was damaged on 9 November when he flew too low during a bombing run and an exploding bomb tore his canopy and damaged a wing- tip. He was escorted back to K-16 and landed safely.

By the end of 1951 the administration of 2 Squadron had become largely a matter of routine. The personnel of Liaison HQ in Tokyo, who had given such excellent service, had been rotated during August 1951, and by the end of September the newly arrived officers were handling the affairs of the squadron just as efficiently as their predecessors. The rotation of pilots and ground crew had continued regularly, the pilots being flown home as soon as their operational tours had been completed, and a steady stream of pilots and ground crew arrived regularly at K-10. The old supply of veteran pilots with experience in the Second World War was drying up and being replaced by young volunteers from citizen-force squadrons.

Jan Blaauw on completing 100 combat sorties

On 10 September the second batch of ground personnel whose tours had expired (one officer and 24 other ranks) and who had served with the squadron during its first year in Korea, left K-10 for Yokohama, where they boarded a ship for the long-awaited voyage home. This completed the first rotation of ground personnel, and they left behind an enviable reputation for a high standard of work under circumstances that had sometimes bordered on the impossible. Their successors became aware of the high standard set when comment was received from an impartial source on 14 October in the form of a letter addressed to the Commanding-General for the Far East Air Material Command by

Messrs Wright Patterson of Ohio, the manufacturers of the Mustang:

> The scope of the engine maintenance work performed by the
> South African Air Force reflects complete knowledge of the
> Packard Rolls-Royce engine and is commendable.'

This letter was passed on to the CO of 2 Squadron with the endorsement:

> 'I wish to state that I am very pleased with the
> maintenance standards and the 'know-how' of your
> engineering section.'

Every pilot who flew with the Cheetah squadron in Korea was aware of the value of the ground crews. Such outstanding results on operations could never have been achieved without the ability and devotion to duty of these men who worked long hours in all kinds of weather to keep the aircraft flying. They were proud of their aircraft and of the men who flew them.

The great event on the ground on 26 September was the celebration of the first anniversary of the departure of the squadron from South Africa for Korea. A party was held at the Special Service Club at K-10. The guests included General Rogers (recently promoted), and the heads of various sections. Toby Moll, the Senior Liaison officer, who had taken over from Jan Pretorius, was there, and the party served as a farewell to Jan Blaauw who had completed his 100th combat sortie and handed over the reins of the squadron to Barry Wiggett. Jan Blaauw was the last pilot of the original draft that had sailed from Durban on the *Tjisadane*. There was a sequel to the celebration that evening, when every officer received a confidential letter from General Rogers expressing the serious view that he took of certain forms of celebration, which included stamping holes in the floor and throwing furniture and glasses about! As the Cheetah squadron celebrated at K-10 everyone could look back on a year during which the squadron had overcome difficulties in administration, operational conditions, inter-air force co-operation and morale, to become a well integrated, highly respected fighting unit. In fact, by the end of the first year a large part of its task in Korea had been accomplished. If the statistics for the entire campaign are taken into consideration, by the end of the first year the squadron had already flown 40 per cent of the sorties, lost 59 per cent of the pilots listed as missing or killed in action, received 36 per cent of its American DFCs and written off 46 per cent of the aircraft lost. Within two months of the first anniversary celebration, the war on the ground was to enter a completely new phase and the intensity and nature of the air war was to change accordingly.

CHAPTER

11

The Pattern Changes

The entire pattern of the ground fighting changed in October 1951, and the front line, except for the occasional tactical offensive, remained fairly static across the entire neck of the peninsula until the signing of the armistice in 1953. The situation might be compared to that of the 1914-1918 war, with the accent on an intricate series of trenches, artillery and mortar fire, patrols and raids.

Air power was the United Nations' main means of applying pressure to influence the peace talks on the ground. The communists had increased their forces by 265 000 men as against an increase of only 57 776 by the UN. The missions carried out by 2 Squadron in the next six months can be divided into railway interdiction, supply and troop interdiction, neutralisation of forward troops, artillery and mortar positions, main route reconnaissance and stand-by rescue patrols.

During interdiction and close-support missions, many of the responsibilities of the squadron consisted of flak suppression. Some operations were often dual-purpose, with rescue patrols and interdiction missions to reconnoitre main supply routes while returning to base. Interdiction missions were flown in far greater number than other types of operations because the main aim of the United Nations at that time was to attempt to reduce the quantity of supplies reaching the communist front line.

The rail interdiction raids of *Operation Strangle* continued according to the mid-1951 pattern, and 18 Fighter-Bomber Wing flew on morning and afternoon missions on a smaller scale, with 16 to 24 aircraft per formation as against the former 32 to 64. The flak-suppression element in each formation was increased to at least one flight armed with proximity-fused bombs. These flights did not always go in first. Often, when the need to locate silent anti-aircraft batteries arose, a normal flight was sent ahead to draw the fire, so enabling the flak-suppression pilots to spot and destroy their targets. The *Strangle* missions flown by 2 Squadron from November 1951 to February 1952 were directed almost exclusively against two short stretches of the double main line between P'yongyang and Sariwon and the secondary line between Sunch'on and Hwadong-ni.

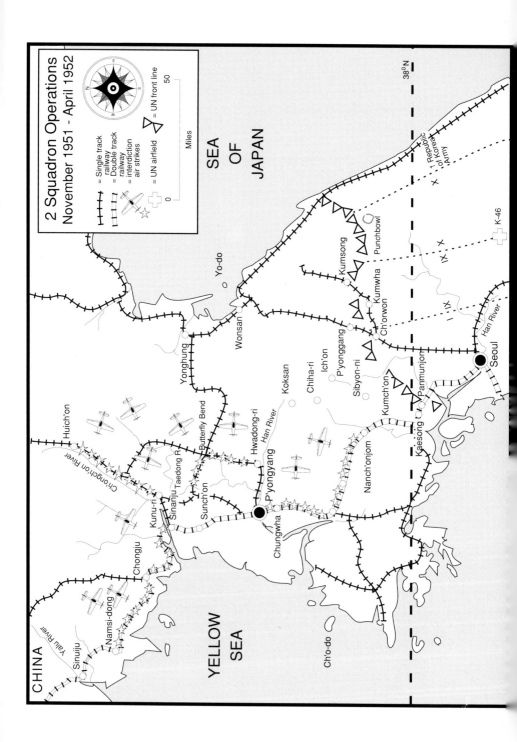

2 Squadron Operations
November 1951 - April 1952

= Single track railway
= Double track railway
= interdiction air strikes
= UN airfield
= UN front line

Miles
0   50

N
E
S
W

SEA OF JAPAN

38°N

Republic of Korea 1 Army

K-46

Punchbowl
Kumsong
Kumwha
Kumhwa
Ch'orwon
P'yonggang
Ich'on
Chiha-ri
Koksan
Sibyon-ni
Kumch'on
Panmunjom
Kaesong
Seoul
Han River

Wonsan
Yo-do
Yonghung

Huich'on
Butterfly Bend
Taedong R
Sinanju
Sunch'on
Kunu-ri
Chongju
Namsi-dong
Sinuiju
Yalu River
Ch'ongch'on River
CHINA

Hwadong-ri
Han River
P'yongyang
Chungwha
Nanch'onjom

YELLOW SEA
Ch'o-do

124

The main danger to fighter-bombers in these raids was from anti-aircraft weapons, which the communists had placed in increased numbers along vulnerable sections of the main supply routes. MiG-15s that occasionally ventured south of the Ch'ongch'on River were another danger. By the beginning of 1952, after more than eight months of *Operation Strangle,* the railway interdiction missions by 2 Squadron had become a routine exercise. The only breaks in the monotony occurred with the loss of a pilot or an aircraft or both.

The unfortunate consequences of a pilot becoming separated from his flight were clearly brought home on 24 November, when George Krohn was posted missing in action. Three Cheetah flights had been briefed to join a Wing formation on a railway interdiction mission against a target south of Sunch'on. A radiator defect had caused George to leave ten minutes after his own flight, and he was seen passing two USAF flights trying to catch up with the Mustangs of 2 Squadron. After they had finished their attacks on the target, George reported over the radio that he intended to attack with a USAF flight. The last American to leave the target reported that he had seen George attacking and had watched his bombs exploding. He had also seen a lone Mustang heading southwards, but nothing more was heard of George.

Amo Janse van Rensburg

Amo Janse van Rensburg was lost a few days later over a secondary target. His flight was briefed for flak suppression on a routine *Operation Strangle* raid. No flak was observed over the primary target, and when pilots did not use all their ordnance, the flight flew on to the secondary target, a village used as a supply dump south east of Suan. This target was duly attacked, and while they were forming up, light flak hit Amo's aircraft, which began to leak glycol. It suddenly dived towards the ground out of control and Jimmy Parsonson, flying No 3, was forced to take evasive action to avoid a collision. Ken Hansen, at No 4, saw Amo slumped forward in his seat as the Mustang began its dive and then plunged into the ground.

Jimmy Parsonson was the next victim of communist ground fire on 6 January 1952 under circumstances similar to those that had led to the loss of Amo. He was hit while making a second strafing run on a secondary target north-east of Kumsong. He flew southwards, but before reaching friendly territory his Mustang caught fire and crashed.

A third pilot in a very similar situation nine days later, escaped with his life but lost his freedom. After attacking the Sunch'on - Hwadon-ni railway, Reg Gasson followed his leader, John Trotter, into an attack against a supply dump east of Sibyon-ni. His Mustang was hit by ground fire during the strafing run. He headed southwards and baled out when

Reg Gasson

his clothes caught fire. As he abandoned the aircraft he was thrown against the stabiliser fin and broke his leg. Ten minutes after he had landed, a helicopter arrived, but the pilot could not rescue him because of the intense ground fire.

Reg spent the next 14 months in communist POW camps and was released during *Operation Little Switch* on 20 April 1953. He was the first SAAF POW to be released, and he was awarded the Bronze Star in recognition of the information that he was able to give United Nations intelligence officers.

Two weeks later Rex Earp-Jones fell into enemy hands while flying No 4 on a railway interdiction mission. After attacking the target between Sunch'on and Hwadong-ni the flight set course for K-46, and when halfway home the engine of Rex's Mustang suddenly spluttered and cut out. He baled out, landed on a thick layer of soft snow near Chiha-ri and was captured. After a preliminary interrogation he was marched in front of a Chinese infantry platoon. He thought he was about to be shot and was greatly relieved when finding that the firing party which claimed to have brought his aircraft down with rifle fire only, wanted to have a look at their prize! Rex spent the rest of the war as a prisoner.

According to UN intelligence reports the communists made a desperate attempt to defeat *Operation Strangle* and they managed to get a fair amount of supplies through to the front line. Apart from increasing flak concentrations and deception tricks, they used their main advantage over the United Nations forces, which was manpower, and it was estimated that half a million military and civilian workers were employed on repairing damage to railways. Aerial photographs confirmed that any damage was repaired within eight hours.

General Ridgeway and General Weyland realised that a different scheme had to be adopted to improve interdiction results, and during February 1952 *Operation Saturate* was adopted. Four sections of railway line were to be chosen and intensive saturation bombing round the clock was to be carried out by fighter-bombers during the day and by B-26 bombers during the night. Until this new operation commenced on 3 March 1952, ordinary interdiction attacks were to continue.

The new operation was to motivate 2 Squadron into new activity, for during March 1952, 470 combat sorties were flown as against 266 in February 1951, the lowest total since December 1950. The area chosen for *Saturate* was between the Ch'ongch'on and Yalu Rivers, mainly because the flak there was limited, the Chinese probably relying on their MiG-15s to keep the area clear of fighter-bombers. But there had been a perceptible lack of enterprise and aggressiveness by the Chinese pilots since the beginning of 1952, and they seldom appeared south of the Ch'ongch'on River.

Dave Taylor

The first of the two South African pilots to be shot down by an enemy aircraft during the Korean war was lost in March 1952. Dave Taylor had been in Korea for only seven days when on 25 February he had a narrow escape coming in to land at K-10 after a training flight. While on final approach his Mustang stalled and cartwheeled into Chinhae Bay. He was rescued by two American master sergeants, S M Starks and R Renaud. The latter risked his life to free Dave from the submerged cockpit and he was awarded the Soldier's Medal for bravery in recognition of this deed.

Dave Taylor's luck ran out on 20 March 1952, when Able and Dog Flights of 2 Squadron took part in three strikes by 18 Fighter-Bomber Wing against the Sunch'on-Kuadong-ni section of the railway. Eight Mustangs led by Commandant Dick Clifton, who had assumed command of the squadron from Barry Wiggett in January, took off on the third strike for a flak suppression mission in support of the rest of the Wing, which followed at a short interval to attack the railway line at BU4665, a section known as 'Butterfly Bend'. On the way to the target one of the second section aircraft developed a rough engine and was escorted back to base leaving only six Mustangs to carry on to the target, where heavy flak greeted them, the gun flashes pinpointing the aiming point.

Dick Clifton wasted little time leading his pilots into the attack. As he pulled out of his bombing dive in a climbing turn to observe results, the sky suddenly seemed full of MiGs, no doubt attracted by the black puffs of bursting flak. Dave Taylor's Mustang was hit by cannon shells while it was pulling out of the dive, and he turned towards the south with his aircraft streaming glycol and black smoke. Joe Joubert, Mac Maclaughlin and Hans Enslin formed up with the leader in tight battle formation covering Dave while Vin Kuhn, managed to fight his way into the safety of a cloud bank.

(L/R) Mac McLaughlin, Dick Clifton, Bruce Barnard after mêlée with MiG-15s

When forced to turn towards two MiGs, which made a series of quarter attacks, the leader's section lost sight of Dave's aircraft, and while Dick was watching the two enemy aircraft, Joe Joubert's sharp eyes spotted another MiG sneaking up quite slowly from behind and below. Joe's warning came in the nick of time, for as the enemy jet opened fire on the leader, the formation broke to port and the MiG overshot in a shallow climb. Hans Enslin, who was in the most advantageous position, fired a long burst into the jet and hit it in the port wing-root. Later these hits were confirmed by gun-camera photographs, and Hans was credited with a 'damaged MiG-15'. This proved enough to discourage the

Hans Enslin

MiGs from further attacks, and the Cheetahs were able to turn their attention to a search for their comrade. But Dave Taylor had disappeared and was never heard of again.

The first *Operation Saturate* missions across the Ch'ongch'on River in which the Cheetah Squadron took part were on 25 and 26 March. The operations officers of the Fifth Air Force had chosen a stretch of railway line between Chongju and Sinanju. It was based on a road-bed built up through swampy terrain which the repair gangs would find difficult to negotiate during the spring thaw. The role of the squadron on this operation was flak suppression. During April 1952 the Cheetahs flew on strikes north of the Ch'ongch'on River along the railway line to Namsi-dong. Raids on 6 April against targets north-west of Sunch'on were the most northerly missions that had been flown for some months by Mustangs, and it was inevitable that they should attract the attention of MiG-15 patrols. Three of the four formations of 18 Fighter-Bomber Wing were attacked in the target area and on one of these occasions 2 Squadron was present.

On the second raid of the day, as the wing approached the target at 8 000ft, a Cheetah flight of four led by Al Rae was attacked by four

130

MiG-15s. Al ordered his pilots to jettison their bombs and turn towards the enemy aircraft, and he fired two machine-gun bursts at one of the MiGs as it passed. The jets did not return.

The attrition rate of the aircraft of the Fifth Air Force during the interdiction campaign had been high, and 2 Squadron suffered proportionately. At the time when Holtzie Holtzhausen's aircraft was lost, the number of Mustangs on the strength of 2 Squadron had been reduced to only 12. Since the end of May 1951, when *Operation Strangle* had been in progress, the numbers of aircraft lost by the squadron were four in June, nine in July, four in August, 18 over September, October and November, two in December, eight in January 1952, four in February and four over March and April, although not all these aircraft were lost on interdiction missions.

(L/R) Al Rae - Jimmy Newton - John Montgomery

The Fifth Air Force had also suffered heavily on the interdiction campaign, and by April 1952 it had lost 243 fighter-bombers, of which only 131 had been replaced. Although the Sinuiju to Sinanju railway line was put out of action during April, there were not enough aircraft available to make interdiction strikes on the alternative rail routes. Since 12 November 1951 interdiction attacks had not been confined to railway lines and installations alone. Supply dumps and troop concentrations were also attacked when they could be accurately located. Some troops and supplies had successfully evaded the strikes against the communist transport system, but they were usually found just north of the front line stretching along a belt across the waist of the peninsula. These strikes were carried out by specially detailed aircraft or by rail interdiction flights seeking alternative targets.

At the beginning of 1952 general purpose bombs were normally used instead of napalm when it was found that because of the static nature of the war the communists had been able to build substantial bunkers for both troops and supplies. On New Year's day 1952 John Montgomery was briefed to lead seven Mustangs on a strike against communist storage areas east of Sibyon-ni and north of the front line. Two of the Mustangs carried proximity-fused bombs, the rest napalm.

During the first strafing run Pikkie Rautenbach, who was flying at No 3 in the second flight, pulled away from the target with his aircraft streaming glycol. It had received a direct hit by an explosive shell on the engine cowling just behind the spinner. Pikkie flew his burning aircraft back to friendly lines determined not to be taken prisoner. He flew low, using the minimum power to keep airborne. He released his harness, unplugged his radio leads, jettisoned the canopy and crouched with both feet on the seat flying by stick alone while peering out of the starboard side of the cockpit, because flames and smoke obscured forward vision.

After passing over the front line he sprang clear, and his parachute opened immediately depositing him safely in friendly territory. At that moment his Mustang struck a hilltop and exploded. As he lay there, winded and covered by the collapsed parachute, he was found by a member of 45 Infantry Division, who told him that he was in the middle of a minefield. He was taken to Divisional HQ and flown back to K-46 in a liaison aircraft.

Two days later Jimmy Newton had a similar but less dramatic experience while flying No 3 in a formation of eight aircraft. The target was a village east of Namch'onjam housing troops and supplies. On their arrival in the area the Cheetahs were kept orbiting for one-and-a-half hours, being passed from one controller to another before the target was at last indicated. The two leading Mustangs had been briefed and armed for flak suppression, so it fell to Jimmy to lead the remaining six aircraft

Pikkie Rautenbach is decorated

into the attack in the face of intense and accurate fire from small-arms and automatic weapons.

His aircraft was hit by a bullet that passed through the cockpit between his neck and the armour plating behind his seat. As he turned towards friendly territory there were holes in the port fuel tank and oil cooler, and the oil pressure indicated nil. He had crossed the UN lines when the Mustang began to burn, and he baled out and landed in a tree beside the command post of an American artillery officer who gave him a mug of coffee and sent him back to the squadron in a helicopter.

It has already been mentioned that interdiction missions were necessary to prevent enemy supplies and troop re-enforcements from

133

reaching the front line. By the same token, although a stalemate situation existed on the front line, certain targets had to be attacked and 2 Squadron played its full share on close-support to the Eighth Army, many strikes being made against fortifications which had been built in the enemy front line during the static situation.

It was after a close-support mission that Frank Grobler had an unusual experience while leading a strike against communist infantry dug in along a ridge west of Ch'orwon. A Mosquito controller had placed a white smoke rocket to mark the target, but it fell too far to the

Jimmy Newton

west and Frank decided that he would indicate the target to the rest of the flight by means of a strafing run. Pulling away from the attack, he found that the enemy's ground fire had caused his Mustang's control column to jam in a central position and the elevators were unusable. He still had aileron control so he orbited south of the target with his No 2 Cliff Collins, until the other pilots had completed their attack. While attempting to turn for base he lost aileron control and was forced to bale out over friendly territory. His flight patrolled above him for ten minutes until a helicopter from an army forward airstrip picked him up. He was returned to K-46 three days later in a liaison aircraft.

A close-support target on 14 January 1952 resulted in the writing off of another Mustang flown by Nic van Zyl. John Trotter had led six Mustangs in an attack on four artillery positions on the north-western edge of the 'Punchbowl'. Their bombs were dropped on the target without incident but after the first rocket run Nic reported engine trouble and turned for home. His engine failed soon after he left the target area, and he made a good wheels-up landing on an emergency strip just inside friendly territory. He was uninjured, but the Mustang was damaged beyond repair.

CHAPTER

12

Ops, Hops and Tributes

While the peace talks were in progress at Panmunjom, 2 Squadron had shared in the task of patrolling the main supply route from P'yongyang to Kumch'on. The primary purpose of these patrols was to keep an eye on the vehicles used by the communist delegates and their personnel while they were on their way to the site of the talks, and by mutual agreement they were to display red panels. The secondary purposes were to collect information and to destroy targets of opportunity. The Cheetahs began flying on these missions on 28 November 1951, and on that day their Mustangs patrolled the main supply route in pairs between P'yongyang and Kumch'on for periods varying from two-and-a-half, to five hours. At first, the aircraft were only armed with machine-guns although later, four rockets were carried for flak suppression. Sightings of red panelled vehicles were regularly reported by pilots enabling UN intelligence to watch the movements of the communist peace teams and ascertain whether their vehicles were being used as a screen for carrying troops and material.

On a mission flown by Holtzie Holtzhausen and Jan van der Merwe to reconnoitre a main supply route near Panmunjom, a clear picture is given of a pilot's task and the variety of information that can be gathered on this type of operation. The report at debriefing disclosed that besides several vehicles displaying red panels, an airfield had been observed near Hwango with a long runway and adjoining parking bays. There were dummy craters in the runway and the genuine bomb craters on the perimeter contained ack-ack guns. The bridge at Sinwon-ni was serviceable; it was estimated that there were six heavy ack-ack guns at Namch'onjam where an uncoupled locomotive was strafed. Three vehicles without red panels were seen at Chomghwa, but they were not attacked because a flak trap was suspected.

Aircraft patrolling the main supply route were exposed to constant anti-aircraft fire, and during January 1952 Shadow Gardiner-Atkinson's aircraft was hit in one wing by a shell that blew a hole in it big enough for a man to stand in. There was no question of baling out, because the moment Shadow released the control column, the aircraft would flick-

136

roll, and he'd have no chance of getting clear of the cockpit. He checked the lowest controllable speed of the aircraft and then reported to base that he would be coming in for a high-speed crash landing. He made a perfect belly landing, there was no fire and it was not long before the damaged parts were replaced and the Mustang was flying again.

From the first week of January onwards, the Cheetahs took part in the general rescue organisation of the Fifth Air Force. If their aircraft were hit, pilots over North Korea were briefed to make for Ch'o-do Island off the west coast or for Yo-do Island in Wonsan Harbour off the east coast. When a pilot baled out or his aircraft made a forced landing in enemy territory, an immediate patrol was provided by the remaining members of the flight until they could be relieved by standby flights orbiting the islands. Most of standby patrol missions by 2 Squadron were made over Ch'o-do Island, where they formed part of a team with a Grumman Amphibian aircraft from 3 Rescue Squadron, also in continual orbit. Two Sikorsky helicopters on strip alert at Ch'o-do completed the rescue team.

When strikes by fighter-bombers of the Fifth Air Force on Ch'ongch'on River region became more frequent, the Ch'o-do 'standby' rescue patrols allocated to 2 Squadron increased sharply from 4 per cent in December 1951 to 23 per cent in April 1952. From mid-April these operations were shared by the four squadrons of 18 Fighter-Bomber Wing, with each squadron contributing one aircraft to each mission. It was while flying in such a composite flight that Gus Baransky was lost on 12 April. The flight was called inland from its orbit position over Ch'o-do to help two downed pilots west of Sonch'on. Gus's aircraft was seen to crash in flames during the rescue patrol.

Next day 2 Squadron flew 15 rescue patrol sorties out of a total of 18 for the day. The first sortie effected the rescue of the pilot whom Gus Baransky had been protecting when he was lost. Wilbur Clark and Wally Hefer took off in the early morning, escorted the Sikorsky helicopter to the spot where the USAF pilot had been shot down near Sunch'on, and while it landed to rescue him, Wally made several strafing runs to keep the enemy away from the area. They then escorted the chopper safely back to base. Their efforts were commended in a signal from the Commander of the Fifth Air Force, General Everest, who said: 'The nature of the operation was not only hazardous but demanded the closest timing and the highest degree of airmanship. I would like to commend the pilots who contacted the downed pilot and escorted the helicopter. It is evident that they used sound judgement and excellent flying technique during the operation.'

The squadron had an odd encounter during the first week of December 1951 after reports had been received that Chris Lombard, who had disappeared after baling out two months earlier, had not been

Wilbur Clark completes 75 combat sorties

captured by the communists but was in the hands of friendly guerrillas, and that a rescue was possible. Frank Grobler was entrusted with the attempt at rescue, and he led three Mustangs in a search of the mountainous area in the middle of the peninsula, midway between Kunu-ri and Yonghung, not far from the spot where Chris had last been seen. They searched unsuccessfully for more than an hour and a half only hearing a shrill radio signal as if someone was trying to make contact with them.

Frank returned to the area the next day in a USAF 'PIG' (a Mustang specially converted to carry a passenger) accompanied by a South Korean Army officer, Lieutenant Hong. This time radio contact was made with a Korean agent on the ground, and Frank arranged for Chris Lombard to be picked up at a given rendezvous the next morning. He duly led a rescue mission of four Mustangs and a helicopter to the agreed area, where contact was made again with the Korean agent who was asked to bring Lombard into the open for identification. He refused to comply, and, suspecting a trap, Frank abandoned the operation. Soon afterwards the communists announced that Chris was being held prisoner.

The mystery was only cleared up 19 months later when Chris was released by his captors, and he told how the particular circumstances of his capture had been exploited by the North Koreans in the hope of using him as bait to capture a United Nations helicopter. The enemy had tried to gain his co-operation for the scheme by the offer of a colonelcy in the North Korean Air Force and a safe conduct for his family to North Korea. The offer was made by the Chief of the North Korean Air Force, General Nam Il, in person.

When interrogation and persuasion failed, he was quartered with a double agent, Kim Dong Shik, and both were set to work on a pig farm near P'yongyang. Acting on instructions from the North Koreans the

Frank Grobler

139

agent had used radio equipment brought from South Korea to transmit the message that Chris was in the hands of guerrillas and that a rescue could be arranged.

From November 1951 until the end of February 1952 the Flying Cheetahs suffered casualties in aircraft and men in a series of unfortunate mishaps. The costliest of these was a collision in mid-air on 3 December 1951. It happened when Peter Norman Smith was leading a mission back to K-46 in poor weather. The flight was short of fuel, so Peter decided to land at K-16. While approaching Seoul in battle formation at 1000ft in good visibility, his Mustang was rammed by Ken Whitehead's aircraft. Peter's aircraft rolled over and crashed into the Han River while Ken's, minus engine and propeller, plunged to the ground. The loss of Ken was particularly ironic, for six days earlier he had walked away unscathed after crash landing his battle-scarred aircraft on an emergency strip behind the enemy lines.

On 26 January 1952, Cliff Collins was taking off on a test flight when the engine of his Mustang cut out seconds before it became airborne. Cliff raised the undercarriage and the aircraft slithered to a stop on its belly before it reached the end of the runway. Dicky Harburn was killed on 11 February on his early return from a railway interdiction mission. He decided to abort when his aircraft sprang an oil leak, and as he approached K-46 he jettisoned his bombs and prepared to land. While in the circuit his engine seized up and the Mustang crashed.

Dicky must have failed to lower his seat before jettisoning his canopy and baling out. Marks on the canopy found some distance away suggested that the canopy had struck him on the 'bone dome' and knocked him unconscious. That was always a danger with the Mustang.

Nine days later Jimmy Newton walked away unharmed from the wreck of his Mustang. Immediately after take-off his coolant gauge had failed, giving a false maximum reading, and he made an emergency downwind landing at full power. Topper van der Spuy had engine failure soon after take-off on 6 March, jettisoned his bombs and crash-landed without injury to himself, but his Mustang was a write-off. Topper has recorded the entire story of his crash landing in Chapter 18.

Two further casualties occurred while the pilots were still under operational training. Bob Staats had recently returned for his second tour of operations, and five days after his arrival he failed to return to K-10 after a test flight. On 20 January the wreck of his aircraft was seen in Chinhae Bay, and his body was recovered by South Korean divers. On 19 February Jack Lellyet arrived at K-10 with 11 other replacement pilots. Towards the end of their operational training period Shorty Leathers led three of them on a 'milk run' rail interdiction strike against a railway bridge north of Chong-du when Jack, flying as his No 2, failed to recover from a dive-bombing attack and his aircraft plunged to the

The squadron ops room - (note furniture made from ammunition boxes)

ground. It is possible that he had not yet used the fuel in his fuselage tank, which would have made the aircraft uncontrollably unstable in the bombing dive.

There was an interesting sidelight during Dick Clifton's term as CO during April and May 1952, when it was touch-and-go whether the squadron would be withdrawn from operations and be relegated to training duties in Okinawa. The Senior Air Liaison Officer, Toby Moll, asked Dick to visit him in Japan to discuss an important confidential matter which was 'top secret'.

It transpired that the authorities back home had become anxious that the war would be over before the promised conversion of the squadron from Mustangs to Sabres. It was of course vital that the Cheetahs should have the opportunity to fly the best jet fighters available on operations. Considerable pressure was therefore put on the Americans behind the scenes to get the squadron converted to Sabres. Toby Moll showed Dick Clifton a signal concerning the intention to withdraw the squadron from operations immediately and send it to await conversion to jets at an unspecified date. Dick was horrified that all the respect and goodwill that the squadron had earned and the high morale of all personnel would be wiped out by a withdrawal from 18 Fighter-Bomber Wing while the other three squadrons remained on operations. Toby Moll agreed whole-heartedly with Dick's point of view, and together they concocted a signal to SAAF HQ, which obviously did the trick because the near disaster was averted.

Shorty Leathers

As it happened, it was not until January 1953 that 18 Fighter-Bomber Wing was withdrawn from operations to convert to Sabres. The original plan to languish for seven months on Okinawa would have been a disaster for the Cheetahs and at the time Dick found it a great strain to keep the matter to himself.

So often in air operations the exploits of aircrew personnel receive far more publicity than the fine work done by the ground crew. It is therefore appropriate to record some episodes that highlight the achievements of the erks and the magnificent part they played in keeping the aircraft flying.

Although never up to full aircraft strength because of a succession of casualties in 1951 and 1952, and despite excessive engine trouble caused by the harsh weather, the serviceability of the available Mustangs allowed the daily sortie rate of the squadron to be consistently better than that of the other three squadrons in the Wing. That was simply because the Cheetah servicing crews were in every way superior to the American ground crews. Most of the Americans had been drafted to

Cpl de Bruyn carries out a daily inspection on the CO's aircraft

Outdoor adjustments made by lamplight

serve in Korea, while the South Africans were volunteers and practically all veterans of the Second World War. That the keenness and efficiency of the erks of 2 Squadron impressed the Americans is illustrated by the following incident.

One day in early February 1952 at Chinhae the CO, Dick Clifton, was chatting to the CTO, Zulu van Rensburg, when he noticed two unfamiliar USAF officers on the dispersal area where there were several unattended Mustangs belonging to the American squadrons. Thinking that they were also enjoying the unseasonable sunshine, the two South Africans strolled over to find out who they were. The strangers introduced themselves as Fifth Air Force Inspectors. At that moment a SAAF Mustang landed and taxied in from the advanced airfield at K-46. Immediately a swarm of SAAF Erks converged on it, and scarcely had the propeller stopped turning when armourers and fitters were opening panels and a tractor was hitched up to tow the aircraft to the servicing bay. The pilot had to get out of the cockpit in a hurry before the tractor began to move. The senior USAF officer, a colonel, turned to Dick Clifton and said: 'Goddamn, Commandant - there's the reason why your serviceability is plain superior!'

Lofty Lance

Lofty Lance crash lands

It became necessary to create a new Mustang to augment the dwindling supply of new aircraft by cannibalising three Mustangs that had been written off as damaged beyond repair. In February 1952, Dick Clifton gave permission, rather reluctantly, when W/O Willard and 14 of his men at K-10 suggested the operation on their own initiative. Dick considered that they were working hard enough already, and he feared that their ordinary work might suffer. However, they argued that they were not fully extended because of the few aircraft on squadron strength. There was no such thing as 'normal working hours' for SAAF erks on operations, so these men kept at it until the job was done, and 325 flew within a month.

The arrangement with the Americans was that South Africa would pay only for aircraft written off. The original 325 had been ditched during its delivery flight from Japan and, although debited to 2 Squadron, it had never been received, so the Cheetahs had no scruples about using its number 'free' so to speak! Mustang 325 was nearly lost on her first mission when Dick Clifton took her on a rail-cutting mission near Sukch'on on 24 March. One magneto packed up after the attack and a very rough engine had to be nursed to the nearest friendly airfield at K-14 outside Seoul, and 325 survived to carry out many more missions.

Yet another example of the professionalism of the squadron erks was the occasion when Lofty Lance came back with a failing engine to a short landing-strip used by light spotter aircraft behind the front line. The unavoidable wheels-up landing on so short a strip damaged the Mustang quite seriously, though Lofty escaped with nothing worse than a cut finger. With the CO's blessing, Engineer Officer Harold Knight went by road to examine the machine, and he returned confident that the aircraft could be repaired and, if stripped to its lowest possible weight, it could be flown off the strip. A working party with the necessary tools and spare parts was assembled and, encouraged by front-line troops within sight of artillery and tank duels, they camped on the strip and proceeded to get the Mustang into a fit state to be flown off.

While this work was in progress, Dick Clifton took the opportunity of visiting the scene during a test flight. This created an amusing and, for him, rather embarrassing scare. As it was only a test flight, he had omitted to inform Operations of his intention or to check by radio with the control centre. After 'shooting up' the working party several times to cheer them up and have a good look at the situation, he switched to an operational frequency in time to hear an excited conversation about an unidentified aircraft 'making hostile passes' at ground positions at a specified map grid reference. It suddenly occurred to him that he was in the exact position that they were referring to! He hastily interrupted

Harold Knight and his ground staff

146

the discussion about whether anti-aircraft guns should shoot him down or fighters should be sent to intercept him, and he sheepishly identified himself.

The work was soon completed, and Attie Bosch was chosen to fly the aircraft off the strip because he was a very experienced flying instructor and also the lightest pilot available. There was a dangerous hump some distance before the end of the strip, but Attie managed to get the Mustang airborne before reaching it, while Harold and the others watched with bated breath.

Recalling their memorable experiences on the little airstrip, Flight Sergeant Eric Burger told of the pride that they all felt while watching the fighter-bombers providing close-support to the ground forces in full view of their camp. Sergeant Thys Greef thought his most interesting observation was the Korean frogs, which are green on top with red bellies. He wondered whether the frogs had survived the earlier communist occupation by floating on their backs! Harold Knight's favourite story was about the occasion when he was stopped for speeding by a black American M P but let off when pleading that he was unable to see the gentleman in the dark!

Recognition by the Americans of the outstanding achievements of the ground staff stands out unmistakeably in the citation of the United States Presidential Distinguished Unit, which reads as follows:-

The 2nd South African Fighter Squadron distinguished itself by extraordinary heroism in action against an armed enemy of the United Nations, from 28 November 1951 to 30 April 1952. Throughout that period the 2nd South African Air Force Squadron demonstrated the highest qualities of devotion to a united and co-ordinated operation, achieving remarkable success in the face of great hardship and difficulty. The organisation not only conducted a brilliant tactical phase in the United Nations operations, but performed the supply and maintenance of its units under exceptional trying conditions. The 2nd South African Air Force Fighter Squadron was maintained in the field at forward airfields and its tactical aircrews were faced with the hazards of flying over extreme mountainous terrain and in adverse conditions of the winter season. Although losses of personnel and equipment were experienced, the morale and esprit of this organisation was exemplary. A total of 1 950 effective combat sorties were flown. The effectiveness of these sorties was evidenced by the destruction of three locomotives, 20 railroad cars, 14 bridges, two tanks, 30 vehicles, ten supply dumps, five marshalling yards,

90 gun emplacements, an estimated 180 buildings and an unestimated number of enemy troops. Repeated acts of valour and personal gallantry marked the aerial accomplishments of the 2nd South African Air Force Squadron, and the extended and continuous efforts of each individual officer and airman made possible the high degree of effectiveness which reflected great credit upon its individual members, the South African Air Force, and the United Nations Command.

CHAPTER

13

Applying Pressure

General Mark Clark took command of the UN forces from General
Ridgeway on 12 May, and he decided to increase pressure on the communist negotiators by increasing air strikes by the UN forces. The
railway interdiction campaign was not proving very successful, and
damage to railways and damaged bridges was still being repaired within
a few hours of attacks, so it was decided to allocate these operations to
the light bomber squadrons and release the fighter-bombers for general
interdiction missions on industrial targets in North Korea by mid-June.

At the end of May General Barcus assumed command of the Fifth
Air Force from General Everest, and the target priorities for fighter-
bombers were clarified. These were listed as aircraft, serviceable airfields, electric power facilities, radar equipment, manufacturing
facilities, vehicles and vehicle repair facilities, locomotives and railway
carriages, ordnance and petroleum products, rail and road bridges,
tunnels and marshalling yards, and military personnel. From mid-June
missions by 2 Squadron were carried out on such targets, and the
regular twice-daily rail interdiction missions were phased out. All missions by the Squadron were to be flown against selected targets as part
of the Fifth Air Force, or 18 Fighter-Bomber Wing, or as small independent formations of one or two sections.

It came as a great blow to the Cheetahs when in May the second-
in-command, Carl Mouton, and the Commander of 'Dog' Flight, Jimmy
Groenewald, were grounded by the Wing Safety Officer. These two had
elected to fly on despite a ruling by the Fifth Air Force that it was unsafe
for a man over 6'2" in height or weighing over 220lbs to fly Mustangs.
Three other experienced pilots, Harold Kirby, Bats Maskell and Gillie
Nell-Shawe were grounded for the same reason. This ruling was based
on the fact that a large pilot wearing bulky flying clothing plus escape
and evasion equipment, including pistol, radio and rations carried in a
waistcoat, would have great difficulty in getting clear of the rather
narrow cockpit of a Mustang if forced to bale out. This came at a bad
time when pilot strength was already low through casualties, and pilots
having completed their tours.

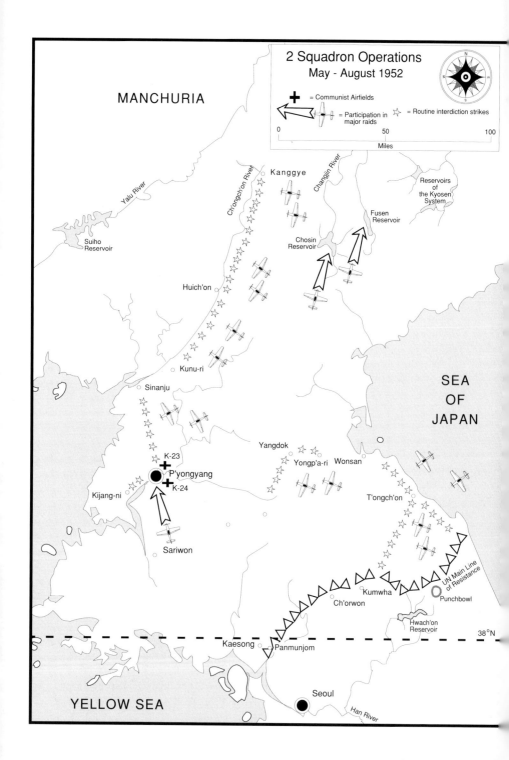

2 Squadron Operations
May - August 1952

✛ = Communist Airfields

= Participation in major raids

☆ = Routine interdiction strikes

0   50   100
Miles

MANCHURIA

Yalu River

Suiho
Reservoir

Ch'ongch'on River

Kanggye

Changjin River

Reservoirs
of
the Kyosen
System

Fusen
Reservoir

Chosin
Reservoir

Huich'on

Kunu-ri

Sinanju

SEA
OF
JAPAN

Yangdok

Yongp'a-ri   Wonsan

K-23
P'yongyang
K-24

Kijang-ni

T'ongch'on

Sariwon

UN Main Line
of Resistance

Kumwha
Ch'orwon

Punchbowl

Hwach'on
Reservoir

38°N

Kaesong   Panmunjom

Seoul

Han River

YELLOW SEA

150

It was fortunate, however, that Joe Joubert had recently rejoined the Squadron for a second tour, so he was a natural choice for Second-in-Command. To the great delight of the other ACF volunteers Commandant Clifton recommended Vin Kuhn to take over 'Dog' Flight, and his promotion straight from second lieutenant to acting captain was approved. He did a splendid job, and morale reached a high peak despite the setback of losing so many experienced pilots. Vin had a brilliant sense of humour. 'Able' Flight had set up a totem pole just outside the entrance to Rorke's Inn labelled 'A' Flight's Touch Pole, which the members of the Flight made a habit of touching for good luck when entering or leaving the Inn. Vin took a bottle of beer and poured some at the foot of the pole with a notice scribbled in chalk: 'Dog' Flight was here!' This healthy rivalry was good for morale.

The continuation of the rail interdiction flights between May and mid-June had taken 18 Fighter-Bomber Wing and 2 Squadron further north than they had penetrated during 1951 and early 1952. They attacked stretches of railway line south and north of the Ch'ongch'on River, venturing into MiG Alley, missions that followed the fixed pattern of *Strangle* and *Saturate*. Depending on the intensity of the ack-ack in the area, one or two flights were usually briefed for flak suppression.

On 8 May, 485 sorties were flown to bomb a supply depot near Suan, to which 2 Squadron contributed 23 sorties. Three separate missions, including two Cheetah flights in each, were flown by 18 Fighter-Bomber Wing, preceded by flak-suppressing F-80s. The large number

Typical Korean weather

of aircraft over the target caused a dust and smoke haze that prevented accurate observation of the results of bombing.

A week later Joe Joubert was a member of a Cheetah flight in a wing formation operating on a railway interdiction mission in the afternoon. The target was the railway line south of Kanggye and because of poor visibility the American leader got lost. Joe, who had almost completed his second tour of operations, volunteered to take over the lead much to the dismay of his compatriots who considered that he was acting presumptuously. In the event Joe did not let the wing down, and he led it to the target without further ado.

Three days later Joe flew four close-support sorties in a single day. After the last mission he was treated to the usual ceremony with a bottle of beer and a wreath round his neck - a custom that marked the end of a tour of duty. This particular ceremony was unique in the South African experience as the number of combat sorties written on the wreath was not 75 but 175; or in other words, one tour of 100 sorties and another of 75.

Whenever fighter-bombers flew across the Ch'ongch'on River into MiG Alley they attracted the attention of MiG-15s patrolling the Yalu River. On 17 May Wilbur Clark was on a rescue patrol in the area with three American pilots when they were jumped by four MiG-15s, and later by another six. A dog-fight ensued, but without casualties on either side. A few days later Sabres came to the rescue of Jan van der Merwe, who was leading a formation of 20 USAF and eight Cheetah aircraft on a rail-cutting target south of the Yalu River. The MiG-15s attacked as the Mustangs were pulling away from the target, and after a brief skirmish the Sabres chased the enemy jets back across the Yalu.

Union Day saw another brush with two flights of MiG-15s in the same area. While leading a flight in a Wing mission of 20 aircraft, Wally Hefer ordered his pilots to jettison their bombs and turn to meet the enemy jets that dived down on them in a series of yo-yo attacks. The Cheetah aircraft edged southwards while turning towards the MiGs which eventually broke away without inflicting any damage and headed northwards.

The previous strikes against North Korean airfields during the summer were revived on 14 June 1952, when Shadow Gardiner-Atkinson led 13 Mustangs in three flights as part of a Wing formation on a raid by the Fifth Air Force. The targets were the two airfields at P'yongyang, K-23 and K-24, the latter having been used by the advance party of the squadron as its first base after arriving in Korea. As Shooting Stars were sent to suppress flak before the arrival of the Mustangs, the pilots encountered little anti-aircraft fire and were able to mark their return to K-24 by dropping most of their bombs on the runway.

When railway interdiction missions had decreased, the emphasis

152

Wally Hefer is decorated

was placed on general targets. The squadron flew eight sorties in two separate group raids on electrical installations south-west of P'yong-yang, followed by eight more sorties to attack a hand-grenade factory in the city centre. The North Korean Hydro-Electric scheme comprised four generating systems: Fusen, Chosin, Kyosin and Suiho on the Manchurian border, with an extensive network of transmission lines linking these systems to industrial and rural centres. The destruction of such a system required simultaneous concentrated attacks on all its main elements. Suiho was attacked in the afternoon of 23 June by fighter-bombers of the Fifth Air Force and naval dive-bombers, with B-29 raids continuing throughout the night and followed by more fighter-bomber raids in the morning.

On 23, 24 and 26 June the Cheetah Squadron attacked the plants at Fusen and Chosin. This was the first raid in which the whole of 67 Squadron took part and six Cheetah Mustangs led by Commandant Hendrik Burger, who had taken over command of the squadron from Dick Clifton on 13 June, was launched against Fusen No 3. Later photographic reconnaissance photographs showed that the powerhouse had been totally demolished. While 67 Squadron and Hendrik's flight were bombing Fusen No 3, 12 Squadron and two Cheetah flights led by Ben Grové and Attie Bosch attacked Fusen No 4. These installations were also destroyed by four direct hits.

Cheetah pilots took part in raids next day against 3 and 4 plants at Chosin. Ben Grové led 16 Mustangs to attack the targets at Chosin, four aircraft carrying proximity-fused rockets, while the rest were armed with 500lb bombs. The target was obscured by fog in the valley, so they attacked supply buildings and flak positions west of Chosin. The weather was better for the afternoon strike when Reg McClure led 11 Mustangs to Chosin. From 6/8th to 7/8th cloud covered the area, but all pilots managed to find the target and launch an attack. An accurate assessment of the damage inflicted could not be made because of the scattered cloud, smoke and dust. Although the production of electric power in North Korea was brought to a standstill, follow-up attacks on both the Fusen and the Chosin plants were made on 26 and 27 June. Jeff de Jager and Barry Kenny each led a flight in a maximum wing strike on the Chosin plants. All bombs fell in the target area, and two large fires were started, with intense smoke billowing from the target area.

During the four days of sustained operations against the electric installations by fighter-bombers of the Fifth Air Force, naval dive-bombers and B-29 night-bombers, more than 90 per cent of the North Korean generating capacity was destroyed. Of the 13 plants in the four main complexes, 11 were made unserviceable and the remaining two were badly damaged and unusable.

Industrial complexes were the next target, with P'yongyang as the main choice. Missions were flown against 30 various targets in the city totalling 1 254 sorties. The operation was called *Pressure Pump*, and fighter-bombers made three strikes. On 11 July George Dodson led two flights on the first raid of the day against ammunition dumps near P'yongyang, and the attack was successfully pressed home in the face of heavy anti-aircraft fire. While he was pulling away from the target Ben Grové spotted an enemy tank firing on the Cheetah aircraft, and during de-briefing he sketched the precise position of the tank. On the next sortie, while attacking the same target, Tubby Singleton was able to mark the last mission of his tour by destroying the tank.

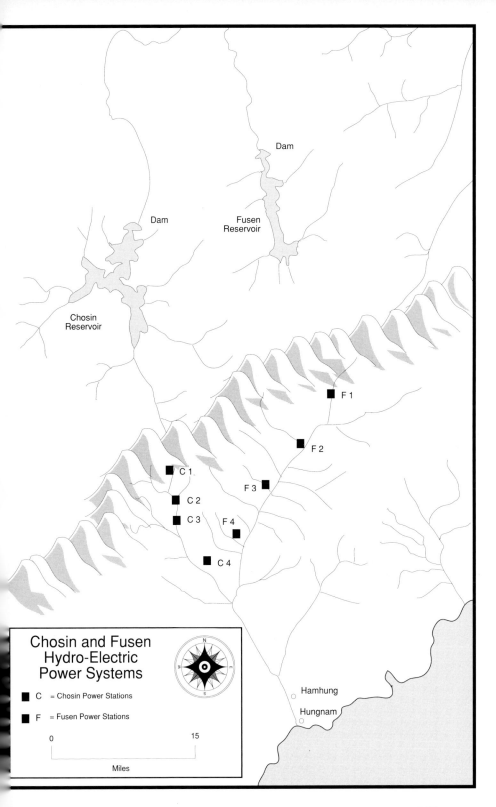

Dam

Dam

Fusen
Reservoir

Chosin
Reservoir

■ F 1

■ F 2

■ C 1

F 3 ■

■ C 2

■ C 3

F 4
■

■ C 4

Chosin and Fusen
Hydro-Electric
Power Systems

■ C = Chosin Power Stations

■ F = Fusen Power Stations

0   15

Miles

Hamhung

Hungnam

Two Cheetah flights took part in the last *Pressure Pump* raid of the day, to complete the squadron's total of 31 sorties out of 1254 for the entire operation. Radio P'yongyang reported that 1500 buildings had been destroyed and there were 7000 casualties. Later photographic assessment of bomb damage showed moderate to severe damage to 31 targets.

Besides their part in the multi-flight railway interdiction raids in May and June and in the more spectacular *Pressure Pump* strikes in July and August, Cheetah pilots continued with tasks that by that stage in the war, had become routine. During July, close-support targets remained the same; the dug-in bunkers in the communist frontline and the artillery and mortar positions to the north of it.

Dick Clifton hands over command to Hendrik Burger

Reg McLure

When the monsoon brought conditions that caused poor visibility over the target areas, the squadron once more took part in radar-directed drops. The radar bombing tested by Lippy Lipawsky had been considerably improved during the intervening year, and from mid-June in 1952 three tactical centres controlled blind strikes against communist frontline positions. With few exceptions these radar-directed close-support missions consisted of individual flights of four aircraft, which were brought over the target in relays.

Not all radar-directed bombing was successful, but the bombs forced the enemy to keep their heads down in winter when the weather was unsuitable for ordinary operations. On 9 July Bill Church led four Mustangs on a radar-controlled drop through a solid overcast. The mission proceeded as briefed, and the controller congratulated the flight on an excellent performance.

From May to August the Ch'o-do rescue patrols developed on lines similar to close-support missions. The fundamental pattern was retained, but variations were introduced to take advantage of technical development. When the rescue alert was started over Ch'o-do in 1952

157

the orbiting Mustangs carried only their machine-guns, and their sole function was to protect pilots in distress. It soon became evident, however, that the rescue patrols could serve a double purpose, and towards the end of April the Mustangs assigned to Ch'o-do missions were armed with four rockets in addition to machine guns. This gave them a secondary task, which was to attack communist artillery and troop positions along the west coast opposite Ch'o-do and Sok-to islands, held by the UN forces.

This pattern was maintained until the end of July, when a further variant was introduced that changed the primary nature of these missions. Some rescue patrols carried bombs and were directed against targets along the coast by a surface controller. Thus from July two

Outside the ops room. (L/R) Ben Grové, Aussie Austin, George Dodson, Tubby Singleton, John Bolitho, A.Q de Wet, Bill Church

different types of missions developed from a rescue patrol over Ch'o-do and Sok-to; first the usual rescue standby, and secondly the more heavily armed missions that were more like armed reconnaissances.

Normal armed reconnaissances along the front line also fell to the lot of 2 Squadron from May to August. The routes patrolled were in the central and eastern sectors. Interdiction of communist troops and supply concentrations in the zone to the immediate north of the front line were also maintained. Occasionally napalm was used against these targets, but usually bombs were preferred. Missions were pre-briefed, sometimes consisting of more than the usual single flight.

On the morning of 23 July Hendrik Burger led three flights against a large concentration of troops and possible ammunition carriers that had been detected south-west of Wonsan. There was intense and accurate automatic fire over the target, and the flight covered the area with bombs and rockets, but with no visible result. The same afternoon three flights returned to attack the same target led by Johnny Eloff. This time the results were spectacular, with one main and two secondary explosions. By the time the Mustangs had left the target area, smoke was billowing to a height of 2 000ft.

From November 1950 until the end of April 1952 the Squadron's losses in aircraft and pilots had been very high (one pilot for every 266 combat sorties), while the Fifth Air Force had lost fighter-bombers faster than they could be replaced. However, from 1 March 1952 the casualty rate in both pilots and aircraft decreased drastically. The reason for this remarkable change was a new policy laid down by the Chief of the Fifth Air Force, General Barcus. Operational analysis showed that fighter-bombers had suffered most damage and casualties when flying below an altitude of 3 000ft, and when a second or third strafing run was made on the same target. The General therefore decided that as long as the ground war remained static, no target was important enough to justify the loss of a pilot and his aircraft. He therefore restricted fighter-bombers to a minimum operational altitude of 3 000ft including recovery from a dive-bombing attack, and to one pass per aircraft at any particular target.

Although this new policy reduced the numbers of pilots and aircraft lost, it did not help Trevor Scott and Piet Kotzenberg. On 19 July Trevor led a flight to a front line target east of Kaesong. On arrival over the area he had difficulty in making contact with the controller on his radio, so he handed over to Tubby Singleton, who was flying at No 3. The controller warned them of the flak, but none was observed, and the strike began. The pilots followed one another down at safe intervals in a dive-bombing attack, and the No 4, Aussy Austin, flying behind Trevor Scott, saw a flame on his aircraft and large pieces breaking away. The Mustang showed no sign of recovering from the dive, and plunged to the ground.

On 22 August Piet Kotzenberg, who had recently been appointed 2 Squadron's deputy commander, was reported missing in action after a dive-bombing attack on artillery positions. The mission, led by John Bolitho, consisted of two flights, with Piet bringing up the rear as No 4 in the second flight. Nobody saw what happened to the Mustang, but when Piet did not report at the rendezvous, a search was launched. Although a secondary fire was seen in the target area, it could not be associated with the missing pilot and his aircraft.

14

'Totsiens' Mustangs

The Communists rejected the United Nations peace proposals for resolving the problem of released prisoners of war, and a recess was declared until either these proposals were accepted or a satisfactory alternative was submitted in writing. Meanwhile both sides tried to force a return to the conference table on their own terms.

During the last few months of 1952 the Fifth Air Force was called upon to give support to the Eighth Army on a scale that had not been seen since November and December 1950, when the Eighth Army had been fighting for survival. In those days the number of close-support sorties flown by the Fifth Air Force had totalled 2 908, but in October and November 1952 it rose to 4 488 and 3 546.

This remarkable rise can be ascribed to the increased activity by both the communist and the UN forces. The limited fighting of the past few months was over, and the battle for the possession of tactically situated outposts along the battlefront erupted in September, after the soaking August rains had ceased and movement became relatively easy. During October some of the hardest ground fighting of the war for more than a year took place.

Besides regular missions to neutralise the growing threat from communist artillery and mortar batteries, the Cheetahs took part in various outpost battles, small and large. The enemy frequently ventured at first and last light from the cover of well fortified bunkers, on small scale reconnaissance probes. To be able to provide immediate air support for these movements, the Fifth Air Force needed to keep a certain number of its fighter-bombers on daily 'strip alert' during dawn and the twilight hours. This duty was rotated among the squadrons of 18 Fighter-Bomber Wing operating at K46 forward base, and this became a feature of the routine of 2 Squadron.

The early morning 'strip alert' is best remembered by members of the Flying Cheetahs for its inconvenience. The pilots of the duty flight were awakened at 04h00. A quick wash was followed by a brisk walk to the mess in the chilly air before dawn for the operational briefing. Then, wrapped in their heavy winter clothing, flying kit and escape and

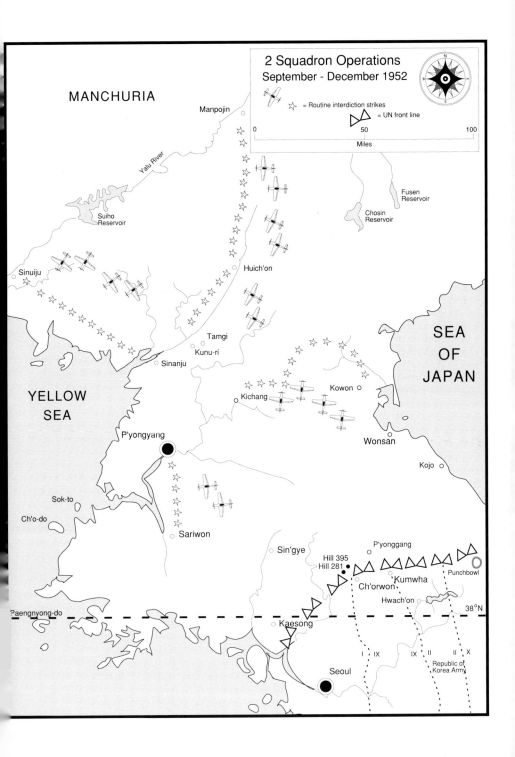

2 Squadron Operations
September - December 1952

☆ = Routine interdiction strikes
△▽ = UN front line

0   50   100
Miles

MANCHURIA

Manpojin

Yalu River

Suiho
Reservoir

Fusen
Reservoir

Chosin
Reservoir

Sinuiju

Huich'on

Tamgi
Kunu-ri
Sinanju

SEA
OF
JAPAN

YELLOW
SEA

Kichang

Kowon

P'yongyang

Wonsan

Kojo

Sok-to

Ch'o-do

Sariwon

Sin'gye

P'yonggang

Hill 395
Hill 281

Kumwha
Ch'orwon

Punchbowl

Hwach'on

38°N

Paengnyong-do

Kaesong

Seoul

I   IX   IX   II   II   X
                        Republic of
                        Korea Army

161

Ground crews waiting for aircraft to be scrambled

evasion gear, they carried out their pre-flight checks on their Mustangs while the ground crew scraped the ice off the windscreens and cockpit canopies. The engines were then started up and the aircraft taxied to the end of the runway.

At this stage the normal procedure was interrupted, for after all the final checks had been made, the engines were switched off and the four pilots sat in their cockpits in the dark, awaiting a call from some desperate front line outpost. This inactivity gave them the opportunity to think about what lay ahead in the immediate and distant future. Many must have wondered why they had volunteered to fight so far from home. The 'strip alert' flight was always backed by another standby flight which would replace the aircraft waiting at the end of the runway if they were called out. Once airborne, a flight was allotted to a particular airborne Mosquito controller who would indicate the target.

The Cheetahs also took a hand in the large-scale outpost battles during October and November. The battle for 'White Horse Hill' and 'Arrowhead' raged between 6 and 15 October and cost the communists 10 000 men. If their goal had been achieved they would have threatened the main supply route to Ch'orwon. During this period the Fifth Air Force flew 669 close-support sorties, of which 676 were night-bombing missions, and 61 were flown by 2 Squadron, although not all of them were directed against the communists in the Ch'orwon area.

It was during one of these missions that Peter Maxwell made a forced landing behind the UN front lines. He took off in the afternoon of 14 October with three USAF pilots from 67 Squadron to support the defenders of 'White Horse Hill'. On reaching the target he found that his radio was unserviceable. The leader indicated that he should circle to the south and stand by. Peter watched the rest of the flight make three passes at a concentration of enemy troops and then decided to follow his American comrades into the next attack. He wanted to join in the action. It was only when committed to the dive that he noticed the gun-sight and all other instruments were not working, and then the engine cut out. He pulled out of the dive, and after an unsuccessful attempt to restart the engine he lined up for a landing on a a short emergency strip just behind the UN front lines. He overshot the strip and the the aircraft was damaged beyond repair, but he himself was unhurt.

Another battle that required maximum support from the air was *Operation Showdown,* an assault on a complex of five hills north of Kumwha. This operation, which began on 14 October and ground to a halt six weeks later, cost the communists 19 000 casualties and the UN 9 000. A total of 2 217 sorties were made on close-support.

During October and November 18 Fighter-Bomber Wing including the Mustangs of 2 Squadron, carried out close-support missions along the length of the front line including an area north of Kumwha where *Operation Showdown* was in progress. The most common close-support targets were mortar and artillery positions although infantry bunkers were also frequently attacked. The persistence with which some of these strikes were driven home was well illustrated by a mission flown on 27 October during which everything seemed to go wrong.

A Mustang's guns receive a final check

Peter Maxwell

On that day a flight of four aircraft was pre-briefed to attack enemy bunkers and trenches north-east of Kaesong. Even before the Mustangs were airborne, technical hitches compelled two pilots to abort. The other two Mustangs, flown by Vic de Villiers and Don Stewart, found heavy smoke over the target area obscuring the controller's markers and as the enemy positions were uncomfortably close to UN troops, Vic and Don had to rely entirely upon the controller's description to locate the enemy positions. Despite strong winds and intense small-arms fire they succeeded in covering 90 per cent of the target with their bombs and rockets.

Another difficult close support strike was made on 10 November by a flight consisting of John Moir, Michael du Plessis, Brian Forsyth and Peter Maxwell. They were directed against artillery positions and infantry trenches near the sector held by the ROK (Republic of Korea) Division east of Kumsong. On reaching the target they found that the Mosquito controller had been forced to withdraw, but John made contact with a ground controller who used artillery smoke shells to mark the target. The difficulties of the flight, however, were not over. Brian's bombs failed to detach on the first pass and he had to make a second run. His own and Peter Maxwell's aircraft were hit by automatic fire and the oil pressure of both engines fell to well below normal.

When they landed at K-46 the pilots were surprised to see a large crowd waiting in the parking area. Brian ascribed the excitement to the emergency landing and battle damage, but when he got out of the cockpit he was relieved to find that the reception had been organised to mark the 50 000th combat sortie by 18 Fighter-Bomber Wing in the Korean campaign which he had just chalked up. It had become the first fighter-bomber wing in Korea to reach this total of which 10 000 had been contributed by the Flying Cheetahs.

The last four months of 1952 saw a general reduction in 2 squadron's combat sortie rate, although the Cheetahs carried out their fair share of general missions including strikes on North Korean industrial plants. On 5 September the Wing sent four waves of 12 aircraft as part of a larger operation by the Fifth Air Force against a mine and ore-processing plant at Tamgi, north-east of Kunu-ri. The first formations consisted of two flights from 12 Squadron and one from 2 Squadron led by Johnny Eloff. The second was made up of two flights from 67 Squadron and one from 2 Squadron led by Don Stewart. All aircraft carried 500lb bombs to break up the target so that incendiary bombs, to be dropped by succeeding strikes, would be more effective.

Since the Mustangs had been preceded by flak-suppressing F-80 Shooting Stars and F-84 Thunderjets, ground fire over the target was negligible, but the rugged terrain and the situation of the target at the bottom of a narrow valley, called for skilful airmanship. The follow-up formations were constituted in the same manner as the preliminary groups, except that they carried the incendiary bombs.

Johnny Eloff led a flight against the same target a second time that day, and later he took part in two more strikes against artillery positions along the west coast and the front line respectively. When he was flying on the fourth strike, Johnny had completed five hours' combat flying in a single day.

In common with the other units of the Fifth Air Force, the main interdiction targets of the Cheetahs towards the end of 1952 were not the supply routes but the communication centres and the concentrations of troops and supplies in the zone to the immediate north of the front line. These strikes were carried out by both single and multi-flight formations.

On 12 September Dick Lewer took part in a particularly successful mission when he led two flights against a supply shelter north of Sin'gye. The target area was almost clouded over, with a ceiling of 600ft, but Dick's navigational skill brought him over the target, and he led eight Mustangs through a single gap in the cloud. The enemy, who felt secure under the cloud cover, was taken completely by surprise and

Dick Lewer

offered little opposition. Dick scored two direct hits with his bombs causing a secondary explosion, and all the other pilots' bombs fell in the target area. Dick Lewer received the DFC for his leadership on this raid.

With the exception of the more vulnerable points along the front line and the sensitive industrial targets where the communists concentrated their anti-aircraft batteries, the Cheetah pilots encountered very little opposition from ground fire during this period. Only one Mustang was lost as a result of enemy action, and it happened during an air-to-air encounter. On the morning of 12 October 1952, three Mustangs were on an armed reconnaissance between Samdong and Kowon. A fourth Mustang flown by the leader, Peter Maxwell, had returned to base with engine trouble. George Allan had taken over the lead and the flight was approaching Kowon for the second time when four MiG-15s attacked in a shallow dive from six o'clock. Chick Fryer's aircraft was hit and flipped over into a spin, bursting into flames as the other two pilots broke to starboard to meet the next attack. The enemy jets made two more passes without scoring any more hits, and the Mustangs returned to K-46 at a low altitude.

Meanwhile Chick Fryer had managed to bale out of his blazing aircraft and had come to rest with his feet just above the ground, suspended by his parachute which had caught on a tree. In the confusion his flight had neither seen him leave his aircraft nor noticed any sign of the parachute. He slipped out of his harness, scrambled to the top of a hill and hid in some foliage. Hampered by badly burnt hands and face and blurred vision and with a metal fragment in the back of his head, he was captured by the North Korean security police and taken to a nearby house where his wounds were dressed and the preliminary interrogation begun. He was later posted missing in action, and the fact that he was a prisoner only became known to the UN authorities in April 1953, when prisoners released in Operation Little Switch reported his presence in a communist POW camp.

Although it was rumoured that the USAF had agreed in principle in July to re-equip 8 and 18 Fighter-Bomber Wings with the fighter-bomber

Peter Allam

Chick Fryer

version of the F-86F Sabre jet, it was only made public during a dinner in honour of the South African Minister of Defence, Advocate F C Erasmus, at the University Club in Tokyo, on 29 October. The Minister's 11-day visit to the Far East had begun the day before when he and his party were met at Haneda International Airport by the British ambassador and the Commanding General of the Far Eastern Air Force. On the morning of 29 October he was received in audience by the Emperor of Japan.

The Korean leg of the tour began on 31 October, when the official party left Japan on board General Clark's personal Skymaster, Bataan, which had formerly been used by General MacArthur. The party arrived at K-10 to be met by the commanding officers of 18 Fighter-Bomber Wing and 2 Squadron. That evening the Minister was introduced to the squadron's officers at a party in Rorke's Inn, and next day he inspected K-10 and the SAAF facilities. On 2 November the party went to K-46, where they attended the briefing and de-briefing of a napalm strike by 24 aircraft led by Dick Turner against enemy personnel and vehicles. They were then taken to a vantage point from where they could see an attack by Mustangs of 12 Cheetah Squadron led by Commandant Ralph Gerneke, who had taken over command of the squadron from Hendrik Burger in September.

From the beginning of October rescue patrols over Ch'o-do Island on the west coast and Yo-do Island on the east coast were once more in demand and these were not without incident. On 19 November Stan Wells orbited Ch'o-do Island with his flight of four aircraft for two hours and five minutes without receiving any calls. He then led the flight back to K-46, where an aircraft crash on the runway kept the Mustangs circling for 30 minutes while the wreck was removed. Permission to land was only granted at 18h40 by which time it was nearly dark. Over and above that there was a power failure, and the emergency lights proved to be too faint to permit a safe landing, so the pilots were diverted to K-16. Stan's aircraft ran out of fuel on the final approach, but he landed safely. The flight had been airborne for five-and-a-half hours, and there was precious little fuel left in the tanks of the other Mustangs.

On Christmas Eve the squadron threw a party in the workshops at which everyone was presented with a beer mug. On Christmas day a church service was held at the base chapel in Afrikaans and English conducted by Captain Olivier and Captain Brown. Unfortunately this special day was a busy one for some of the pilots, who had to fly on combat

Dick Turner (right)

Ralph Gerneke (right)

missions; and on one of them John Moir was lost. He was shot down and killed while flying as wingman to John Nortje on a search along the bomb line for a communist light aircraft dropping propaganda pamphlets. They were over Hwach'on Reservoir when they spotted an unidentified aircraft below them flying very low. John Nortje dived down to investigate, but unknown to him the strange aircraft was an American Marine spotter plane engaged in directing strikes in the area.

As John Nortje descended, he was followed by a Marine Skyraider that had broken away from a circling flight, and to cover his leader John Moir followed the aircraft down, drawing another Skyraider on to his own tail, the pilot opening fire and shooting him down in flames. John Nortje then called for help over the radio, only to hear a message to the controller from the American pilot: 'I have just shot down a drab grey aircraft which was making passes at us.'

On Christmas afternoon, 12 South Africans, including Colonel Danie du Toit, the new senior liaison officer, who had taken over from Toby Moll, and Commandant Ralph Gerneke, visited the orphanage in Chinhae. Thousands of children in South Korea had lost their families and had been abandoned to wander among the streams of refugees, and they had been taken into orphanages wherever possible. These institutions were adopted by various fighting units, and the Cheetahs had become associated with the Chinhae orphanage soon after arriving at K-10. Bringing joy to the children during Christmas had been a rewarding experience in 1950 and 1951, and the same pattern was followed in 1953.

The Cheetah party was met by a Korean missionary, Pastor Lee, the father of the orphanage. The events that followed were recorded by an anonymous member of the squadron:

Indeed, we felt, I think, rather like clumsy giants blundering about in a doll's house, an impression which was heightened by the doll-like appearance of its exquisite little inhabitants. Rows and rows of tiny little people, the boys with cropped hair and the girls with straight black hair cut in a short bob, sat crowded together, yet very orderly, dressed neatly in brightly coloured clothes made for them at the orphanage out of bundles of old garments and material received from America. The youngest of them, a fat solemn little boy dressed in a yellow knitted outfit with cap to match that had recently adorned some bonny 'junior' in the States, broke ranks and gave us an unrehearsed clown-act that went on intermittently the whole afternoon. Pastor Lee handled the introductions, and then the children entertained us with songs, recitations and a mime show

SAAF officers with Korean orphans

with dancing, all obviously long prepared and practised, and yet with a delightful gaiety and charm and a distinctive quality all of its own. One tiny person in particular delighted us with her natural grace and feather-like lightness as she pranced about in unselfconscious enjoyment. Some of the older children sang songs. The Koreans are musical people, and the youths have strong, resonant voices which they use to great effect. Then came the big event of the afternoon, as each child came forward in turn to receive the presents we had brought for them. A polite little bow, and back they went to their seats on the floor clutching a little bundle of American candy, a writing block, a pencil and other small items. We were surprised to see that none of them ate the candy. It would have been considered impolite. The restraint was too much for us to bear and we urgently asked Pastor Lee to tell them to tuck-in, a request which was granted. When the time arrived for us to leave, the children were photographed with us, and they cheered as we drove away. I am sure that we all departed with a lump in our throats and feeling that a Christmas afternoon in Korea could not have been more profitably or happily spent.

Jimmy Groenewald with a little Korean lady

The festive season of 1952/1953 saw the Flying Cheetahs part with their Mustangs, which had served them in combat for the past two years. On 27 December two Cheetah flights of four Mustangs apiece took off in a formation of 24 aircraft to bomb personnel shelters north-west of the 'Punchbowl'. On this occasion Baker Flight consisted of Porkey Rich, André du Plessis, Shorty Dowden and Brian Forsyth, all of whom completed their operational tours on this last mission. Able Flight consisted of J J Kruger, Frank Grobler, Stan Wells and Lionel Dixon. They placed all their bombs successfully on the target, and on reaching base both flights made an impromptu formation fly-past. This was followed by aerobatics by Baker Flight. These spontaneous gestures marked the end of the Mustang era for the Flying Cheetahs.

Two days later a fly-past of all 22 surviving Mustangs was staged at K-46 after which they landed at K-10 to be serviced before being flown on 31 December to Kizarazu in Japan for delivery to the 6 408th USAF Maintenance Supply Group. The pilots made use of the opportunity to join the officers of the SAAF Liaison HQ in Tokyo for a memorable New Year party at the University Club.

Altogether the SAAF had bought 95 Mustangs from the USAF of which 74 had been lost or written off in Korea, with 34 pilots listed as killed or missing in action. Various statistical sources give a variety of figures for the number of combat missions and sorties flown. The 2 Squadron war diary records that 2 890 missions and 10 597 sorties were flown.

While the pilots were seeing to the delivery of the Mustangs to the USAF, the removal of the entire squadron and its equipment to Osan (K-55) got under way on 30 December.

Training the Sabre Pilots

One of the greatest advantages that 2 Squadron derived from the relocation of 18 Fighter-Bomber Wing was that there was no longer any need for an advance and rear base. It meant that the squadron would no longer have to operate in two sections with an advance detachment at K-46 and the rest of the personnel and equipment at K-10. The moves from K-10 to K-46 and then to K-55 at Osan are remembered for three good reasons: the remarkable carrying capacity of the C-119 Flying Boxcars, the biting cold of the Korean winter, and the need to settle once more in new unfurnished accommodation. The Cheetah personnel had to repeat all the improvisations that they had made when the first detachment arrived in 1950 to create comfortable quarters from which to operate effectively.

With the physical move completed by 8 January, the squadron was reorganised to conform with the requirements of the new operational arrangements. Instead of four flights, it was divided into two flights with the key appointments as follows:

Commanding Officer - Commandant R A Gerneke
Deputy Commander - Major J S R Wells
A Flight Commander - Captain A D Lawrenson
A Fight Deputy Commander - Captain E A C Pienaar
B Flight Commander - Captain J F Nortje

The Deputy Commander of B Flight was not appointed until 26 January 1953, when authority was received for Lieutenant J J Kruger to assume the post.

Both 8 and 18 Fighter-Bomber Wings were equipped with the new ground-attack version of the Sabre known as the F-86F-30. The difference between the two types was that the latter was fitted with bomb shackles and a modified bomb-gun-rocket sight, and it could carry two 170-gallon long-range fuel tanks. These modifications were made for a versatile aircraft, for besides effectiveness in ground attack, ordnance and extra fuel could be jettisoned at the touch of a button and the pilot could switch over to interception. The jets could carry two 1 000lb bombs, had a combat radius of 570 miles and were fitted with General Electric J47-GE27 engines giving them a climb rate of 10 000ft a minute and a service ceiling of 50 000ft.

The Sabres compared favourably with the best aircraft available to the communists. The MiG-15 had a higher ceiling (56 000ft) and a superior rate of climb, but was slightly slower in level flight at sea level, and in the dive. It also tended to be unstable at slower speeds and to go into a spin without warning.

Although the pilots of 2 Squadron were confident that their new aircraft could match the best that the enemy could send against them, the disparity that worried them during January 1953 was not that between the MiG-15 and the Sabre but between the Mustang and the Sabre. They were faced with the task of converting, under operational conditions, from a piston-engine aircraft to a high-performance jet fighter; though fortunately all but two of them had previously flown Vampire jets during training in South Africa.

Nevertheless the task facing Stan Wells, as OC Flying, was a formidable one, especially as 2 Squadron was the first of the squadrons of 18 Fighter-Bomber Wing to convert to Sabres. As the pioneer in this undertaking Stan had to draw up the training syllabus, handling notes, lecture précis and briefing guides. He tackled the job systematically and collaborated with the USAF instructors, who had been detached from 4 and 51 Fighter Interceptor Wings, in compiling the training material. He ensured the closest co-operation by sharing billets with them and holding nightly discussions on the progress of the Cheetah pilots.

Ground training began on 4 January with the preliminary jet introduction, which consisted of lectures on a multitude of relevant subjects by the Mobile Training Detachment, and on 7 January the same detachment began instruction on the technical aspects of Sabre jets. The instructors, a captain and nine senior NCO's, gave lectures lasting four hours a day for ten days. The pilots then wrote a fifty-part multiple-choice test on the technical details of the Sabre.

The first Sabre was delivered to the squadron on 27 January, an event that caused great excitement, and for the next few days, curious personnel crowded round the aircraft. The diarist of 2 Squadron noted:

If we had charged ten cents admission to view the
aircraft, the squadron and the Air Force fund would not
need donations for years!

The arrival of the new jets gave the Cheetah pilots the opportunity to complete their ground training by spending four hours in the cockpit familiarising themselves with the lay-out. A blindfold cockpit-check fol-

Sabre in the snow

Airfield Radar

Cheetah Squadron Sabres

lowed. The actual flying training had already begun on 7 January with dual instruction on a T-33 jet trainer, in which each pilot received instruction until he was ready to fly solo in a Sabre. On 30 January Ralph Gerneke and Stan Wells were the first to fly solo, and the event was celebrated in the customary manner with a squadron party. Within eight days, all 28 Cheetah pilots had flown the new jets.

Developments in Manchuria led to great changes in the flying training syllabus. By the beginning of 1953 the strength of the Chinese Air Force had increased considerably, and it now totalled 1 485 aircraft, including 950 jet fighters and 100 1L-28 jet bombers with a radius of operation of 800 miles carrying a bomb load of two tons. This challenge caused the Commanding General of the Fifth Air Force to issue a directive to the CO of 18 Fighter-Bomber Wing to the effect that when all pilots in a squadron had been trained in fighter-interception tactics and had flown sufficient interceptor missions, training in fighter-bomber tactics must be proceeded with.

The decision to use the newly converted squadron first as fighter-interceptors affected the syllabus, which now included formation flying, combat formation and air-to-air ciné. The combat formation exercises, which were flown between 35 000 and 50 000ft at speeds varying from

An introduction to a Sabre engine

Mach 0,8 to Mach 0,92, taxed the pilots' flying and formation-holding abilities to the utmost. There was little surplus power available at such altitudes or speed for repositioning in the event of error. The most difficult of the whole conversion proved to be air-to-air ciné, for the high speed and various other factors of the unfamiliar equipment made it difficult for pilots to aim shots other than from dead astern, although as training progressed there was a steady improvement.

All this training was undertaken from a base that was still under construction. Bulldozers, lorries and other assorted vehicles drove about the runway and taxiways while flying was in progress, but there was only one flying accident and one near accident during the training period. Stan Wells attributed this safety record to sound technical training, good traffic control, the long runway and close and strict supervision by two very experienced flight commanders. Rodney van Rooyen was the first pilot of 2 Squadron to eject from a Sabre. While returning from an air-to-air exercise he lost his leader as they descended through the overcast; his radio compass failed to work and he ran out of fuel before he could find the airfield. He ejected successfully and landed in a rice paddy south of K-55. A few days later Rodney gave the pilots a talk on his experience followed by a practice of ejection procedure on a seat provided by the Mobile Training Detachment. The conversion training ended during the second week of March 1953, with individual pilots averaging 30 hours' pre-operational training on Sabres.

On 22 February Ralph Gerneke flew the first operational sortie in a Sabre as No 2 to the CO of 67 Squadron, Major Hagerstrom, while the new CO of the Wing, Colonel Martin, and the CO of 12 Squadron, Major Evans, comprised the rest of the flight. They sighted numerous MiG-15s, but no contact was made. On 11 March Stan Wells and John Nortje flew with two USAF pilots on a sweep of the Yalu, and the next day the squadron became fully operational on Sabres when four counter air patrols were flown along the Yalu River. These missions marked a turning-point in the history of the SAAF as the Flying Cheetahs became the first South African squadron to go into action with jet aircraft.

(L/R) Stan Wells, John Nortje, Tony Lawrenson

CHAPTER

16

Armistice

As in the two previous years, one of the main features of 1953 was the uncompromising attitude of the communists towards a peace settlement, although there was a marked change after Joseph Stalin's death on 5 March 1953, when towards the end of the month Kim Il Sung told General Clark that the communists would agree to an exchange of sick and wounded prisoners of war, at the same time suggesting that this would smooth the way to peace. The exchange was duly carried out, and when on 9 April the communist negotiators wrote to their opposite numbers proposing that men not repatriated should be handed over to a neutral state, the UN replied by proposing that negotiations at Panmunjom should be resumed; and the proposal became a reality on 26 April.

Before that, the stalemate in the fighting along the front line had continued, but as soon as the talks resumed, both sides intensified their activities, the communists on the ground and the UN in the air, with the intention of putting themselves in an advantageous position when the armistice was signed. That is proven by the increase in communist casualties over the last four months of the war. In April they were estimated at 10 000, in May 16 454, in June 36 346 and July 72 112.

As usual the familiar pattern of delay and stall had appeared by the first week of May when the parties failed to agree on a neutral nation to deal with repatriates, so the UN decided to exert more pressure from the air. Two important dams north of P'yongyang were attacked, and the rush of flood water destroyed large stretches of the routes between P'yongyang and the Yalu River, including railway lines, bridges and marshalling yards, which were swept away by the raging water.

On 8 June the documents for a truce were completed, and during the intervening period the Flying Cheetahs played a versatile role with their Sabre jets while making their contribution to the operations of the Fifth Air Force. The Sabre was not only more effective than the Mustang as a fighter-bomber but it also gave 18 Fighter-Bomber Wing a formidable counter air capability. As a result 2 Squadron was tasked with the full range of missions during the last few months of the war,

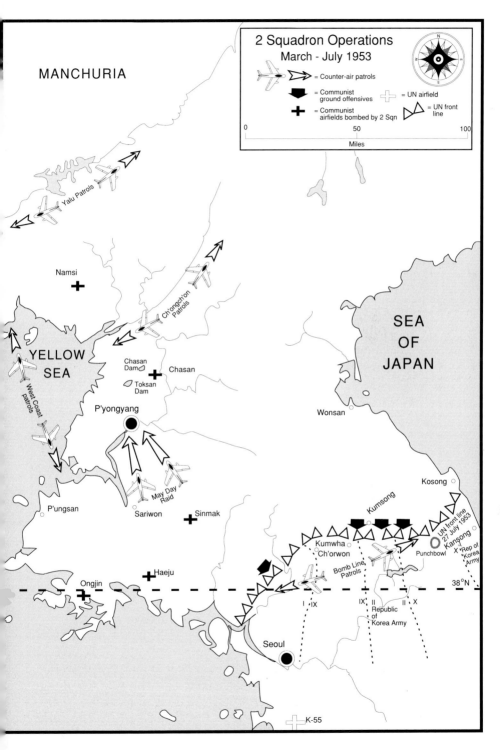

MANCHURIA

2 Squadron Operations
March - July 1953

= Counter-air patrols

= Communist ground offensives   = UN airfield

= Communist airfields bombed by 2 Sqn   = UN front line

0   50   100

Miles

Yalu Patrols

Namsi

Ch'ongch'on Patrols

SEA
OF
JAPAN

YELLOW
SEA

West Coast patrols

Chasan Dam

Toksan Dam

Chasan

P'yongyang

Wonsan

May Day Raid

Kosong

P'ungsan

Sariwon   Sinmak

Kumsong

Kumwha

Ch'orwon

Punchbowl   UN front line 27 July 1953   Kansong

X Rep of Korea Army

Haeju

Bomb Line Patrols

38°N

Ongjin

I   IX   IX   II   II   X

Republic of Korea Army

Seoul

K-55

181

Cheetah Sabres in formation

The business end of the Sabre

including counter air interdiction, rescue patrols and close-support. They also took part in attacks on irrigation dams and in the airfield neutralisation programme, this being of high priority to prevent the Chinese from using airfields to gain air superiority, not only while the war was still being waged but during the period that followed the armistice.

Between March and mid-April all the combat missions carried out by 2 Squadron were counter air patrols that either took the form of sweeps along the Yalu River or air alerts along the west coast and the front line. The Yalu sweeps were made with elements of the Wing in an attempt to lure MiG-15s across into Korea and engage in combat. The air alerts were simple flight missions to provide top cover for Thunderjets engaged in front line close-support and interdiction tasks. Barely a week after the first sorties on Sabres, the Cheetahs were considered fully ready for air-to-air missions, and flights consisting exclusively of 2 Squadron pilots, instead of mixed South African and American flights, became the normal practice.

The first mission of this kind was carried out on 18 March by Ralph Gerneke, Neil Stocks, Eddie Pienaar and Jean de Wet. Eddie had an encounter with MiG-15s five days before when he was flying No 2 to the Wing leader on a patrol of the Yalu River. He followed Colonel Martin in pursuit of two MiG-15s, and after the Colonel had expended his ammunition on one of the jets he handed over to Eddie, who also fired a few well-placed bursts. Shortage of fuel compelled the two pilots to break off the pursuit, and they saw their quarry disappear into the cloud. Immediately afterwards a bright glow appeared, which suggested that the damaged MiG-15 had exploded. This kill was confirmed later, but the Pentagon gave full credit to Colonel Martin.

On 16 April the squadrons of 18 Fighter-Bomber Wing were ordered to begin air to ground training, and next day dive-bombing practice commenced. Within a week the squadrons were ready for their first ground attack, and on 14 April Colonel Martin led 12 aircraft, including four Sabres of 2 Squadron, to attack stockpiles hidden in a village on the west coast south-east of Haeju. All bombs were dropped in the designated target area, but the pilots found that the minimum altitude restriction was as much an impediment to accurate bombing with the Sabre as it had been with the Mustang. After that, operations by 2 Squadron during the second half of April were confined almost exclusively to regular morning and afternoon group raids on troop concentrations and supplies along the transport routes west of the P'yongyang-Kaesong main supply route. This pattern continued until the last day of the month, when variations were introduced in ordnance, targets and types of mission. Jaap Krige began the day's operations by leading a close-support mission against mortar positions and trenches along the IX Corps front. Unfortunately Jaap became separated from his flight, which proceeded to bomb a road west of Ch'orwon.

The next mission was a flight led by Ralph Gerneke, loaded with 1 000lb bombs instead of the 500lb variety. This was the first time the Sabres had carried the heavier load, and they made good the occasion by dropping six of their eight bombs on the runway of Sinmak airfield. This mission was also Ralph's 86th sortie, and he handed over command to Stan Wells on 5 May. John Nortjé added to the success of the day by leading eight aircraft on a raid against enemy troops concentrated west of P'yongyang. All 16 bombs were placed in the target area.

The first months of operations on Sabres were not without loss, but fortunately there were no casualties among the pilots. On the afternoon of 19 April, nine Cheetah Sabres flew in a group formation of 24 aircraft against a troop concentration south of the Sarwon-Sohung railway line. The dive-bombing attack was successful with the last pilot over the target, John Koekemoer, scoring a direct hit on two large buildings. On returning to K-55 Piet Visser discovered that his Sabre did not respond when he attempted to lower the landing gear, speed-brakes and flaps, and he had to make a belly landing on the runway. The aircraft was

1 000 lb bombs (left) and 500 lb bombs

John Nortjé completes 100 combat sorties

damaged beyond repair, and on investigation it was discovered that burnt-out field windings on the generator had caused a total electrical failure.

While 2 Squadron was winning its spurs on Sabres, two batches of replacement pilots arrived at Osan. Four of them, Jean de Wet, Shag Morris, Ian Gow and Al Rae, had already completed a tour of operations on Mustangs. Their training on Sabres proceeded smoothly, although one aircraft was written off when the pilot baled out after losing direction on his return from a practice mission. His aircraft ran out of fuel, and although he tried to make it to K-2 he was forced to eject at 3 000ft and parachute to safety.

The last rotation of squadron ground personnel took place on 2 April. New arrivals were welcomed with a party at the NCOs' Hizikazimba club, which was temporarily housed in a tent. On the same evening a squadron tradition was revived when a newly constructed 'Rorke's Inn' was handed over by the CO of 839 Aviation Battalion Engineers. There were 55 American officers at this function. Two other notable events during this period were the South African general elec-

John Koekemoer

tions and the first release of prisoners of war from communist camps. The solemn registration of votes on 14 April was offset by news that Reg Gasson was among the first UN prisoners to be released. Up to that moment no one knew whether Reg had survived after being posted 'missing in action'.

April was the lull before the storm of the heavy fighting that took place during the last three months of the war. The reduced tempo of operations and the coming of the Korean spring made it possible for personnel to spend a little more time than usual on recreational activities. Although relations with their American comrades were excellent, the nature of the team games preferred by South Africans did not invite participation by Americans, and the Cheetahs had to use their Commonwealth links to get some outside competition.

On 7 March the squadron called a halt to training and stood down to play rugby against a New Zealand team in Seoul. Later in the month a South African team again went to Seoul to play against a team from a British Field Maintenance unit on the soccer field. On 28 March a New Zealand rugby team visited Osan and fought the SAAF team to a draw

K-55, the squadron's Sabre base

in a muddy paddy field. The season was completed with a rugby tour of Japan, when at the end of April Stan Wells left for Tokyo with 17 Cheetah players, who won against a Commonwealth team at Ebisu (37-3), but lost against the students of Waseda University (13-21).

By the end of April the combat squadrons of 18 Fighter-Bomber Wing were capable of carrying out the whole range of operations expected of a fighter-bomber unit. During the last months of the war the 2 Squadron missions were evenly distributed between counter air, interdiction and close-support, with an occasional rescue patrol. The month of May began with an operation designed to upset the communists; an air raid on May Day on their principal propaganda organ, Radio P'yongyang. This target had survived an attack by B-29s in January and had gone off the air for a short time after another strike by B-29s on 15 February that cut the power to the long-range transmitters.

During the May Day strike, 4 and 51 squadrons of the Fighter Interception Wing provided top cover while the attacking force, consisting of 8 and 18 Fighter-Bomber Wings, including eight Cheetah Sabres led by John Nortje, passed P'yongyang as if heading for the Yalu

Pilots on way to the flight lines

River, but suddenly let down and dropped their bombs on the radio station. The enemy flak batteries were taken completely by surprise and proved ineffective. After the last bomb had fallen, General Barcus, who had personally commanded the operation, circled over P'yongyang and, using a radio frequency known to be monitored by enemy intelligence, promised further raids in retaliation for propaganda directed at the Fifth Air Force.

Two days later the squadron took part in the first of a new series of strikes against the North Korean airfields. Six Cheetah Sabres carried 500lb bombs to Sinmak airfield and succeeded in placing eight out of 12 on the runway. Other operations during May consisted mainly of group raids on concentrations of enemy troops along the P'yongyang-Kaesong railway line and the west coast, air alert patrols between Ch'o-do Island and the Yalu River mouth, and close-support missions against artillery and mortar positions and bunkers along the front line.

Two Sabres came near to being written off during this period. At the end of the month Mike Gedye had a lucky escape. When taking off with 11 other pilots to rehearse for a mass fly-past over Seoul to celebrate the coronation of Queen Elizabeth, the control tower informed him that he had lost the outer cover of a tyre. Undismayed, he carried on with the exercise, and when the formation returned to K-55 it was welcomed by fire engines, ambulances, crash tenders and a tense crowd. Mike made a perfect landing on the inner tube, which stayed intact. Ironically, the fly-past itself, which was to have taken place on 31 May, was cancelled because of bad weather. However, the squadron was later given its chance to take part when on 2 June, ten Cheetah Sabres marked Coronation Day by flying over the Commonwealth Division's Sector of the frontline in 'E' formation.

Operational flying by the pilots reached a peak during June with a total for the month of 400 combat sorties. Most of these were flown in direct and indirect support of XI ROK Corps which was in the front line of the resistance to a last communist offensive to the south of Kumsong. When the ground situation on the ROK Corps front deteriorated in mid-June, the newly-appointed Commander, General Anderson, waived the minimum altitude restrictions and ordered an all-out support for the ground troops. Together with the other squadrons in the wing the Cheetahs responded with direct close-support along the front line and with reconnaissance patrols along the north-south supply routes in the rear of the attacking communist divisions.

Mike Gedye

Lionel Dixon

A mission flown by Lionel Dixon, Mickey Delport and two USAF pilots on 13 June was typical. Their targets were four heavy anti-aircraft batteries north-east of Kumsong. No ground fire was observed, and they had no difficulty in placing all their bombs in the target area. Lionel's Sabre was hit in the nose by shrapnel and the radar equipment was damaged. In June four more Sabres were damaged by flak. The squadron also took part in the airfield neutralisation programme. On 10 June four Sabres dropped their bombs on the revetments and taxiways of Chasan airfield, followed up with an attack by eight Sabres on Haeju airfield, and a day later eight aircraft flew as part of a 36-aircraft Wing formation to attack Onjin airfield. With one possible exception, all the North Korean airfields had been neutralised by 23 June 1953. June ended with numerous missions by the Fifth Air Force to give close-support in poor weather. The radar control received more aircraft than they could handle, and the excess missions were directed to make 'free drops' well behind the enemy lines. Cheetah flights had this somewhat disconcerting experience on 27 and 29 June.

As the squadron entered its last month of operations in Korea, the summer monsoon began. Operational flying was impossible from 2 to 9 July, so Stan Wells and John Koekemoer took advantage of the lull and visited the Commonwealth Division, with whom they enjoyed the hospitality of Australian, New Zealand, Canadian and British officers. They also attended the GOC's briefing, visited the front line, and discussed various ways of improving close-support techniques. When the weather improved, close-support, interdiction and air alerts continued, with radar making missions possible in doubtful conditions.

On 20 July Stan Wells led nine Sabres to attack the runway at Sinuiju airfield, and all bombs landed on target. Two days later Stan again led five Sabres to bomb Namsi airfield. Only one Sabre was lost to enemy action in Korea and that was on 21 July. George Thom was on his 72nd combat sortie, which was an armed reconnaissance patrol from Wonsan to P'yongyang, when the leader aborted and he took

Stan Wells addresses his men

George Thom

over. He continued the patrol with Barry Ross and Henry Ludick. On the home run George saw some vehicles through a gap in the clouds and decided to attack. There was heavy anti-aircraft fire in the vicinity and he told Barry and Henry not to follow. As he pulled out of his strafing run he felt a thud, the fire warning lights came on and when Barry warned that the Sabre was alight behind the cockpit, he ejected.

His parachute carried him safely on to a hillside north of P'yongyang, from where he made contact with Barry on his URC/4 radio, explaining that the parachute had been left on the slope of the hill as a marker and he was heading for cover in the ravine. Ross called for help on the emergency channel, and two Cheetah flights were diverted from an interdiction mission to cover George. A helicopter was dispatched, but poor weather and lack of fuel resulted in the Sabres having to leave the scene before a rescue could be effected. In any case, an attempt to rescue would have had little hope of success, because George had already fallen into the hands of a North Korean militia section commanded by a Chinese officer.

During the week that followed, George underwent a number of field interrogations while he and his captors were billeted in North Korean houses. On 28 July he noticed that the ever-present UN aircraft had disappeared from the North Korean skies. That evening his hosts left the house and returned later in a jovial mood. He concluded that the war had ended, although he could not induce his Oxford-educated interrogator to admit it. George's story appears in Chapter 18.

For those pilots and ground crew who were serving with 2 Squadron during the last week of the war, time dragged by interminably, and by mid-July the feeling that peace talks would never be decisive caused a decline in morale. The future seemed very uncertain. Each morning and afternoon the pilots flew on regular radar-bombing missions, which seemed impersonal and lacking in challenge. At last on the afternoon of 25 July, the world received the news that a truce would be signed at 10h00 the next day and that it would take effect 12 hours later. While Colonel Danie du Toit and his liaison officers went to Panmunjom to attend the signing ceremony, the Fifth Air Force prepared for a final operation to prevent the last-minute transfer of a communist air force from Manchuria to North Korea.

The ground crew of 2 Squadron did not spare themselves, and on the morning of 27 July, 14 of the 16 Cheetah Sabres stood ready for the last day of combat. The squadron flew four missions on that last day of the war and established a new record for operations in Sabres with 41 combat sorties during a single day. From 11h00 to 13h20 a formation of 14 Cheetah Squadron Sabres patrolled the Yalu River, followed later by

Len Wilmans (left) - He flew the last 2 Squadron sortie of the war

a similar patrol of 14 aircraft along the Ch'ongch'on River. At 17h00, four Sabres took off for another Yalu patrol and at 18h00 two more flights plus one reserve were the last flights led by Stan Wells. When they returned to base at 20h00, Len Wilmans was credited with the last 2 Squadron combat sortie of the Korean War.

The war had ended for the Flying Cheetahs with a remarkable performance. The squadron had averaged 2,93 sorties per aircraft on 27 July compared with 1,92 by 12 Squadron and 1,76 by 67 Squadron. That evening all personnel at K-55 joined in celebrating the cessation of hostilities.

The war is over

CHAPTER

17

After the Armistice

On the first day of peace in Korea all ranks of 18 Fighter-Bomber Wing were addressed by the Wing Commander, Colonel Martin. As he spoke, a solitary Sabre represented the Flying Cheetahs in a formation fly-past. Post-war flying training began immediately, for the squadron was to remain operational in Korea until 29 September. During that period the Cheetah pilots would not only take part in a training programme but also maintain a watch over the communist air forces.

It was during a naval affiliation exercise with HMS *Ocean* that the squadron suffered its only post-war casualty. Four Cheetah Sabres were engaged in this exercise, which took place off the west coast on 28 August. On completing his dummy run Mike Botha reported to the leader, Stan Wells, that his aircraft was not responding normally to the controls. When instructed to climb towards the coast, Mike reported that the controls were locked on both the alternative and emergency systems. He ejected at about 15 000ft over land, but he was blown out to sea and his parachute was seen to hit the water about a mile from the shore.

Meanwhile Stan Wells had run short of fuel and returned to base. Taking another aircraft, he led helicopters, amphibians and two naval units in a fruitless search for Mike. The air-sea rescue operation continued for two days and was called off only after thorough questioning of the inhabitants of an island in the vicinity had failed to yield any useful information. Ironically, Mike had returned from an escape and evasion course only the day before his sad disappearance in the Yellow Sea.

The UN was wary of a sneak attack across the armistice line by communist air and ground elements, and a constant watch was maintained by flights of four to eight aircraft patrolling the area immediately to the south of the demarcation line. Similar missions also kept a vigilant eye on the east and west coasts, and 2 Squadron was engaged in both defensive measures until stood down on 29 September and placed on ground alert, which meant keeping a flight of four aircraft on 15 minutes' standby from before sunrise until after sunset. This flight was supported by eight more Sabres placed on call at first light.

Occasionally the waiting aircraft would be scrambled, and when that happened on 9 August three Sabres managed to get airborne in 12 minutes, but the fourth member had to ground-abort because of a technical defect. Relieved of the physical demands and psychological tensions of daily combat, and averaging just over nine sorties a day on training and patrols, the pilots and ground staff of 2 Squadron found time on their hands. That, together with the prospect of a return home on a date as yet unannounced, made it necessary for distractions to be devised. Among other diversions, musketry-training was arranged during August, but the highlight of the month was a visit by the Combined Services Entertainment Unit, which gave a much appreciated concert at K-55.

During the first two weeks of September excess energy was channelled into the levelling and preparation of rugby and cricket pitches

SAAF memorial in Korea

The Commonwealth sector of the UN cemetary

that were put to good use during the second half of the month. On 19 September the squadron played cricket against 77 Squadron RAAF, and six days later a Cheetah team left K-55 to play a match against 10 New Zealand Transport Company. The last sporting event in Korea was a rugby match against 77 Squadron RAAF followed by a traditional braaivleis. Among the occurrences that gave heart to everyone who was waiting to go home, and to the nation in general, were the intermittent releases of the 2 Squadron prisoners of war. On 5 August, the officer who had been held longest was released first: Hector MacDonald, who had been captured on 1 June 1951, and been a prisoner for 26 months.

The last of the seven South Africans to be returned to the UN during Operation Big-Switch, as this exchange of prisoners came to be called, was George Thom, who had been held for only nine weeks. He regained his freedom on 6 September and was in sufficiently good health and spirits to visit his comrades at Osan before leaving for South Africa. The returning airmen were thoroughly interrogated by UN Intelligence officers after being handed over at Munsan. The various accounts of their experiences while in the hands of the communists, have several features in common. They found that the Korean militia or civilians who captured them were invariably hostile and had to be restrained by Chinese officers and NCOs.

At first interrogations took place in the field or en route to the main interrogation centre, the so-called Coal Mine Camp. During the first few

197

months of captivity these interrogations were frequent and seemed interminable. They were conducted by well-educated Chinese and Korean officers who had a good command of English and displayed a remarkable knowledge of South African history and politics. Europeans, perhaps Russians, also took their turn at asking questions. Attempts to acquire information from prisoners often took the form of spells of solitary confinement, deprivation of food, threats of summary execution and various other persuasive techniques, depending upon the interrogating officer.

The information sought by the communists included details of operational training, organisation and strength of the Squadrons' armament, tactics, call signs, tactical control systems, base organisation and airfield facilities. The prisoners either remained silent or resorted to various ruses to avoid giving away useful information to the enemy. As far as possible they colluded to invent plausible stories to deceive the interrogators. One officer used the layouts of well-known South African taverns as models for fictitious ground-plans of air bases, while another gave Afrikaans obscenities as the names of senior Squadron personnel.

Mutual support in these circumstances was important. That was typified by an incident during April 1952 when Chris Lombard received

Rex Earp-Jones

much needed encouragement from his fellow prisoners. He was placed in solitary confinement for unco-operative behaviour during an interrogation, when he heard the traditional South African songs from the adjoining stockade. Four Cheetah pilots, Hector MacDonald, Denis Earp, Rex Earp-Jones and Mike Halley, as well as some British officers, knew about Chris's predicament and decided to stiffen his resolve with a serenade!

The treatment received by sick or wounded officers such as Hector MacDonald, Reg Gasson and Chick Fryer, was comparable to the medical care given to the enemy soldiers in a similar condition, but the shortage of medical supplies caused by the UN bombing was evident.

The prisoners often saw other evidence of the effectiveness of the UN air strikes, and on one occasion, a night raid by B-29s was used as cover for an attempt to escape. It was one of four made by Mike Halley, Denis Earp and Chris Lombard and although escaping was fairly easy,

Allies bid farewell

escapees were invariably recaptured because of their distinctive facial features, stature and gait.

The North Korean camps were situated north-east of P'yongyang and the Chinese camps in a belt south of the Yalu River. The ground between these camps and the sea was inhabited by an unsympathetic population. When they identified Westerners they either handed them over to the authorities or compelled them to give themselves up by refusing any sort of help or succour.

One of the worst experiences of South African prisoners was the 'Death March' from Kangdong, north-east of P'yongyang, to Pyoktong on the Yalu River. Denis Earp and Mike Halley set out on this journey on 14 November with 41 other prisoners. The relentless pace of the march, general weakness, dysentery and ill-treatment by the guards and passing civilians all took their toll. Some of the UN prisoners died on the 12-day march and some of the survivors arrived in Pyoktong in a serious condition. Mike Halley, who died in Durban on August 1954 from the effects of the treatment that he had received, testified to the personal courage of Denis Earp. He said that the support given by Denis to his comrades on that terrible journey, strengthened them, both morally and physically, and enabled them to withstand the harsh conditions.

While the repatriation of the prisoners was in progress, the Cheetah personnel made tentative arrangements to return their equipment to the USAF. As early as 1 August the Senior Liaison Officer, Danie du Toit, had ruled that the draft that had left South Africa in September 1952 would be the first to return home, and they would enjoy the bonus of air travel. The time-table of the withdrawal of the squadrons was announced on 2 October. In response, the stores personnel worked late into the night to complete the return of all the various items that had been issued by the USAF. Between 5 and 7 October, five different groups of 2 Squadron personnel left for Japan en route for South Africa, until at last a rear party of only five officers and 19 other ranks remained in Korea.

These departures were accompanied by a variety of farewell gestures. On 6 October Stan Wells, Jean de Wet and Lionel Dixon went to the UN cemetery where they performed the sad duty of paying the respects of the surviving members of the squadron to those South Africans who would not be going home. A more joyful farewell took place next day when 18 Fighter-Bomber Wing held a dinner party for the officers of the departing Cheetah Squadron, at which Stan Wells was presented with a squadron plaque; and two days later Stan and John Koekemoer bade farewell to their Commonwealth friends by flying in formation with two Meteors of 77 Squadron RAAF.

As a last tribute to the SAAF, 18 Fighter-Bomber Wing organised a Retreat ceremony on 28 October, when the SAAF flag was to have been lowered by the squadron CO, but unfortunately torrential rains pre-

The flags of South Africa and America on parade for the last time

vented the parade from taking place. As an alternative the CO of the Wing issued a policy directive that ensured that the association between his Wing and the SAAF would not be forgotten. It read:

> During the United Nations action in Korea, 2 Squadron South African Air Force served as an integral part of 18 Fighter-Bomber Wing, United States Air Force. In memory of this living evidence of United Nations solidarity and of our gallant South African comrades, it is hereby established as a Wing Policy that all retreat ceremonies shall be preceded by the introductory bars of the South African National Anthem, 'Die Stem van Suid Afrika'. All personnel will render the honour to this anthem as our own.

This signified the end of the SAAF engagement in the Korean War, and the senior Air Liaison Officer in Tokyo, Colonel Danie Du Toit, sent a simple message to Defence Headquarters, Pretoria: 'The squadron has been withdrawn from Korea.

A last farewell

The Commanding General of the Far Eastern Air Force paid this farewell tribute to the Flying Cheetahs: 'I need not dwell on the gallantry, fighting qualities or co-operation of the SAAF - these have been indelibly engraved in the hearts and consciousness of your comrades-in-arms in my command. It has been a privilege and an honour for me

Korea is added to 2 Squadron's colours

to command your forces in the field, and I have the same pride in your SAAF squadron as in any American Unit.'

This last tribute came from the South African Chief of Staff, Brigadier H J Willmott in a special Order of the Day issued on 28 July 1953:

> The history of the Flying Cheetahs in Korea will remain a proud and significant chapter in the more general history of the SAAF. The signing of a truce in Korea yesterday marked yet another milestone in the proud history of the South African Air Force. For nearly three years we have maintained a fighter squadron at full strength in a war theatre halfway across the world. It is not necessary for me to enlarge on its achievements or the renown which it has brought to us as a service; that is common knowledge. But it is with a feeling of deepest pride that I now take the opportunity of congratulating all those who have been connected with this meritorious effort. Our thoughts go out first and foremost to those who have laid down

their lives in the cause of freedom. Glory can never be earned without some sacrifice. Next we must remember the 264 officers and 555 other ranks who have seen service in the Far East and who have upheld the great tradition of 2 Squadron. They, however, could never have achieved what they did without the solid backing of each other and every other member of the Air Force. This, as always, has been a team effort, and the South African Air Force, as was expected, has come up to scratch again. Every member has, in some way or another, contributed towards the success of the squadron and it, in turn, has played its vital part in bringing this long-drawn-out campaign to a close. My heartiest congratulations to you all.

An outright victory in the Korean war was not achieved by the United Nations, so were the horrors of war and the tragic loss of life worthwhile? General Ridgeway gave the answer to his war-weary, demoralised forces in a letter circulated to every man on 21 January 1951. The letter was titled: 'Why are we here and what are we fighting for?' It concluded as follows:

> In the final analysis, the issue joined here in Korea is whether communism or individual freedom shall prevail; whether the flight of the fear-driven people we have witnessed will be checked, or at some future time, however distant, engulf our own loved ones in all its misery and despair.

South Korea would not have remained a free, democratic nation if the war had not been fought.

CONTENTS TO CHAPTER

18

18

The Cheetah Squadron Remembers

Three's Enough

Dick Lewer

Dick was awarded a well-earned American DFC in Korea, and 30 years later he became the only SAAF pilot who had survived that war to fight in the Border war as a fighter-bomber pilot, winning the Honoris Crux (Silver) for one of the most courageous air operations in the records. In his Impala jet he rocketed and strafed an enemy ambush at night by the light of parachute flares, saving an army reconnaissance unit from heavy casualties.

By the end of August 1952 I had already completed 45 sorties of my tour of operations in Korea which included many dangerous close-support missions. These consisted of low-level dive-bombing, rocket and strafing attacks made under the direction of either an airborne Mosquito controller or a ground-based forward controller. The targets were mainly troops well dug-in, artillery and mortar positions along the mountainous front line, often so near our own men that unless they were marked by small smoke rockets known as 'Woolie Peters' fired from the marker aircraft, or smoke shells from the ground, attacks could inadvertently be made on our own troops. The pre-marking of targets ensured accurate results, and a useful bonus from using an airborne controller was his ability to report on the damage inflicted in the attack. An observer in the rear seat used a powerful pair of binoculars.

Heavy ground-fire was aimed at attacking aircraft, and in addition every enemy soldier was equipped with an automatic weapon (the so-called burp-gun, a Russian sub-machine-gun), so that an impressive barrage of red-hot lead and a spectacular array of bursting shells and passing tracers greeted aircraft during an attack.

Dawn on 29 August at K-46 forward base heralded a crisp cloudless morning, and at briefing we were told that 18 Fighter-Bomber Wing was to attack a variety of military targets in the centre of P'yongyang. After take-off at 08h30 we formed up into our normal 'finger four' formation and set course for the target, a large storage dump alongside the river flowing through P'yongyang. Our progress along the route was uneventful, except at one point when a cluster of shells suddenly burst round the formation, but there were no further disturbances; and suddenly in the distance we could see the sprawling metropolis of P'yongyang which appeared to be covered by a layer of scattered cloud. To our horror, as the distance melted, we realised that the supposed cloud layer was in reality caused by the bursts of flak lambasting the formations attacking ahead of us.

All pilots had been reminded at briefing that the big guns in this area were radar-controlled and that their shells could lock on to aircraft flying straight and level for more than ten seconds, so in the circumstances our aircraft fell back into a loose line-astern formation while we approached the outskirts of the town and began weaving, bobbing and jinking all over the sky. Trying to navigate and at the same time reconcile landmarks on the ground with those on the map while performing such wild manoeuvres was difficult, especially with flak exploding on all sides, bright flashes followed by dense puffs of smoke creating a macabre spectacle. My Mustang was frequently buffeted by near misses.

I located the storage dump near a conspicuous bridge crossing the wide expanse of river, and after selecting the appropriate arming switches I dived to the attack and released my two bombs in salvo when the cross of the bombsight was covering the target and the minimum release height had been reached; then, yanking back the stick and opening the throttle against the gate, I zoomed up and away before the blast of my bombs blew my Mustang to bits.

It was a nightmare flight once more battling through the heavy flak until we were clear of the town. A disturbing thought was the unpleasant reception we would get from the soldiers and civilians in P'yongyang if by chance an aircraft was hit and the pilot was obliged to bale out. Once clear of the flak it was an exhilarating feeling to have survived such a frightening experience, and we headed back to K-46, relieved that the attack was over. However, when landing and reporting to the ops tent for de-briefing we were in for a rude shock. The Ops officer congratulated us on the operation and immediately announced that as the general attack had been so successful it had been decided that the raid would be repeated on a similar target in P'yongyang. It says much for the courage and tenacity of the Cheetah pilots that when a request was made for one of them to fly a Mustang to our safe southern base at K-10 for a routine overhaul, only one volunteer stepped forward.

The rest of us went back at 12h30 to the nightmare of the P'yongyang flak barrage; and, needless to say, on returning to base we were sent out for a third time at 16h00 to attack the Secret Police Headquarters in the middle of the town. We left it in flames. Three missions of that sort in one day were enough; and luckily nightfall prevented a fourth dice with death.

The Drinks Were On Me

Al Rae

'The irrepressible Al would keep smiling even though he was unhappy,' said his CO, Dick Clifton. He was one of the few Cheetah pilots who completed a tour of operations on Mustangs and then returned for another on Sabre jets. He was awarded an American DFC.

I hadn't the slightest idea where Korea was situated geographically when I volunteered to fight in the war, an adventure which began at Palmietfontein Airport, Johannesburg, when six of us *sprogs* flew off to tackle the commie scourge. Here are a few incidents that remain indelibly in my memory. The first story is against myself!

As leader of a flight of Mustangs for the first time, I had been tasked for a close-support mission, and I was told by the controller that the target would be marked by 'Woolie Peters'. I was under the impression that 'Woolie Peters' was the 'call sign' of the marker aircraft that would mark the target area with rockets, so I awaited the appearance of a T6 aircraft in which 'Mosquito' controllers normally flew. While circling behind the target area, I noticed that it was becoming totally obliterated by smoke, and only then did it occur to me that 'Woolie Peters' were the white phosphorus smoke shells fired from the ground to mark target areas. Because of this blunder I was obliged to buy a few extra drinks in the Pub that evening!

De-briefings after missions were memorable occasions, especially when the squadron doctor was present and produced a bottle or two of hard tack for post-sortie therapy! Unfortunately the Doc had no idea of the capacity of 2 Squadron's pilots who turned the de-briefing into a party at every opportunity. The amount of Scotch consumed reached such high proportions that the Doc was obliged to ration further supplies, which put a stop to these parties.

An incident involving Mac MacLaughlin and Tubby Singleton occurred early one morning, which Mac was lucky to survive. Often a dawn standby was required in case an emergency operation was called for. Aircraft would taxi from the revetment to the runway in the dark. On this occasion Mac happened to be leading, and when he reached the runway he stopped his aircraft and switched off the engine. Tubby, following behind, ploughed straight into the stationary aircraft. His propeller chewed up its tail and left poor Mac sitting forlornly in half a Mustang.

I can still picture the occasion when I returned to my quarters after a good evening in the Club to hear a high- pitched voice blaring forth from my bungalow. When I went inside, there was Topper van der Spuy brandishing a glass of brandy and listening to the portable record player that I had won in a game of bingo. The record was of my favourite singer, Doris Day, but Topper had selected 78 instead of 33 rpm, and I am sure that Doris had never sung so fast or at such a high pitch in her life. But Topper thought she was magic!

I remember the occasion Lofty Lance's Mustang was shot up during a mission. When he selected 'undercart down' before landing, only the right wheel locked down and it refused to retract. So Lofty had to land on the one wheel, keeping the left wing up as long as possible after touch-down. The expected ground-loop took place, and the aircraft slithered to a gentle halt; but before the dust settled the fire-fighting service, which had followed the Mustang down the runway, began spraying foam. Suddenly someone yelled!: 'Get the pilot out of the aircraft,' but Lofty had already jumped clear. He said later that he had no intention of staying in the cockpit until the Mustang stopped, so he leapt out and became an interested spectator while the foam was sprayed.

Lofty joined the RCAF twice after the war, then the RAF and ultimately the RAAF. He was shot down and killed in a helicopter operation in Vietnam.

I was to lead four Sabres on a 'target of opportunity' mission with George Thom as my No 3. George had decided that he didn't need maps, and as we walked out to the aircraft I said to him: 'George, when you get shot down today, give my regards to Rex Earp-Jones.' Rex had been a fellow-pilot during my tour on Mustangs. He'd been shot down and was a POW in a commie camp near the Yalu River. As it happened, I ground-aborted because of a faulty aircraft, and George took over the lead. Twenty minutes later he was shot down by ground fire and ended up in the Yalu River POW camp.After the war Rex told me an amusing story about George's arrival at the camp. They hadn't served together in the SAAF and therefore didn't know one another, so Rex asked George to identify himself. 'How d'you do?' he replied. 'I'm George Thom, and Al Rae sends his regards.'

Our base at K-55 housed many different detachments of 18 Fighter-Bomber Wing, and in the middle of a square a totem pole had been erected on which the plaques of the different units were hung in order of merit. I understood that points were awarded for the various activities each month, which determined the ranking, but for some reason or other 2 Squadron was always somewhere near the bottom of the pole. That incensed one of our pilots, Johnny Roberts, who decided that this blot on the squadron's good reputation must be erased.

He requisitioned an axe from stores, and after an evening in Rorke's Inn he decided that the time had come to fell the pole. Luckily Johnny was not a drinker, and the few beers he consumed spoilt his swing and his aim. He missed the pole, and before he could take another swipe, Major Pierrie Retief came out of his bungalow to see what all the noise was about. When he saw what Johnny was trying to do he shouted: 'Roberts, you chop that pole down and you are under arrest!' Needless to say, the totem pole stayed up and Johnny stayed free. He was killed after the war in a Tiger Moth accident in Rhodesia, as Zimbabwe was then known.

Guff Gow and I participated in one of the early Sabre missions led by Major Hagerstrom and his deputy Pat Buey of the USAF. While on the way to a MiG hunt along the Yalu River, Guff lost the flight and was chased back to base by a couple of MiGs. The remaining three of us crossed the Yalu River into China while chasing four MiGs but a shortage of fuel forced us to break off the chase and head for base with the MiGs becoming the chasers and closing in on us. Hagerstrom went his own way while Buey and I put our Sabres' noses down towards the south passing over the main Chinese air base. At one stage we thought that the MiGs had been outpaced but they were still there right behind and shooting at us until we turned into them when they broke away and disappeared.

Fuel was now critical and radar guided us back to a US forward base where both aircraft flamed out while landing. Hagerstrom was grounded for two weeks after this sortie. He ended up as one of the air aces of the Korean War with five MiGs to his credit. Buey and I could thank our lucky stars that the MIGs were such unstable gun platforms and their pilots so inexperienced.

Dangerous Cargo

Dick Clifton

Dick was no stranger to 2 Squadron when he took command in January 1952. He had been a flight commander in the same squadron ten years earlier during the Second World War when 'Fiffi' Stahlschmidt, one of the top scoring fighter aces in the Luftwaffe, shot him down. Seriously wounded, Dick baled out, and landed in the sea near El Alamein. He was rescued by an Australian soldier as he was about to pass out from exhaustion and loss of blood.

Fate is always the wild card in the dangerous environment of operational flying, and strange things happen in war that defy rational explanation. In the story I am going to tell, it would be presumptuous to talk of Providence or my guardian angel, so let's just say that Lady Luck saved my bacon. The fact is that John Naude, only half a wingspan away, was near enough to see the arming vane spinning off the bomb under the starboard wing of my Mustang. If he hadn't noticed and warned me, I would probably have been blown to smithereens in my dive-bombing attack, if not sooner. It was just a coincidence that he was there at all. Naturally at that particular stage of a mission he would have been in open battle formation, much too far off to notice. On the spur of the moment I had decided to bend the rules a little, but let's begin at the beginning.

The date was 3 May 1952; the place K46 airfield in South Korea; the mission close-support of United Nations ground forces near the 39th Parallel. Ostensibly a perfectly normal operation. But unknown to the participants, a plot had been hatched to sabotage one of the aircraft involved. It might have succeeded if that invisible power that governs the destiny of mortals had not decided to intervene and reshuffle the cards, so that a whole series of chances would combine to produce a quite different result. My decision to fly with B Flight that afternoon was purely arbitrary. Mustang 334 was allocated to me merely by chance. I would lead the section with Wally Hefer, John Naude and Wilbur Clark flying as No's 2, 3 and 4. These were three very experienced pilots who could be relied upon to fly in immaculate tight formation, even in those hot bumpy conditions. Take-off was to the south, and it suddenly struck me that this was a golden opportunity to give the erks a morale-booster while showing the 12th, 39th and 67th USAF Squadrons - our comrades in 18 Fighter-Bomber Wing - how South Africans could fly what the Yanks called 'show formation'.

After take-off I turned slightly to starboard, then to port, letting the section cut the corner to join up in the turn. A check with airfield control confirmed that there was no other traffic in the vicinity; then, after ordering the selection of fully fine pitch, I brought the section back in a shallow dive low over the strip with the Packard Merlins roaring at close on 61 inches of boost and 3 000rpm. As we sped past in tight finger formation and began climbing I was about to order: 'Battle Formation - Go!' when I heard Naude's quite casual voice: 'Cheetah Red Leader, Red 3, the arming vane on your bomb seems to be rotating.' My instinctive reply: 'Roger, watch it and let me know if it spins off,' was, of course, quite superfluous, as I knew instantly that the vane was going to come off. Obviously for some strange reason, the arming wire wasn't doing its job. A few seconds later Naude confirmed that the vane had flown off. Now I knew for certain that I was carrying a bomb fused live which was apt to explode at any moment if I didn't treat it ever so gently.

Most fighter-bomber pilots couldn't care less what goes on inside a bomb. They have a rough idea, of course, but their job is simply to deliver it accurately on target, so they are usually quite content to leave the details to the armourers. My good fortune was that I had been trained, many years before, as an armament specialist, and I knew only too well at that moment that nothing but a weak creep spring was holding the inertia striker off the highly sensitive detonator. Any sudden deceleration caused by firing the guns, throttling back quickly or a violent change of direction might be enough to explode the 500lb bomb.

In the turbulent air near the ground I could imagine the striker jolting back and forth within a hair's breadth of the detonator. Needless to say, I lost no time in climbing up to escape the bumps in the smoother air above. I had already opened up the formation, so there was no danger to the others. I had considered dropping the bomb immediately but as there was no way of making it safe, that would have been an unfriendly thing to do on our side of the front line. There was a designated area near K-46 for jettisoning bombs in an emergency, but the drill was to drop them safe for demolition later, so I also dismissed that possibility.

As we climbed the air became less turbulent, so there was no great urgency to shed my dangerous cargo. 'No problem now,' I thought; 'I'll just take it into North Korea and give it to the 'Gooks', dropping it straight and level, nice and gently, and I'll keep the other bomb for the target.'

What I hadn't bargained for was the enthusiasm of the forward air controllers. While approaching the prebriefed area I checked with

'Palomino', who immediately passed me on to 'Mosquito Snowflake 7', an airborne forward air controller. He was so keen to put us on to a hot target that he had lined up that I hadn't the heart to tell him there was a small problem. While listening to his excited directions, I decided it was too late to jettison this damned bomb, and in any case if it went off there would be some explaining, which might give the bloodthirsty Yank the wrong impression of the Cheetahs' operational expertise. So the decision was more or less made for me. I was not, however, going to take any unnecessary chances, so I made what must have been the gentlest wingover into a bombing dive that has ever been executed. That was followed by the smoothest possible aileron turn to line up the target and an ever so delicate backward pressure on the stick to get the aim right. What a pleasant relief it was to feel both bombs leave their carriers without any trouble! A hang-up of that live cookie would have been fatal - the pullout from the dive would almost certainly have set it off.

Feeling much better, I then led the way as we beat up the target with rockets and guns. The 'Mosquito' controller liked what we did, as is evident from my logbook entry for the mission: 'Attacked troops and supplies at CT 836537 under control of 'Mosquito Snowflake 7' after diversion from Palomino. Arming vane spun off tail fuse of my bomb shortly after take-off. Dangerous cargo!! 'Snowflake' gave us 90 per cent coverage and 80 per cent effectiveness.' These airborne forward air controllers attracted a lot of flak because the Gooks knew what they were up to, so I suppose one could hardly blame them for being bloodthirsty.

There was an interesting sequel to this incident. After my experience, the American Service Police kept a discreet watch on the flight line, and a day or two later they caught the saboteur red-handed. He was one of the locally recruited Korean labourers. The Mustangs were parked with their flaps fully down to relieve the hydraulic pressure in the actuating mechanism. When the aircraft were bombed up, the lowered flaps screened the tails of the bombs so that one had to stoop and peer under the flaps to check the fusing arrangements - something I had skipped that day. This commie 'Gook' mingled with the armourers during the hustle and bustle of re-arming, and when he thought no one was looking he quickly slipped off the safety clip on the tail pistol arming wire and withdrew the wire from the hole in one of the blades of the arming vane.

Perhaps I should explain that when a bomb is released in flight and its arming wire is locked electro-magnetically to the carrier, this wire is withdrawn and the vane, which is now free to rotate in the airstream, spins off when the bomb is a safe distance from the aircraft. However, in the case of a 'safe' jettisoning, the arming wire is released, thus preventing the vane from rotating and locking the striker so that it cannot fly forward under its own inertia on impact with the ground.

As might have been expected, the Americans dealt with the saboteur appropriately. They suspected that he might have had some success, as there had been a few occasions when USAF aircraft had disintegrated on bombing attacks over targets where there was little flak. This was even more likely because in the American squadrons it was common practice to fire the six 50-calibre machine-guns during a bombing dive to keep the flak gunners' heads down. It was also supposed that the vibration of the guns firing would prevent a hang-up if the release slip was iced up.

'Johnny Naidoo' - the nickname Naude earned while he was with 35 Squadron on Sunderland flying boats at Congella in Natal, where Indian surnames are plentiful - was wide awake to see that vane turning, and he earned my very special thanks. All the same, I can't help thinking that rather too many coincidences were happening that afternoon and that perhaps I should also direct my gratitude elsewhere. What do you think?

Thirteen - My Lucky Number

Topper van der Spuy

Topper distinguished himself in World War II when flying 161 operations in a Spitfire. In Korea he was a valuable member of 2 Squadron not only as a combat pilot but for his contribution towards uplifting morale, resulting from his humorous disposition and his talent while singing and strumming his guitar.

It was the first week in October 1951. My father had suffered a crippling stroke that had affected his brain, and the worst was expected. I was granted compassionate leave and my departure for Korea was extended by 14 days. While my father tenaciously held on to life, the time drew near for me to report for duty; and when I bade him farewell he sat up in bed, gathered enough strength to give me a hug and then pointed to the sky. 'Don't worry, son,' he murmured. 'I'll be seeing you up there one of these days.' His sudden burst of energy and his lucid words were totally unexpected, and I was devastated by the implication of his farewell.

214

I left Palmietfontein with one of the legendary pilots of the SAAF, Pikkie Rautenbach. We spent six days in Rome together waiting for John Montgomery, Jack Tindall and Shorty Leathers. Eventually the four of us arrived at K-10 in Korea, and as it happened we all survived the war.

On 6 March 1952 I flew on five combat missions, although the last one didn't progress far from the airstrip and turned out to be an experience never to be forgotten. The first mission of the day lasted an hour and 20 minutes. Our bombs left six vehicles in flames and a rail bridge destroyed, and three rail cuts after four runs. Two railway bridges were cut with rockets, and what appeared to be a huge haystack exploded when it was strafed with black smoke billowing up to 1 000ft. While we were leaving for base with all ammunition expended there were several additional explosions from the supposed haystack.

After three more missions, aircraft were refuelled and re-armed and while I was taxiing to the end of the airstrip for take-off I felt happy about flying my fifth sortie of the day as the maximum permissible number of sorties for my tour would soon be reached and I would be on the way home.

Shortly after becoming airborne I switched over from the left main fuel tank to the reserve tank, for the distance to the target area was not too far and it was necessary that most of the fuel in the reserve tank should be used before the target was attacked. An overfull tank altered the Mustang's centre of gravity, which could cause a flick over to the right or left when there was an increase in G force, and this was not a pleasant thought when a pilot was pulling out of a dive-bombing attack with intense flak bursting round him.

I could hardly have been more than 150ft above the ground when my engine cut dead. Instead of selecting the reserve tank, I had selected the wing tanks' position by mistake, and these tanks were not fitted. There was a deathly hush in the cockpit, thanks to a dead engine, and a mental bolt flashed through my mind and body when I realised that within a few seconds I should be crash-landing my aircraft loaded to capacity with fuel, bombs, rockets and ammunition. 'This is it.' My father's farewell words seemed prophetic.

The first priority was to jettison the bombs. The selector switches were on a panel, and they could be selected either singly or together. Near these switches there were two more tumbler switches to arm the bombs, and in my haste I not only selected both of the former switches but accidently flicked on one of the arming switches. The bombs fell clear when I pressed the release button, and a few seconds later there was a sharp shudder and a muted metallic thud as one bomb exploded somewhere close behind.

I was far too low to bother about re-selecting the main tank for the engine was starved of fuel and wouldn't pick up before the inevitable crash. Two huge trees loomed up ahead, but without power there was no hope of climbing over them, and fortunately the Mustang only hit the smaller branches as I selected full flap to reduce speed. The terrain was mountainous, rugged and undulating, and a river ran past some small paddy fields terraced towards it.

The aircraft dropped abruptly into a paddy field, ploughed to the end of it and crashed over a low retaining wall. Alas, the next paddy field was much lower, the Mustang breaking behind the cockpit on hitting the ground and as it aquaplaned through the adjoining field, the left wing was torn off. Fire, the fear that haunts all pilots during a crash landing, was uppermost in my mind for the aircraft's fuel load, rockets and ammunition could explode into a huge fireball.

The cockpit's canopy would not budge, so I tried the emergency release; and praise God it worked to some extent, and I hastily extricated myself from the cockpit, stumbled across the paddy field and dived behind a retaining wall that was high enough to protect me if the aircraft caught fire and exploded.

My sense of relief was overwhelming, and I remember putting my hands together and thanking the good Lord for his great mercy. My shattered nerves called for a cigarette, and, fishing out a packet from an overall pocket, I found it drenched with aviation fuel; indeed all my clothing was soaked in 120 octane! I could feel it stinging my backside. Unknown to me, the reserve tank had ruptured, and at first I had been protected by an abundance of clothing, including two pairs of long underpants, two pairs of long trousers, two thick T-shirts, a leather lumber jacket and an overall.

When I ventured back over the wall I saw a sorry sight. The Mustang lay there, a complete write-off. The rockets had been sheered off and were lying scattered behind the path of devastation like huge earthworms. It was sad to see the aircraft with its tail section buckled and torn apart. The fuel from the reserve tank was still dripping out of the tangled wreck and the left wing was lying near by, bent and resembling a grotesque monster. I had grown attached to that machine, for we had been through some frightening and exciting times together.

This was a dramatic finale. When looking at the cockpit I wondered how I had ever got out. The canopy was almost closed and would hardly budge. I saw my watchstrap lying on the cockpit floor but couldn't find the watch; and to this day I have never worn one again. (I lost my first Zobo watch in 1942 while flying upside down in a Tiger Moth. It slid out of my top overall pocket. And in World War II, after baling out of a Spitfire over Italy, I lost my second watch.)

Apparently when one of the bombs had exploded it had ripped off the eastern side of a large part of the roof of a Catholic church. Later I met the hardened priest of that church in the officer's mess at K-46. He had been in Korea since 1936. He was a tough, squat Irishman. His Irish accent was loud and clear when he called me a careless fool for damaging his church. He said that his flock had been confused, as the blast of the bomb had rocked the bell tower and the bell had rung a few times! We made our peace over a few snorts later on and parted good friends.

Three vehicles arrived virtually together at the scene of the crash, for no doubt the exploding bomb had been heard at base, or my flight must have alerted the control tower. An ambulance, a fire tender and a truck full of 2 Squadron mechanics stopped near the paddy field in which my aircraft lay, and more trucks arrived with both Cheetah and USAF pilots. It felt good when they shook my hand and I was aware that I was still alive. I thought again of my father's prophetic words. The number of my Mustang was 373 and its figures totalled 13. My casualty number for the day was 13, my two-way radio was 13W and the numbers of my 67 missions totalled 13!

John Montgomery, Harold Knight and 'Zulu' van Rensburg escorted me back to base. After a hurried de-briefing and a number of drinks, the maintenance staff strapped me in a harness from the parachute section, hitched it to the hook on the arm of a 'cherry picker' crane, and dangling aloft I was paraded down the main street of the village, Wonju, swaying over the low roof tops of the houses lining the streets. Children were waving, laughing and screaming at me. I was spiritually and physically elated, and so glad to be alive. Whenever I was lowered to the ground I was immediately topped up with a snort!

After a short rest at Chinhae I went back on to ops to complete my tour; but after one more sortie the CO, Dick Clifton, grounded me. I was thankful that my share in the war was over. The Americans gave me the sizzler of a farewell at K-10 which I shall never forget. It is a memory to cherish as long as I live.

'Doempie'

K B Mcdonald

Much credit goes to KB for this excellent sketch of the highly respected Doempie Cloete. KB was among the first volunteers to serve on a tour of operations with 2 Squadron in Korea. During World War II he operated against the Japs, flying Hurricanes and Thunderbolts. He was well known in the SAAF for his expertise as an aerobatic pilot and was the leader of the Central Flying School's aerobatic team before and after the Korean war.

When South Africa decided to send 2 Squadron to Korea in 1950, a Padre was an essential member of the detachment. The person to be selected caused much speculation among the members of 2 Squadron. When the name was published only two of us, 'AB' de Wet and I, knew him. He was Captain Michiel Daniel Victor Cloete MC. Both of us had served with him at the Permanent Force Training Centre, Voortrekkerhoogte in 1947. We were inundated with questions, and our assessment was that he'd have every member of the squadron eating out of his hand before the ship reached the Mocambique Channel; and we were right.

He was a great sportsman who excelled at all ball games, was an exceptionally fast left wing at rugby and a robust hockey player in any position. Tennis and squash were naturals. To portray some idea as to the calibre of the man, the citation to his immediate award of the Military Cross reads as follows:

'On the morning of the 13 October 1944 at 05h00, 'A' Company of the Wit/de la Rey Regiment formed up on the start line prior to an attack on the strongly held position of Mount Stanco. The enemy brought down a heavy concentration of shell fire, killing eight men including the company medical NCO, two stretcher bearers and wounding most of No 3 platoon. Captain Cloete, the Battalion Padre, who was with them, immediately worked his way towards the casualties under continual heavy fire and assisted the wounded. Here, despite the Red Cross flag he came under accurate spandau and sniper fire that pinned him down for an hour-and-a-half before he was freed. He then went on to re-organise the remaining stretcher bearers, personally rendering first aid to every wounded man and evacuating almost the entire platoon, only four of which had escaped unscathed. Shells were falling all round, but he struggled on over the difficult terrain and reached the village of Stanco where, entirely on his own initiative, he established a forward Regimental Aid Post, rendering aid to the casualties of all three forward companies and seeing to their evacuation.

'Finding the steep trench impassable he reconnoitred a route to 'B' Company HQ where 12 badly wounded men lay. Shell and mortar fire were raking the area but he successfully evacuated these casualties. He worked incessantly throughout the entire day under fire dragging the wounded to safety from highly dangerous areas, organising the jeep ambulances, keeping the stretcher bearers going with his superb example of unflagging energy and dauntless courage. 'Through his out-

218

standing and exemplary conduct under constant enemy fire, his untiring efforts, quick initiative and complete disregard for his own safety, saved many lives and were a vivid inspiration to all.'

This then was the man whom we were privileged to have with us in 2 Squadron. He once told me a story against himself, concerning an episode in Italy. The Wit/de la Rey were relieving a British Battalion in the Monte Casino area. It was a dark moonless night and during a hold-up, one of the 'Poms' standing near him, ignorant of the fact that he was talking to a Padre, said: 'I believe you are South Africans.' After Doempie had replied in the affirmative, the Pom said: 'And I believe that you're all volunteers.' Doempie answered once more in the affirmative and the Pom said: 'Well you must all be f...... mad!'

The first Sunday at sea, Doempie held a church service in the lounge of the *Tjisidane* which was not all that well attended, but word soon got round that here was something different. His services were completely interdenominational. There was none of the sing-song monotone that so many men of the cloth adopt as a pre-requisite to a church service. Here was a man who spoke about THE MAN and his teachings. By the end of the voyage there was standing room only at his services and that remained the norm throughout my stay in Korea.

It was a great morale booster for the pilots to see Doempie standing on the edge of the runway giving his ever famous thumbs-up sign before take-off, a time when a silent prayer must have been said for each pilot as he opened the taps and the pre-mission butterflies abated. During de-briefing, there was always a glass - yes, a glass of Doempie's coffee, but never has coffee tasted so good, accompanied by a subtle wise-crack or a gentle leg pull about a bad landing. It was uncanny how Doempie was able to understand the idiosyncrasies of each pilot and approach them in the right manner. He possessed the incredible ability of being able to sum up each individual mission - and there were thousands of them.

At the end of the day, in Rorke's Inn where Bob Monroe held court, Doempie would put in an appearance so as to keep a finger on the pulse of his boys, only disappearing when a drink was forced upon him.

Perhaps the best summing up of Doempie's contribution to the Cheetah saga in Korea is the Citation to his American Bronze Star: 'Captain Michiel D V Cloete distinguished himself by meritorious service in connection with military operations against the enemy as Chaplain to 2 Squadron SAAF, 18 Fighter-Bomber Wing, from 17 December 1950 to 1 December 1951. Capt Cloete's remarkable grasp of situations and his ability to furnish mature advice and constant inspiration to all ranks was invaluable to all personnel of the squadron. His diligent efforts resulted in a direct strengthening of the morale and social behaviour within the squadron. Through his outstanding devotion to duty which required a high degree of personal endeavour, Captain Cloete reflected great credit upon himself, the Far East Air Force and the South African Air Force.'

Upon his return to the Union, Doempie continued to serve in the Permanent Force until 1960 when he transferred to the South African Police as their Chaplain-General, being responsible for the initiation, development and organisation of the Police Chaplain Service. His distinguished work in this role was recognised by the award of the South African Police Star for Distinguished Service (SOO) and the Police Star for merit. He retired from the Police Force in 1977 with the rank of Major-General.

He is without doubt the greatest man of the cloth that I have had the privilege to know.

Diversified Talent

Willem van den Bos

Willem served with a Spitfire squadron in Italy during the Second World War and was shot down over Yugoslavia. He spent the last two months of the war as a POW. In Korea he was also shot down, but on that occasion he was rescued and completed his tour of operations.

On Saturday 18 August 1951 I was one of four Cheetah pilots sent on a close-support mission in the 'Punchbowl' area. Poor weather had hampered operations for several days and compelled 18 Fighter-Bomber Wing to abandon its forward base at K-16 which meant that the squadron had to fly direct from K-10 to its targets. On this occasion the controller decided that a close-support attack in such bad conditions might endanger our own troops, and since a shortage of fuel prevented aircraft from waiting for a break in the weather, the strike was called off.

We therefore decided to search for targets of opportunity north of the front line, and attacked the harbour at Changjon inflicting heavy damage on wharf installations and warehouses. My radio suddenly went dead, and as the weather to the south was deteriorating rapidly we landed at K-18, a newly established airfield on the east coast, south of Changjon, where the visibility clamped down soon after touch-down.

K-18 was being prepared as an operations base for 12 Marine Air Group USMC, and US Army, Air Force and Marine Corps personnel were working together to finish the job. They gave us a hearty welcome, and we spent the evening in the officers' club downing a few beers and chatting about Korea, the war, the US Armed Forces and the SAAF. Sunday dawned wet and gloomy, with no chance of flying so we had more beer and more talk. Monday brought a slight improvement in the weather but my radio was still temperamental in spite of some tinkering by 12 Marine Air Group, and it was ascertained that the weather further south had not improved; so any attempt to take off for K-10 was ruled out.

Just before lunch a Dakota of the Hellenic Air Force flew through a break in the cloud carrying a party of four girls from the American United Services Organisation (AUSO), who turned out to be talented entertainers. They put on a show for base personnel in the afternoon under difficult conditions. Julie acted as MC and sang a variety of popular songs in the style of singers who had made them famous; Peggy combined singing and dancing; Rosanne was an acrobatic dancer, while Terry accompanied them all on the piano accordion. The applause that they received was well deserved.

That evening the US liaison staff with the South Korean Army in the nearby village of Kangnung invited us to a party at their billets, so we and the four girls piled into a jeep and headed for the thrash. Whisky flowed freely and there was much singing by the girls, the American officers and ourselves. I have a vague recollection of solemnly making the commanders of the Army, Air Force and Marine Corps honorary members of 2 Squadron provided they could sing 'Ai Ziga Zumba'. Our drive back to K-18 in the pouring rain was somewhat erratic and included a breakdown, an involuntary sojourn in a ditch beside the road and the collapse of the canvas roof of the jeep which left us soaked to the skin. However, none of these mishaps dampened our spirits, and we eventually crawled into bed before dawn, waking up late in the morning feeling much on a par with the weather that was still lousy. At midday we sought consolation with beer, and with whisky when the beer ran out.

That evening there was a party in the K-18 Officers' Club with us 'Southafs' as the star performers. With Zulu songs, war dances and mock stick fights we managed to split a number of newly-laid floorboards though nobody seemed to mind. On Wednesday the weather improved, so after saying our farewells, heartily to the base personnel and fondly to the girls, we took off at 10h00 for K-10 and although my radio played up again and the weather deteriorated on the way south, we reached Chinhae before a total clamp down.

On Wednesday 5 September I was shot down north-east of Sunch'on, rescued by a US Navy helicopter and deposited on a US Navy

Landing Ship Dock off Wonsan. Four days later I was transferred to a minesweeper going south and put ashore on the beach near K-18 at 21h30 that evening. I was taken to the Officers' Club by jeep, and arrived in the middle of a party. The pilots of 12 Marine Air Group were enthusiastically singing a garbled version of 'Ai Ziga Zumba' and performing an equally amateurish version of a Zulu war dance! The team responsible for preparing the base had gone but they had left behind a tale of the four 'Southafs' and their singing and dancing. On learning that I was one of the four, the pilots of the Marine Air Corps requested some dual instruction, a request that I could hardly refuse.

That night I was given a bed in a tent occupied by three hard-core Southerners, Captain Hembree (Alabama), Captain Love (Texas) and Captain Rector (Virginia). Their capacity for hard tack during the two days I spent with them left me gasping, both figuratively and literally. Each had a case of rye whisky under his bed, and when the time came to quench their thirst, one of them would ceremoniously produce a bottle, unscrew the cap while muttering an incantation in which 'Magnolias', 'Southern Belles' and 'Damn Yankees' occurred at frequent intervals. Then unceremoniously the cap would be thrown through the open tent flap and the bottle would be passed from hand to hand tilted for a long swig. It was followed at intervals, which increased as the level in the bottle decreased, by a pannikin of water from which each man was invited to sip. The emptying of the bottle was followed by another incantation when it was dispatched to join the cap.

After two of these sessions I felt that if my liver was not to suffer permanent damage I had to get back to K-10 quickly, and I managed to hitch a lift on a Dakota flying to K-1, another Marine Air base. There I talked a pilot into flying me to K-10 in an Avenger. Three days and five missions later I landed back at K-10 just in time to see our four lasses from AUSO put on their show in the camp cinema. They were intrigued to learn of my second visit to K-18 and the impact that our 'Southaf' song and dance routine had made, perhaps, I suspect, more than their own show, despite their professionalism!

I didn't visit K-18 again during the rest of my tour with 2 Squadron, but I met the AUSO girls again during a leave in Tokyo a short while later. I often wonder what happened to those four lovely damsels and the three Marine Corps pilots during the passing years. I hope their lives have been as happy as mine.

Some Odes from Rorke's Inn

THE CHEETAH SQUADRON

Oh! It's easy to see it's not the Roosters (67 Squadron USAF)
For the Roosters only crow.
It's easy to see it's not the Cobras (39 Squadron USAF)
For the Cobras never put up such a wonderful show!
It's easy to see it's not the Foxes (12 Squadron USAF)
For the Foxes are too Few.
It's easy to see - who else could it be?
It's the Cheetahs every time.

- the 2nd South Afs -
- it's on your mess bill...
The Cheetahs every time!

'MUSTANG'

Mustang - jy moet nou huis toe gaan,
Mustang - jy moet nou huis toe gaan,
Mustang - jy moet nou huis toe gaan ....

Want die MiGs hulle skiet vir jou Mustang,
Die MiGs hulle skiet vir jou Mustang.
Daar by Sonch'on sal die koeels vir jou slaan.
Mustang, jy moet huis toe gaan!

Nee, nee nee my Mustang nee,
Nee my Mustang nee - nee my Mustang nee,
Nee, nee, nee my Mustang nee,
Ek gaan nie terug na Sonchon nie!!

'THE BLUES OF CHINHAE'

(Theme Song of 18 Fighter-Bomber Wing)
From Chinhae to P'yongyang,
From Taegu to Seoul,
Wherever our Mustangs go;
I've carried some napalm,
I've fired a few rockets,
But there is one thing I know:
The Chinese are two-faced -
A worrisome thing that'll
Lead you to sing:
The Blues of Chinhae.

Chorus: Hear the Flak a-blowin'
See the MiG's a-goin'
WILDWEST! I can't get my tanks off,
Well, laddie, you've had it,
But there is one thing I know:
You can't do a thing,
But sit here and sing,
The Blues of Chinhae.

We call into Mellow,
He knows we're not yellow,
And on to the target we go;
The weather is stinkin'
The engines are clinkin'
But there is one thing I know:
The 80s can't do it,
They're bungling things
That lead you to sing
The Blues of Chinhae.

Chorus: Up and down the Yalu
Hear the pilots yellin' - HEY YOU'.
By order MacArthur,
We can't go no further;
We can't do a thing,
But sit here and sing,
The Blues of Chinhae.

We call a controller,
Start beating our molars,
His answer is 'Stand by, please!'
I'm working some 84s,
I do wish they'd carry more,
They're only fanning the breeze,
They'll be through in a minute,
Then you can come in
And do the right thing,
For the Group from Chinhae.

Chorus: Coming down the Nak-tong,
Pilots sing but one song,
'I've finished my missions,
Now let me go fishin'.'
But the first thing he does,
Is come in to buzz,
The strip at Chinhae.

Now this ends my story
Of fame and of glory,
Together we've known hectic days;
We've had many good laughs,
The 18th and South Afs,
For whom we have nothing but praise.
Oh, I'm going to the ZI,
And tell one and all
Of the deeds large and small, Of the Group from Chinhae.

BESIDE A KOREAN WATERFALL

Beside a Korean waterfall, one bright and sunny day;
Beside his shattered Mustang a young pursuiter lay;
His parachute hung from a nearby tree, he was not yet quite dead;
So listen to the very last words the young pursuiter said:
QUOTE:
I'm going to a better land, a better land, that's right;
Where whisky flows from telegraph poles, play poker every night.
There isn't anything to do but sit around and sing.
There will be lewd nude women:
Oh, death where is thy sting?
Oh, death where is thy sting? ting-a-ling,
Oh, death where is thy sting? ting-a-ling,
The bells of hell will ring, Ting-a-ling
For YOU but not for me!'

IT'S A LONG, LONG WAY FROM PUSAN TO P'YONGYANG

It's a long, long way from Pusan to P'yonyang,
And the mountains are high and wide;
If my engine quits, you can write off a Mustang,
'Cause I'm fixin' to go over the side.
Now close-support is a damn fine mission,
'Cause you work so close to the troops,
But fifties and forties will get you in the coolant,
Then she'll cough and she'll splutter and poop;
So you bail right out while your buddies circle around you
As the Commies blaze away,
And the 'Copter comes in and picks up your elbows,
Registration boys will get the rest some day.

It's a damn fine war and we love every mission,
And we hope we're here to stay,
For we'd rather fight than go out fishin'
They can keep the R and R and the pay.
Now Commandant ..... is a damn fine leader,
But he leads you into the flak,
Then it's 61 - 3 000, as we clean out the engines,
And the drinks are on the last man to get back.

'ON TOP OF OLD P'YONGYANG'

On top of old P'yongyang,
All covered with flak
I lost my poor wing man -
He'll never come back!
For flying's a pleasure
And dying's a grief
And a quick-triggered commie
Is worse than a thief.
For a thief will just rob you
And take all you save.
But a quick-triggered commie
Will send you to the grave.
Now this story's moral
Is easy to see
Don't go to Sinanju
Or old Kunu-ri,
Steer clear of old P'yongyang
All covered with flak,
Stay south of the bombline
If you want to come back!

Split S on to my bomb run
I got too goddam low,
I pressed the panic button -
Let both my babies go,
Then pulled the stick back too damn quick,
And hit a high speed stall,
Now I won't see my mother -
I think I'll see damn-all
Chorus
MUSTANG LAMENT

Once I was happy and I flew a jet,
At 35 000 how fat can you get?
But now I'm a retread and bolder I grow,
So I fly a Mustang - it's old and it's slow.
Chorus:
Sinuiju and Anak, Sinanju and Sinmak,
They'll drive you crazy, they'll drive you insane.
Quad 50s and 40s and 100 sorties,
They'll drive you crazy, they'll drive you insane.
I went to Saldanha for six weeks to train,
They gave me a Spitfire - that's no aeroplane.
Then I came to Korea to fly with this group,
My hair's turning grey and my wings have a droop.
Chorus:
I flew my first mission and it was a snap,
Just follow the leader - don't look at the map.
But now I've got 30 and lead a sad flight,
Go out on armed recce and can't sleep at night.
Chorus:
Went up to MiG Alley, S2 said 'no sweat',
If I hadn't looked round I'd have been up there yet.
Six MiGs jumped my tail and the leader yelled 'BREAK'!
61 and 3000, how my knees did shake.
Chorus:
If I live through a hundred and they ask for more,
I'll tell them to shove it ; my back is too sore,
They can ram it and jam it for all that I care,
Just give me a ground job, a desk and a chair.
Chorus: Loud and Clear.

'MAYDAY - MAYDAY - MAYDAY'

It was midnight in Korea
All the pilots were in bed
When I spoke to General Rogers,
And this is what he said:
'Mustangs, gentle pilots, Mustangs old and slow,
Mustangs, gentle pilots, and all the pilots shouted 'No!!'
Then up stepped a young lieutenant
With a voice as harsh as brass -
'You can take those goddamn Mustangs Jack,
(Concluding line as appropriate)
Chorus:

Oh, Hallelujah! Hallelujah!
Throw a nickel on the grass
Save a Fighter Pilot's (Life)
Oh, Hallelujah! Hallelujah!
Throw a nickel on the grass
And you'll be saved.

Cruising down the Yalu
Doing three twenty per,
Called the Cheetah Leader:
Won't you save me, Sir?!
Got two big flak holes in my wing.
My tanks ain't got no gas
Mayday - Mayday - Mayday
There's Six MiGs on my (tail)
Chorus:
I flew my traffic pattern
To me it looked all right,
My airspeed read 130,
Goddam, I racked it tight
I turned on to the final
My engine gave a wheeze,
Mayday, Mayday, Mayday:
Spin instructions, please!
Chorus:
Fouled up my crosswind landing
My left wing hit the ground,
Came a call from Tower:
'Pull up and go around!'
I racked that Mustang in the air
A dozen feet or more -
I'm on my back, it's worse than flak,
Why did I use full bore!

A Friend to All

Pottie Potgieter

Pottie is a cheerful, unforgettable personality who served in the Cheetah Squadron from 26 September 1950 to 8 May 1951. He had won a DFC in Italy during the Second World War and in Korea he was awarded the American Purple Heart, the first South African pilot to be wounded in action.

The camp and the surrounding countryside were still and quiet. Everyone, including the birds, seemed to be asleep except the shadowy figures of the erks busy with their Mustangs in the bays. Another day was about to dawn and the camp would be woken by the roar of Merlin-Packard engines as they burst into life to be tested for take-off on a mission over North Korea. Inside the ops tent a bright light illuminated a topo-cadastral map surrounded by sleepy-eyed pilots listening to Thys Uys, the ops officer, as he briefed them on the first mission of the day. In the background stood the Padre, Captain M de V Cloete MC, a veteran of World War II, who was usually present at all briefings and de- briefings; in fact he would rather have missed a night's sleep than one of those occasions that kept him in touch with the operational dangers and difficulties facing the Cheetah pilots.

Doempie, as he was affectionately called, stood in a characteristic pose listening to the proceedings, his hands stuck deep in the pockets of his pile jacket, with a blue woollen scarf round his neck. When the briefing was over he chatted to the pilots, cracking jokes with them to ease the tension, and he would stand by the side of the runway to bid them luck and God speed, giving them the thumbs-up as they sped past on their way to battle. When the Mustangs returned he would watch them land and chaff the pilots as they climbed out of their cockpits; and so to de-briefing, where once more he stood quietly in the background listening to the account of unfolding dramas. After the de-briefing had been completed and Thys had said, 'OK, chaps, that's all for now,' Doempie would hand a mug of coffee to each pilot and then conduct his own version of de-briefing. Jerks McClean, Ian Gow and I were all in the firing line as Doempie said: 'Jerks, is that the way to land a Mustang, dropping it so high above the ground? I'll have to show you how we did things in Italy during World War II, my boy.' Everyone roared with laughter, for Jerks was no monkey as a pilot and had won a DFC in Italy. 'What about my landing?' Ian asked Doempie, and was promptly told: . 'Ag man, jy's sleg. Jy kan nie 'n kruiwa land nie - jy's sleg!'. This brought further gales of laughter; and then he turned to me: 'Pottie, hoe het dit vandag gegaan?' to which I replied: 'Nie te sleg nie, Doempie, ek het darem terug gekom.' 'Top line!' he replied.

Much to Thys's relief, the grinning bunch of pilots left the ops tent and he suddenly found himself shouting over the telephone that Doempie was an R & R (rest and recuperation) case!

While I was strafing an enemy tank after my 73rd mission, a bullet passed through the side of my windscreen and knocked off my goggles as I pulled out of the bombing dive. This was the second occasion when I had been fortunate enough to escape with my life, for on 30 March 1951 I had been injured during an operation near Munsan while I was leading a mission of two aircraft. My machine was hit by anti-aircraft fire; a bullet pierced the radio control box and hit me in the right elbow and chest but I managed to complete the mission before returning to base.

After the second lucky escape Doempie took me to see the CO, S V Theron to whom he said: 'Commandant, this is Pottie's second narrow escape and I don't want to conduct his funeral service. He has flown 73 of the 75 missions of his tour, so may I suggest that you send him home immediately.' Three days later I was on my way.

Everyone who served in the Cheetah Squadron with Doempie had the greatest respect and affection for this compassionate Padre who was everybody's friend.

Our Erks Were The Best

Harold Knight

Harold was one of several first class engineering officers whose services the Cheetah Squadron were fortunate enough to enjoy during its three years in Korea. Certainly the ground crews were 'the best', but without the leadership, know-how and enthusiasm of men like Harold, this would not have been a fait accompli.

A contingent of some 60 men under my leadership arrived in Korea during late 1951. From K-10, a number of us were flown to the squadron's forward base at Wonju (K-46).

The discipline amongst our South African ground staff was far superior to that of the Americans, but this can be understood for our men were all Permanent Force members who took a great pride in their work, whereas the Americans were conscripted members of the USAF and a rotation system of service was adopted. On several occasions I was approached by American Officers to loan them some of our Squadron NCOs to knock their men into shape but of course this wasn't allowed.

I was fortunate to enjoy the services of men who could repair unserviceable parts, which was one of the reasons why the Squadron's rate of serviceability was always so good. Normally new parts would be used to keep aircraft flying but these weren't always readily available, so to avoid extensive delays, repaired parts filled the gap.

Our ground crews always showed a great interest in their aircraft and the pilots who flew them, imbuing confidence in the pilot's who knew only too well that their lives depended on well cared for aircraft. When a pilot landed from an operation, a member of his ground crew was always waiting for him and climbed on his aircraft's wing next to the cockpit to enquire how the aircraft had behaved during the mission.

Operations under the extreme cold conditions in Korea promoted many problems and rough engines were amongst these. This was caused by the lead in the highly-leaded fuel separating and depositing on the plug points. No stone was left unturned in smoothing out the running of the engines. The cold at times was so bitter that water was not available for washing or shaving. On one occasion the diesel in the stove turned to a treacley goo and the stove went out. I remember our CO Dick Clifton trying to blow diesel through the pipes and seeing the tell-tale black marks on his lips next morning.

The story of the repair to Mustang 348 has been told in this book but I would like to mention the names of some of the men who worked under me on that occasion and carried out a fine job under the eyes of the communists. Those who come readily to mind are Sonie Barber, Horace Hudd, Eric Burger, Jan van Wyk, Andries Visser, Doug Brown, David Bouwer, Claude Collocot, Fritz Ditmer and Thys Greef. All credit should go to these men for their outstanding achievement in repairing the Mustang so that it could be flown off the short strip by Attie Bosch who excelled when taking off using only 5/6th of the distance available.

The spares required for the repair were taken to Kumwha by truck. Some were new, others were taken from grounded aircraft and some were our own repaired parts. The USAF were extremely helpful and allowed me to rob serviceable parts from their out-of-commission aircraft.

One of the highlights of our life at K-46 included the occasion when Shadow Gardiner-Atkinson was badly shot up and made a one-wheel landing at K-46. This he did with meticulous precision and only a minimum of further damage to the Mustang occurred.

I also remember the time Lofty Lance had to be talked into a one wheel landing by Tex Lyons. We listened to the radio intercom as Lofty explained why he should bale out, but Tex wouldn't hear of it.'You bale out and you'll face a court martial,' he told Lofty, so Lofty circled for a while to use up the fuel and then made a perfect one-wheel landing. Both aircraft were repaired and placed back in service.

There is no doubt in my mind that the morale of 2 Squadron, in spite of the trying conditions under which we were obliged to work, was of a very high standard and this in no small measure assisted the Squadron towards its award of the American Presidential Citation.

Delayed Rescue

Mike Muller

Mike completed his tour of operations in Korea during a drama-packed four month period in 1951 when ten Cheetah pilots were killed in action. He was fortunate to escape with his life on a number of occasions. In 1979 he reached the summit of his professional career when promoted to Lieutenant-General and appointed Chief of the South African Air Force.

On 3 October 1951 I was one of the leaders of two Cheetah flights in a Wing formation briefed for a rail-cutting mission deep into enemy territory. En route to the target there were two loud explosions under my aircraft and glycol began spewing from the engine and streaming past the cockpit.

Capped by my No 3, Amo Janse van Rensburg, and the other two members of the flight, Eric Keevy and Frank Grobler, I headed eastwards towards the coast but the engine temperature was soon off the clock. Bearing in mind the occasions Vernon Kruger and Frank Grobler had been burnt as flames were sucked into their cockpits when opening the canopies to bale out, I was determined to escape before my aircraft began burning.

Scrambling over the side, my right foot got trapped in the cockpit and my body hung in space flapping back and forth against the fuselage like a puppet on a string. After some frantic wriggling of the foot it came free and I shot away from the Mustang missing the tailplane by a fraction and waiting until clear, I pulled the ripcord. What a wonderful feeling to look up and see the parachute mushroom above me. I landed in a tree, the 'chute draping over its branches acting as a perfect beacon for the enemy to locate my position.

After removing the 'chute from the tree I decided to climb up the slope of the hill and position myself on the ridge where the capping pilots would have a better chance of observing and protecting me. On the way I stumbled into a clearing and when waving my scarf at the capping pilots they spotted me and made a number of low passes. Frank Grobler came so low that I recognised him despite his mask and helmet. Automatic rifle fire opened up nearby, presumably at the low flying aircraft and I feared for the pilots' safety, but I was also afraid that the 'Gooks' would use the surrounding bush to close in on me unseen from the air so decided to descend into an open area in the valley where the pilots would have an easier task spotting the enemy.

233

While sliding down a ravine hidden by bush I lost my .38 revolver but didn't bother to look for it. Widening the gap between myself and the nearby enemy was top priority. In the valley I sheltered in a rocky outcrop and used my survival signal mirror to attract the attention of the capping pilots, a move that I was to discover later had almost blinded them.

By this time a USAF flight had taken over capping duties from my flight and this was followed by another Cheetah flight led by Brian Martin, but still no sign of a rescue helicopter, and I became uneasy. The rescue organisation in Korea was fantastic, a great morale booster to pilots, and although I was far into enemy territory I calculated that the rescue should have been effected within two hours, yet three hours had already passed.

My heart almost dropped into my combat boots when the leader of a third flight of capping aircraft made a low pass in a southerly direction waggling his aircraft's wings. This was the standard procedure to inform a downed pilot that a helicopter was not available and he must make his own plan to escape following the direction in which the aircraft was pointing. I was about to start walking when I heard the welcome sound of a Sikorsky helicopter flying up the valley and to my surprise a naval chopper appeared. It was a pleasing sight to see a bearded sailor lowering the rope for me and a blessed relief when he pulled me inside. The pilot glanced at me, gave a smile and thumbs-up and we were away with four Panther jets escorting us.

The helicopter had been hit by small-arms fire during the rescue and the damage caused some problems when landing back on the ship. A physical examination revealed no other injuries apart from an abrasion on my chin. Less fortunate was the Corsair pilot, Leslie Downes, who I'd met on board the helicopter. He'd been rescued after baling out of his burning aircraft and was treated for 2nd degree burns on his face, neck, wrists, knees and ankles. I was to learn later why I had been forced to spend over four hours on the ground before the rescue. The first helicopter detailed to rescue me was shot down, along with one of the supporting aircraft, and the Naval chopper was sent from USS Gunston Hall as an alternative. The machine had a limited range so the Gunston Hall moved south down the coast to cut down on the return distance.

That afternoon I was taken to Yodo Island off Wonson harbour as the guest of a commando unit of the Royal Marines and stayed until the following evening. The unit was carrying out an operation that night so the men were dressed in combat gear and their faces blackened.

I was taken to an airfield where a Dakota flew me back to K-10 on 5 October. When I walked into OC Barry Wiggett's office he said: 'Welcome back Mike, pack your bags. Your operational tour is over.' 'I still have three sorties to go,' I replied. 'You've had enough,' retorted Barry. I think he was right and no further persuasion was offered!

A Legendary Deed

Vernon Kruger

Thirty-seven years after the Korean War ended the SAAF still remembers the occasion Jan Blaauw won the highest American award for bravery. For the first time here is the story of this heroic event, as told by Vernon Kruger, for whom Jan risked his life. Vernon was shot down on the 74th sortie of his operational tour.

At 07h00 on the morning of 11 May 1951, a flight of four Mustangs took off from K-10 for a road interdiction mission in the Kaesong area north of Seoul. Jan Blaauw was the leader, I was No 3 and Pat Clulow and Martin Mentz No's 2 and 4. The flight was to be made from the forward air base at Suwon, so there was every chance that three more sorties would be flown before we returned to K-10, meaning that the total number of sorties for my tour of operations could reach 75 and I would soon be on my way home to South Africa.

Two hours later our Mustangs landed at Suwon, and after the aircraft had been refuelled and rearmed, we were ordered on a second interdiction mission in the same area. That was carried out without mishap, and to my delight we took off again later that afternoon, which was my 74th sortie with only one more to go. It was a road reconnaissance in the Kaesong area, and I was flight leader with Jan Blaauw as my wingman.

At first the recce passed without mishap, and I seem to remember that we bombed a small dam with the intention of breaching it and flooding the road beneath. Continuing the search for targets of opportunity, Jan and I flew low while Pat and Martin provided top cover. Before long I spotted what appeared to be some ack-ack guns, and as I pulled up and turned to take a closer look, Jan reported that they were firing at us. I ordered the formation to attack, peeled down on to a gun pointing in my direction and plastered it with rockets and shells. While I was about to open fire during a second attack a shell hit my port wing and nearly turned the aircraft on its back.

After recovering, I pulled out of the dive, climbed to about 2 000ft and turned towards the south. The aircraft seemed to be flying normally, but the port wing was on fire and there was a large jagged hole right through it. The time had come for me to get out quickly. The bale-out proved to be simple enough until the canopy was jettisoned, when flames were drawn into the cockpit. The sequence of my movements as the flames scorched my hands and face are vague, but I remember tumbling through the air, pulling the ripcord and floating earthwards.

The parachute opened at no higher than 1 000ft, and my left shoulder hit the ground while I was trying to stop the 'chute's oscillations. As I was struggling to release the harness, it was obvious that my shoulder was broken and only one arm was usable. While hopping and hobbling towards a shallow donga I found that my ankle was sprained and my left hand and forehead were badly burnt.

My feelings at that time are difficult to describe; but I believed that if the communists captured me I would probably not survive. It was about four in the afternoon and I could hear the guns firing at the three aircraft circling above. They must have been short of fuel, and when they left, that would be it, for already there was movement in some of the trees nearby. Every now and again Jan would make a strafing run to discourage the possibility of enemy soldiers creeping towards my position. I had been on the ground for about half an hour when two of the top cover aircraft disappeared leaving Jan who continued to circle and strafe the area from time to time.

After another 15 to 20 minutes, some American aircraft arrived; then to my utter astonishment and horror, Jan's Mustang approached flying very low and slow, with its canopy open and flaps down. I watched in disbelief as the aircraft crash-landed, wheels up, in a small paddy field nearby. The engine broke away from the fuselage, and seconds later Jan came running towards me through a cloud of dust. There was blood on his face and he seemed to have gone out of his mind shouting 'klippe, klippe!' and darting about like a maniac picking up stones and piling them in a heap. A short while later he explained that a helicopter was on its way and the stones were needed to adjust the centre of gravity of the chopper when it picked us up.

Jan helped to dress my burns, and he told me that Pat and Brian had been sent home when he realised they wouldn't have sufficient fuel to reach Suwon if they stayed to cover me; yet Jan chose to remain knowing full well that he would not be able to return to base and that a bale-out or crash-landing was inevitable. It was that decision, which endangered his life to save mine, that in my opinion made him the bravest of the brave.

I can't remember how long we were on the ground, but there was a lot of firing going on in the vicinity, mostly directed at the covering aircraft. There seemed to be at least a dozen of them overhead, and as daylight was fading rapidly it was a relief when a S-51 helicopter arrived and landed nearby. The pilot and crewman helped Jan and me to climb inside, put a few of the stones in the baggage compartment and made a hasty take-off. They offloaded us at a forward army medical unit at last light when I was taken to the operating tent for treatment. I was flown back to K-10 the next day and then on to an Australian base hospital at Hiroshima in Japan.

My 75th and last sortie was therefore flown in a helicopter and ambulance Dakota. I was in hospital for about three weeks when Jan visited me. When I tried to thank him for his heroic deed, he refused to talk about it and brushed it aside saying: 'Vergeet dit. Ons vlieeniers moet mos saamstaan.' (Forget it - we pilots must stand together). Incidentally, Horse Sweeney who had been wounded by ground fire, was in the ward when I was admitted. A few days later Piet Cilliers who had been shot down and then wounded by Chinese troops on the ground before being rescued by helicopter, joined us. Being together in the same ward was a real morale booster.

The Thunder-Box

Don Parker

Don has enjoyed a distinguished career in aviation and during his 25 000 flying hours, he flew many different types of aircraft from Spitfires in World War II to Comets and Jumbo jets for South African Airways. A tour of operations on Mustangs in Korea was but a short interlude during his eventful life.

The Koreans were known for their fertile and high crop-yielding paddy fields - after all, their staple diet is rice, and the better the harvest, the richer the farmer. Their fertiliser came from a communal toilet, built at the corner of a paddy, and during the night they would scoop the contents out of the 'long drop' with a wooden 'honey bucket', and spread the evil-smelling mixture over the fields.

At K-10, a perennial stream flowed through the camp. The Americans diverted this to one of the nearby Korean toilets and along its course built a 40 seater thunder-box over the swiftly running water. The result was water-borne sanitation for the officers, and luscious green fields with bountiful crops for the Koreans!

There was no privacy on the thunder-box as users sat shoulder to shoulder, cheek to jowl, on the wooden structure. During peak periods, all holes were occupied with an impatient queue forming nearby.

This proved too much of a temptation for one South African - I think it was Mickey Rorke - who constructed a wooden float, placed some paraffin-soaked old newspapers on it, ignited them and launched the flaming float from an upstream position. You can imagine the screams of agony as the victims had their tender regions singed by the

237

passing flame. The only reason that the perpetrator escaped was that the injured had their pants round their ankles!

There was much jollity and back-slapping at Rorke's Inn that night, but the Yanks, despite an intensive search, never discovered the identity of the flame launcher!

A Promise Fulfilled

Gordon Marshall

Gordon (known as Gus in the Squadron) completed his tour of operations in July 1951. He won the DFC for leading an attack on enemy positions so heavily defended that he and his flight were fortunate to escape unscathed. This moving story confirms that good is often derived from the horrors of war. As a missionary over the past 37 years Gordon has brought hope and comfort to the underprivileged throughout Africa.

I volunteered to join 2 Squadron in Korea because I thought it would be an exciting adventure and it certainly was. After a month of operations I had an experience that was to change the entire course of my life.

I was one of two Mustang pilots taking part in a reconnaissance mission and on the way back to base at Chinhae we became separated and I was flying alone below a cloud base of about 1 000ft.

A strange sight appeared to starboard that looked like a long line of army ants moving slowly in the snowbound countryside. I was fascinated and flew low over the strange scene, and to my amazement observed thousands of people walking along the main railway line that runs from Seoul towards the south. They were carrying bundles on their backs and were dressed in white clothing. The men wore tunics and trousers like jodphurs and the women long white dresses. When flying closer I could see that they were plodding through mud and were barefooted. It was a pathetic sight and far behind they had left their homes and most of their worldly possessions. What tragic thoughts must have been passing through their minds. Yes, they were refugees without any promise for a future livelihood or existence.

I scanned the 'sea of snow' round me and realised that these poor refugees were inadequately dressed for the terrible weather they were experiencing. The children and the aged must have been suffering dreadfully. This scene was soon behind me as I sped south in my Mustang, but it was an experience that was to haunt me forever.

Something happened to me that day that related to my own spiritual life and future. I had become a Christian believer at the age of six and had deep convictions about the reality of God and I knew that HE had a plan for my life. This, coupled with the experience of seeing those thousands of people in dire need made me vow that I would offer the rest of my life to serve God and help such people. The day would come when I would no longer fly warplanes but devote my time as either a missionary or a minister.

I was not a pacifist because I knew that the enemy had to be severely dealt with to save South Korea from godless communism. This was only the first month of my operational tour with many sorties still to be flown. I knew that 'G' flight would take to the air everyday to help stem the tide of communism and I thought of my friends who had already given their lives for this cause. There were Elmer Wilson and Foxy Ruiter and so many others. As No 2 to Lippy Lipawsky I had learnt one day through an experience of near disaster that this was a merciless WAR. Lippy lectured me in no mean fashion when we got back to Chinhae. I never forgot his words.

War is tragic but out of its horrors come experiences that change us, especially in our relationships with other human beings. There were those who risked their lives with you every time a flight of four departed on a mission. There were the Marine Commandos who camped with us for a while and listening to their gruesome story of the evacuation of Hungham made us feel so very fortunate not to have been there in the mud and snow on that occasion.

At the end of my tour 'Horse' Sweeney and I were sent home on BOAC via Rome where we connected with SAA. Due to the unserviceability of aircraft we spent eight days in Rome when there was time to reflect on the war in Korea. Horse had been seriously wounded in action but had recovered well. The wonderful city of Rome was so far removed from Korea and the war that it was hard to believe our experiences hadn't been a bad dream.

Back home I found myself at the Central Flying School once more and then one day I became restless. It was the memory of those miserable Korean refugees trudging through the snow, not knowing when they would eat again. I kept my promise to God and by March 1952 started flying missionaries in Southern Sudan.

Liaison with the Cheetahs

Jock Lello

Jock, who is now the President of the Korean war Veterans Association, volunteered to fly with 2 Squadron in the Korean war. He was accepted as a replacement pilot, and he completed his OTU training on Spitfires with a conversion to Vampire jets. Shortly before leaving for Japan and Korea he was declared unfit for operational flying because he wore corrective lenses. He desperately pleaded with the Chief of the SAAF at that time, Brigadier Bennie Viljoen, to send him to Korea in any capacity, and he was appointed administration officer to the Senior SA Liaison Officer in Tokyo, Colonel Danie du Toit. It was the good fortune of the Cheetah Squadron that such a capable and friendly officer was available to help organise their movements between South Africa, Japan and Korea and to look after their 'rest and recuperation' arrangements when on leave in Japan.

Shadow Gardiner Atkinson was the temporary administration officer when I arrived at SALO HQ in Tokyo. He had completed a tour of flying operations in Korea and had been helping out before his return home. He showed me the ropes and told me who should be approached at Haneda airport to get incoming aircrew through customs and immigration without trouble. It was no less important to find out how to shepherd a bunch of none too sober tour-expired pilots on to a homeward-bound aircraft in the early hours of the morning. It was also my job to take arriving pilots to the transit billets in Tokyo, book them in, and then next morning to pick them up and take them to Danie du Toit for briefing. While that job was in progress I would book seats on a 'Military Air Transport Schedule' flight from Tatchikawa airport to Korea, and once the seats had been confirmed and flight numbers known I would put through a radio phone call to the Adjutant of 2 Squadron, Japie Smits, giving him the details so that the new draft could be met at a Korean air base.

I spent many hours at Tatchikawa airport waiting for delayed aircraft bound for Korea or for Cheetah pilots due to arrive in Tokyo for a ten day 'rest and recuperation' break from operations. On their arrival pilots would invariably book in at one of the numerous transit messes and then wallow in a long, luxurious hot bath. The 'Onson' Tokyo was a popular rendezvous, with Turkish baths where one could relax for many hours. This treatment would rejuvenate the battle-wearied pilots who would often be waiting for me at my billet when I returned from work, hoping that I would show them the hot spots; which I usually did. There were many shows, restaurants and night clubs-cum-bars waiting to catch the big money spenders. The Nicki Gieke, or Round Theatre similar to the Lido in Paris, was a favourite spot. It ran 23 hours a day, and I never saw it empty.

When they were on their way home the pilots were more circumspect in their behaviour, and they liked to spend their brief interval in Tokyo shopping for presents. I would often receive a letter or a radio phone call asking me to buy an electric train set or arrange for a Mikimoto pearl salesman to come to the SALO HQ so that they could buy jewellery to take home. A little Japanese man would arrive on appointment carrying a battered leather briefcase. He would lay a green baize on my desk and up-end two or three chamois leather bags filled with pearls of every size, shape and colour, rings, earrings and bracelets, a king's ransom and a sight to behold. For as little as 200 dollars you could buy a double string of perfectly matched cultured pearls. Such gifts must have brought joy to many a girl's heart, and they are no doubt still their pride and joy.

Communication between races was often beset by hidden potholes that could lead to embarrassing situations. Soon after I arrived in Tokyo I needed an eraser, so I went to a shop and asked the Japanese girl at the stationery counter for a rubber. Imagine my surprise when she said: 'So solly Lootenant, no keep lubbers, you tly the toiletly counter.' I asked at the toiletry counter and was told by another girl: 'So solly, only sell packets of tlee.' Only then did the penny drop and I beat a hasty retreat. I then sent Abie Botha to the shop with strict instructions to ask for an eraser, as the word rubber in American phraseology meant condoms!

As with all airmen away from home, receiving mail was important to morale. In South Africa all mail for the Far East was delivered to the SA Army Post Office where it was bagged and sent by air via Rome and Hong Kong to Haneda airport in Tokyo. From there the British Army Post Office took it for sorting at Ebisu. Kirie Prinsloo would go to Ebisu three times a week, pick up the South African Air Force bag and return to SALO HQ, where he would deposit the mail for 2 Squadron with the American post office and bring our mail back to our billets. It usually took about three days in transit from South Africa but up to a week from Tokyo to the squadron, which was considered too long. During a Sunday lunch at the British Officers' mess, at Ebisu, the only place in Japan where a genuine roast beef and Yorkshire pudding could be found, I mentioned this delay, and learnt that the mail from the British Commonwealth left Tatchikawa airport every midnight on a special flight to Pusan and Seoul.

Next morning I arranged with the British Army Post Office at Ebisu to fly our mailbags to Seoul and to take them from there in their mailvan to K-55 on the way to the British Commonwealth HQ. Feeling very proud of myself, I told Danie du Toit that delay in mail between Japan and the squadron no longer existed. He replied: 'Godt jong Jocks, it sounds all right, but you'd better send a bag of old magazines and news-papers first just to check that all is well.' I had already told Kirie to send the Wednesday night's bag to Korea through the British Army post office, but what with meeting and sending pilots home plus Kirie being away on Monday and Tuesday I failed to change the instruction.

On Thursday morning Danie passed through our office to his own office, as was the usual procedure. Obviously the storm flags were flying. His cap was at an angle on his head and our chorus of 'Good morning, sir' was returned with a grunt that indicated a bad mood and that someone was going to get a rocket before the day was out. About 09h30 there was a roar from the Colonel's office - not the usual 'Jocks' but 'Lello', to which I reacted like a startled rabbit. His first question was: 'Did the mailbag with the newspapers go off last night?' With my heart in my boots and watery knees I admitted that I had forgotten to change my instruction, and for a moment I thought the Colonel was going to blow his fuse; but although he was red in the face he said with icy calm: 'Godt jong Jocks, you bloody slipped. If that bag is not with the squadron tomorrow morning you'll be court-martialled.'

A frantic call to Ebisu ascertained that the mailbag had been dis-patched and had passed through Seoul, so there was nothing to be done but to wait. While I was contemplating what defence could be offered at my trial, the telephone rang; it was Japie Smits from the Squadron. Before I could ask where the mailbags were there was a roar from Danie's office: 'Put him through to me!' which I did. I unashamedly eavesdropped, and you can imagine my relief when I heard 'Ja, Japie, I told Jocks to pull his finger out and use the British Army Post Office to get the mail to the squadron quicker. He will use that system from now on.' Nothing more was ever said about the mail incident but that afternoon 'Godt jong' and I played an enjoyable 18 holes of golf together, and in the evening I enjoyed the rare privilege of being invited back to the Senior Officers' Club where we relished an excellent T-bone steak with French wine, all on the boss.

With the end of the war in sight, the work at SALO HQ increased. Plans had to be drawn up for handing back equipment bought from the American forces, and when the armistice was signed and our POWs released, each one of them had to be met, kitted out, back-paid and the fatted calf had to be killed. When at last the squadron withdrew from Korea I organised a farewell thrash in Tokyo at the British Embassy which may have been the start of the cooling of diplomatic relations between

Britain and South Africa! At 06h30 in the morning the Embassy girls called a halt to celebrations, as they had to start work. We rounded up most of the men but found that two were missing. One was eventually found asleep in a bath and the other, with an angelic smile on his face, clutching his guitar to his bosom while sleeping soundly behind a sofa!

Ridgeline Attack

Joe Joubert

Joe flew on two tours of operations in Korea, totalling 175 sorties. He was awarded the American DFC and cluster, and at one period he was second in command of the Squadron.

On 4 May 1951 I was briefed to lead four Mustangs on a road cutting mission, but when we were airborne the Fifth Air Force controller diverted us to a close-support target south of Koksu-ri on the north side of the Han River. The pilots, besides myself, were John Swanepoel my wingman, Mickey Rorke No 3 and Albie Gotze No 4.

The weather was poor in the target area, with low cloud capping the surrounding ridges. The airborne Mosquito controller marked the target with coloured smoke, and after the dug-in enemy positions along a ridgeline were identified, we made several rocket and machine-gun attacks. The cloud base was about 1 000ft which necessitated a flattish approach that could have led to mistaken recognition of the target during the attack: but apart from that possibility I was worried that our rockets might fall short and cause casualties among friendly troops near the target.

The controller assured me that our ordnance was 'spot on' and kept repeating that all rockets and shells were concentrated in the target area, and we should continue the good work. There was, however, still cause for concern, especially when friendly troops jumped up to one side of the line of fire waving enthusiastically, no doubt intending to encourage us to give the 'Gooks' hell.

When the cloud began to descend lower and lower I decided on one more attack before calling it a day. We had to fly up the slope towards the enemy positions below the ridgeline and, after attacking, peel away to starboard skimming the tree-covered slope while diving

243

down to the road curling through the centre of the valley. Eventually, by flying from valley to valley we found an outlet and set course for base. Mickey and Albie lost us during the attack and, instead of sticking to the valleys and roads, Mickey pulled up directly into the cloud with Albie formating on his aircraft like a duckling tucked under its mother's wing. After flying through the cloud on intruments for an undetermined period Mickey flew into a gap, and he couldn't believe his eyes on seeing K-11 immediately below.

The good news at base was that the attack on the enemy positions had neutralised the area, and there had been little difficulty in capturing the ridge.

From my Notes

Dick Turner

Dick flew on a tour of operations in Korea with the Cheetahs from May to November 1952. The notes scribbled in his flying logbook mention some facts that have not been included in the pages of this book. He was awarded the American DFC.

After 38 years it is hard to recall many details of my tour of operations in Korea, but I kept a few notes that may be of interest.

On 9 July 1952, 18 Fighter-Bomber Wing completed its 45 000th sortie in the Korean War. An American pilot chalked up this score. There was a large crowd present to watch him land, and many photographs were taken. The Cheetah Squadron's 'B' Flight missed this honour by four sorties, pilots Bill Church. Dan van Vuuren, John Botes and I having flown the 44 996th sortie earlier that day.

Over a period of 52 hours, 16 inches of rain was recorded between 26 and 31 July 1952, which washed out all flying operations.

On 2 August 1952, John Bolitho and Doug Lock flew on a rescue patrol led by an American pilot and his wingman. Shortly after setting course the canopy of the leading Mustang blew off and apparently stunned the pilot. His aircraft was seen disappearing into cloud, and he was later found in a North Korean village, having no doubt baled out, but his mind was blank and he could not remember what had happened.

On 5 August, after a game of volley ball, I was enjoying a refreshing cool drink when my flight was scrambled on a rescue patrol. Bill Church was the leader and the other two pilots were Fred Clausen and Mike Cairncross. We took off at about 18h00, located the rescue helicopter, escorted it to the downed pilot, and then to the east coast. There was an abundance of flak as the chopper crept along the valleys, and at one point the pilot reported that the main rotor blade was vibrating as a result of hits received. Our flight landed at K-46 in the dark when a message was received from the Marine Wing thanking us for helping to rescue their CO!

An amusing incident involved one of our pilots who aborted 10 minutes after take-off because of radio failure. He turned back, lost his way, and after stooging round for a while, spotted a Skymaster on which he formated holding the back of his map against his aircraft's canopy with the word 'LOST' scrawled with grease pencil. The crew of the Skymaster led him to an airfield on the east coast.

Unsung Heroines

An Anonymous Contributor

Many wives are left to play both mother and father to a growing family when their husbands go to war. For the sake of the children they show a smiling, cheerful face but behind this facade lies the nagging fear that their husbands may not return and that they will be left to face the future with broken hearts and a never-ending sense of loss, added to the worry about what the future may hold.

Among the brave wives who lost their husbands in Korea were Bobbie and Carmel, two lovely young girls for whom life was still in the melting pot of dreams; yet they overcame their difficulties, put the broken pieces of their lives together again and reared their children. The petite Carmel lost her first husband, Dirkie, in the Second World War, and when Montie was killed in Korea she was left with four children to bring up.

Bobbie, a former beauty queen, with laughing eyes and a lovely smile, met Badie in 1942, when he was a flying instructor in the SAAF. It was love at first sight, and they were married in 1943. In 1944 they had a son, and soon after Badie was posted to a Spitfire squadron in Italy. He survived the war, and in 1946 another son was born. Their third child who they hoped would be a daughter, had completed four months of the journey into this world when the Korean War began and South Africa undertook to send a fighter squadron to help stem the communist tide. Badie was appointed one of the flight commanders.

Most of the pilots of the SAAF were delighted at the opportunity to return to operational flying. The peacetime air force had become boring, and there was the additional excitement of a visit to the mysterious East. Badie was of a more serious bent, and his responsibility to his family weighed heavily on his mind. He could have avoided a posting to Korea by not volunteering for service overseas, for the regulations stipulated that no member of the forces could serve beyond the borders of South Africa unless volunteering to do so. Use of this loophole was something that Badie could not have lived with, so he was one of the SAAF party that embarked for the Far East on the *Tjisadane* in Durban harbour on 26 September 1950.

Bobby didn't want to leave Badie a day earlier than was necessary, so she went with him to Durban to wave farewell from the quayside. She still remembers the hot humid day when the *Tjisadane* slipped her moorings and slowly pulled away leaving behind distraught wives, mothers, fathers and fiancees. Here was a ship that would sail halfway across the world carrying men to fight in a war in which politics would overrule all other considerations and cause the death of millions.

Bobbie managed to control her emotions until the ship had left the quayside and the gap had widened, when the tears began streaming down her cheeks. She dared not wipe them away as she didn't want Badie to see that she was weeping, so she stood silently and waved feeling terribly alone, forlorn and burdened with grief and forebodings. She was left with two little boys and was expecting another child in four months' time. The responsibility was now hers alone.

Badie was one of the first South Africans in action in Korea in November 1950, and he led many outstanding missions which resulted in the award of the DFC. In January 1951 he was overjoyed to hear that the little girl whom he and Bobbie had prayed for had been born and would be christened by the name that they had chosen, Beulah. Then Bobbie received the news on 3 March that Badie had been posted missing, and in 1953 he was officially declared 'killed in action'. Badie's death was a heavy burden for Bobbie to bear, both emotionally and financially. Women are undoubtedly the unsung heroines of war, and the nation salutes them.

The Passing of a Legend

Albie Gotze

Albie was seconded to the RAF during World War II and flew Typhoons and Spitfires on operations. His fighter-bomber experience with bombs and rockets stood him in good stead in Korea.

It wasn't difficult to find a legend amongst the pilots who volunteered to serve with 2 Squadron in Korea. One such person was Mickey Rorke whom I first met in 1946 at Waterkloof Air Base where he was well known for his drum beating, his apt and cryptic remarks and his wild parties.

It was in Korea that he became a legend when instrumental in creating 2 Squadron's famous pub, Rorke's Inn, named after him. All those who drank in the Pub during 1951 will remember Mickey sitting in the corner playing his favourite Chinese records on the gramophone, never-to-be-forgotten songs like Kang Kang Mosime and Chiinana Yoru.

The passing of this brave, popular personality and friend was a tragic episode that happened under horrifying circumstances. On 15 May 1951, Mickey was taking off for an interdiction mission from our advance base, K-16, near Seoul. Halfway down the PSP runway was a bump that more often than not seemed to assist a Mustang loaded with bombs or Napalm drop tanks, to become airborne.

Willie Marais, our Telecom Officer, and I, were watching the take-off and when Mickey's aircraft reached the bump, it became airborne. Instead of gradually climbing away, the Mustang commenced nosing upwards, possibly because Mickey hadn't trimmed the elevator correctly. He must have realised that a stall was imminent, so jettisoned the two napalm drop tanks which hit and set fire to a B-26 that had recently crashed on the end of the runway and was being dismantled.

Mickey's Mustang, now in vertical attitude and totally out of control, collided with the blazing inferno. Willy and I drove over to the crash but the heat was so intense that we couldn't get near it. We stood in total mortification and sheer horror watching the funeral pyre of our friend and comrade-in-arms. Nothing except a few chips from his flying helmet was recovered.

Humorous Incidents

John Inglesby

John Inglesby was the first 2 Squadron Intelligence Officer to serve with the Cheetahs in Korea. His tour ended in early October 1951.

A Diplomatic Blunder

Early in November 1950 the first contingent of 2 Squadron, consisting of some 206 personnel arrived in Yokohama Bay, aboard the Dutch Royal Interocean Line's *Tjisidane*. As the vessel was berthing, an American military band provided a rousing welcome, marching along the quayside in full regalia playing their instruments with much verve. It was indeed a warm welcome to the shores of Japan and a fitting introduction to the United Nations Forces. After a speech we disembarked and were transported to Johnson Air Force Base near Tokyo to be equipped before moving to Korea. Once again a lavish welcome was provided.

One evening I was enjoying a few drinks with two USAF officers and expressed my views about the welcome we received both at Johnson Air Base and at the Yokohama quayside. I emphasised how much the military band had impressed me. One of the officers looked at his colleague enquiringly and said: 'Should we tell him the full story?' I replied in a surprised tone, that I would very much like to hear it.

He then related that the band had been a diplomatic blunder as its entire complement had consisted of blacks. He went on to clarify that all units in the United States Air Force were fully integrated, and that a considerable effort had been made to assemble an all-black band by gathering bandsmen from American bands throughout Japan and Korea to welcome their brothers from Africa. The organisers were most embarrassed when they noticed that all the members of 2 Squadron were white, as they had expected a squadron from Africa to be black!

A Measure of Anxiety

The night before the evacuation of the advance elements of 18 Fighter-Bomber Wing from P'yongyang (K-24) in late 1950, all ground personnel were briefed that air transport would arrive at first light the following morning to commence the evacuation. Prevailing weather conditions were variable and there was a measure of anxiety as regards the aircraft arriving in time before P'yongyang was overrun by the advancing Chinese troops.

Sergeant Larson, an American in the Wing's Intelligence Section, asked Captain Slide Trumbo, head of the section, what he would do should the aircraft not arrive in time. Captain Trumbo replied: 'I'll get me a 45 and a bottle of water, sergeant, and head south. What will you do?' Without blinking an eyelid Sergeant Larson said: 'Capt'n, I'll be so close behind your tail you'll think you've got a brand new arsehole.'

Frustration
Early in 1951, 18 Fighter-Bomber Wing was temporarily moved from Chinhae (K-10) so that the airfield could be re-constructed. 2 Squadron was moved to Pusan (K-9). Tiny le Roux, a member of the Squadron's technical staff who was in the sickbay at the time of the move, was transferred to a Swedish hospital ship anchored off Pusan. A few days later Tiny and a batch of American servicemen were discharged from the hospital ship to resume normal duties, and were conveyed to Pusan. After landing ashore they were ushered into a building and issued with new service kit, underclothing, toiletries and an M1 rifle. Tiny refused to accept the rifle but was told: 'Guy where you're going you'll need it!' On leaving the building the party found themselves on a railway siding and they were duly ushered onto a train, when Tiny told the officer in charge that he was a South African, a member of 2 Squadron based at K-9 - but to no avail. He was ordered to remain on the train.

Meanwhile, 2 Squadron was notified that Air/Corporal le Roux had been discharged from hospital to return to his unit. After a three-day journey heading north the train arrived at Yongdong Po, near Seoul; the passengers were transferred to a replacement depot from where American units that had suffered casualties, were brought up to strength by available personnel. Needless to say 2 Squadron, not knowing what had happened to Tiny, had him posted AWOL.

At the replacement depot Tiny tried to convince the authorities of his bona fides, and ultimately the penny dropped that he was not an American, probably due to his accent. A USAF pilot, Jim Lawrence who had rescued John Davis after he had crashed-landed behind enemy lines and had flown him back to 2 Squadron, interviewed Tiny and asked: 'If you claim to be from 2 Squadron how is John Davis keeping?' When Tiny replied that John had been killed a few weeks after the rescue, Lawrence would not believe him.

He was then interviewed by officers of a French Battalion but as he had no knowledge of French, the Froggies reported that he was not one of them. Fortunately two burley military policeman from the British Commonwealth Division who arrived at the depot had heard of Tiny's plight. They knew of 2 Squadron's location and while on their way to Pusan to collect four deserters, they volunteered to take Tiny to the squadron and return him to the depot if this story proved to be false. Imagine the Adjutant's reaction when Tiny was escorted to his office by the British MP's.

Air Control
Brian Martin

Brian retired from the SAAF after 48 consecutive years' service. Apart from his tour of operations in Korea, he flew in Italy on night intruder operations during the Second World War. Recalling episodes after nearly 40 years seemed to be a tall order for Brian until he put pen to paper, when a few amusing stories of his tour in Korea came to mind.

A Measure of Embarrassment

At one of our bases there was an ablution block that served a number of Nissen huts used for accommodating our pilots. In the latrines there were 12 seats side by side, and alongside them there was a cubicle with six showers. Early in the morning the seats were usually fully occupied, but that didn't deter an elderly Korean cleaner woman, who would arrive at that critical period with her mop and bucket to clean the block. Without fail she would stop in front of each occupant who was seated on the latrine and bow in a polite and dignified manner. The men each returned the compliment by rising off the roughly constructed bogholes with their trousers round their ankles and bowing to her with great aplomb and solemnity!

She would then walk into the shower cubicle while some of the men were soaping themselves. At first, especially in the case of the new arrivals, there was a measure of embarrassment as they hastily covered their vital parts, but after a while, like the rest of us, they calmly accepted her presence.

A Lack of Moral Fibre

We were tasked for a low level attack on P'yongyang, which was no picnic, for the town and its surroundings were heavily defended. There were about 200 aircraft attacking the target at the same time that day, some at high level, some at medium level and others, including 2 Squadron, at low level. It was a raid that gave all pilots the jitters, for over that target death was our constant companion. When we returned to base we did not rejoice to be told that another raid was to be made on P'yongyang within an hour or so, particularly as these raids were believed to have a political rather than a strategic purpose.

En route for the target, we heard a discourse over the radio between two American pilots flying in another fighter-bomber squadron. The No 4 in one of the flights asked his section leader whether he was receiving him. The latter replied in the affirmative, and then No 4 called again, to receive the same reply. There was a pause, and No 4 announced that he was returning to base with an unserviceable radio. Another pause followed and the section leader piped up suggesting that he should act as escort. 'Roger, I would appreciate that,' replied No 4. Numerous cat-calls followed branding the pilot as a lack of moral fibre case.

Tension

When we were operating from a forward base there was always tension in the air, but at the same time a sense of fun often prevailed. Our pilots were very professional, and when they were waiting to fly on operations during a three day stage there was little drinking or wild living. In the evening we would walk into a marquee that housed 15 to 20 beds and find a couple of bridge or poker schools on the go, or some bods writing letters, while others were sleeping. Briefing took place before dawn so it was necessary to keep sober and go to bed early.

On one occasion silence reigned in the marquee except for the bidding calls, when suddenly one of the sleeping pilots sat up abruptly in bed and shouted: 'Great God, this is rough!' and promptly fell back in a deep sleep. This was an example of how the tension affected some chaps. There was a stunned silence, until the bridge players dissolved in laughter.

A Mistake Leads to Success

We were on a close-support mission against enemy bunkers a short distance ahead of our own troops. Our Mustangs were carrying napalm and rockets, and after the Mosquito control aircraft had marked the target with white smoke I led my flight into the attack. The usual procedure was to dive on the target with guns blazing to keep the enemies' heads down before we dropped the napalm. Each aircraft adopted the same procedure until the leader was eventually diving behind his No 4, and in that way, all four aircraft protected one another in a circle, using guns and Napalm on the first pass, guns and rockets on the second and after that guns alone if necessary.

251

However, on this particular mission I obviously suffered a mental aberration, for instead of pressing the gun button on the first run I released the napalm tanks prematurely, and to my horror it appeared that they had fallen among our own troops. The attack proceeded, and as I led the flight back to base with a sinking feeling of despair the controller told me that the napalm had fallen 50 yards ahead of our troops and had in fact given them perfect cover for their advance. Despair turned to elation as I was congratulated on my remarkable accuracy!

Air Control

One young pilot who slept in the bed next to mine was noted for his remarkable ability to control his farts. Once when he consented to demonstrate his virtuosity he produced 48 short reports resembling pistol shots. Another bedmate picked up the rhythm and joined in with a whistle between each one. The sound effects were hilarious!

Flak Ahead

When we returned to base from a dive-bombing attack we usually carried out a reconnaissance patrol along the supply routes to find another target. On one occasion we were about to fly over a position where a particular flak gun had bothered me on a previous mission, so I warned my pilots to keep their eyes peeled for it. All our aircraft were well spread out when I saw a puff of black flak burst ahead, and immediately shouted 'Flak ahead!' The urgency in my voice must have given my wingman a hell of a fright, for a rocket suddenly passed between my cockpit and the port wingtip. Obviously he had forgotten to turn off his rocket arming switch, and my abrupt warning had made him squeeze the rocket-firing control. There was no joy in locating the troublesome flak gun: I was far too busy making uncomplimentary remarks to my wingman.

Fêted by the Marines

After an operation on the east coast our flight was heading for a forward base on the western side of Korea. However, during the operation the cloud had gathered ominously and was rapidly descending. Our chances of crossing the high ground between the east and west coasts became remote, and I decided to fly at low level down the east coast to K-10. It wasn't long before that became impossible: the cloud was right down on the water and it was raining heavily. Suddenly to starboard I saw an airfield, and all the Mustangs scrambled in to a quick landing.

Leaving the aircraft in the parking area, we walked towards the stockaded camp and found a large tent which turned out to be the officers' mess where four US Marine officers were playing poker. They completely ignored us and were most inhospitable. Nosing about the camp we found a storeman who allocated a tent with four beds and one blanket each. Not a drink nor a morsel of food was offered to us, and we spent a cold, uncomfortable night in that dismal tent.

In the morning the weather had deteriorated further, but we gave our aircraft a daily inspection in case there was a change that would allow us to fly back to base. While we were tinkering with the Mustangs, a Lieutenant-Colonel who had been one of the poker players the previous evening, walked through the gate of the stockade and saw the insignia on the aircraft. 'My God!' he said, 'Are those your F-51s?' and when it dawned on him that we were pilots of the formidable Cheetah Squadron, his whole attitude changed.

From then on we were fêted and spoilt with food, drinks and anything we could wish for. The Colonel said he had long desired an opportunity to meet pilots from the squadron with the 'jumping goat' insignia on their aircraft, for he reckoned they were the best operational pilots in Korea; and that included his own Marine Air Force pilots! We were well partied into the next morning, and it was probably just as well that the weather remained 'clampers' for four days. I don't think any of us would have been fit enough to get into our aircraft, far less fly them. We were made unofficial honorary US Marines. I still have a Marine collar badge among my souvenirs.

Relaxation

Amid the tension of this vicious war there was little to relieve personal feelings other than Rorke's Inn. Not far from the base at Chinhae there was a beautiful spot where we could swim and relax. In earlier days the Japs had used the area as a seaplane base, and they had built a large slipway to the water's edge. The surroundings were covered with fir trees and the sparkling blue water was crystal clear. When I was off duty I would often retire to this little paradise to relax, and I would eventually fall asleep under the shade of those magnificent trees.

That spot will always remain in my memory as a haven of peace, where the harsh realities of war were forgotten.

'Chappie'

K B Mcdonald

Many South Africans who served in Korea have talked about that fantastic guy Chappie, one of the finest Americans they had the pleasure of working with. It is apt that KB should write about this dynamic personality.

When 2 SAAF first joined 18 Fighter-Bomber Wing in Korea, S V Theron and Colonel Louw, the OC of the Group at that time, decided that 2 Squadron should in the initial stages fly 'wing' to USAF pilots who were experienced in that theatre of operations. It was an interim arrangement until we got the hang of the theatre but good sound thinking, for after all, the Americans had been at it for some time before we arrived. Although most of our pilots had at least one tour of operations under their belts from World War II, this was a different ball game in many ways.

One of three American leaders who showed us the way was Chapman L James Jnr. Chappie, a BA & LLB at California University and an ex World War II Thunderbolt pilot in the European Theatre of operations, was destined to become the first black four-star General in the USAF. His father was the first black Brigadier in the US Marines. In 1950 Chappie was a tall, lean, easy-going humourist with an infectious zest for life. He took a liking to the 'South Afs' as he called us and we to him.

He was particularly fond of Lippy Lipawsky - 'the best gaw-damned wingman I ever did see' - although Lippy probably hadn't flown as his wingman on more than two or three occasions and one of these was rather a hairy one. It was a prebriefed anti-personnel strike with rockets and napalm. T6 'Mosquito' spotter aircraft directed the flight that was close to the front line. The mission should have been a snip.

Winter had already set in with a vengeance. Temperatures were way below freezing at ground level and under these conditions the Mustang's napalm pylons and release mechanism were, to say the least, temperamental. The method of attack using napalm was to dive at an angle of 30 degrees at 300 knots and release at approximately 300ft. This gave the maximum spread and target coverage. If there was a hang up due to one of the release mechanisms freezing up, an aircraft immediately tended to flip over into a roll resulting from 1 000lbs under one wing and nothing under the other. At 300ft this wasn't funny!

Chappie went in and dropped his napalm. Lippy followed but only one napalm came away with the result that his aircraft flipped over onto its back. A desperate battle took place between man and machine but the Mustang responded to Lippy's expertise and he made another run over the target releasing the hung-up napalm. At debriefing Chappie said to Lippy: 'Ole man Lip, what were you doing down there cutting fancy capers and trying to show those commies a thing or two?'

On another occasion when I was flying as Chappie's wingman we were prebriefed for a real snip of a mission. The ground forces had isolated a large pocket of 'gooks' and had called for air support. The commies were surrounded by UN troops, so if a pilot was hit, all he had to do was pull up and fly for a couple of miles before hitting the silk knowing that he would be over friendly territory.

At debriefing, Slide, the Air Liaison Officer, asked Chappie how the mission had gone. Chappie replied: 'Slide, this was a real snip. KB and me is goin' round and round like in a traffic pattern, givin' those commies a squirt here and there, and all the time I'm saying to that ole engine, quit you son-of-a-bitch, see if I care.'

Not long after this, about January 1951, Chappie completed his tour and was posted back to the States or 'Usajima' as he put it. His farewell party was quite a thrash, with the 'South Afs' there to the death. Thank goodness I was stood down the next day. When Chappie said farewell to S V and the rest of us the next day, he unashamedly cried and his parting remark was: 'You bunch of South Afs are the best bunch of bastards I've ever met.' He was truly a great character and one I'm proud to call a friend.

An Experience to be Cherished

Mike Gedye

Mike's zeal for operations as a young man is typical of the qualities that have established the reputation of SAAF pilots at war.

We were young, enthusiastic and inexperienced in the ways of the world, but our spirit of camaraderie and boundless energy produced a fighting unit typical of the SAAF down the years. Life was one long adventure, and we lapped it up without more than a passing thought for the resulting damage.

Our contingent of replacement aircrew left Johannesburg at the end of November 1952 on a SAA Constellation bound for Rome. As a token of appreciation of the excellent service provided, all stocks in the bar of the aircraft were consumed before it reached Nairobi! The flight on to Tokyo was made in a BOAC Argonaut. When the aircraft landed at Karachi Airport to refuel, firm action was necessary to prevent our more volatile fellows from creating an international incident when confronted by a huge sign that read: DOGS AND SOUTH AFRICANS NOT ALLOWED.

At Chinhae air base in Korea the harsh winter was in full rigour and astonished those of us who had never seen snow before. The temperature was well below freezing, and the days ahead brought icy winds from Siberia with temperatures below minus 30 degrees C. The SAAF ground crews proved to be the best ever, for they kept the Cheetah aircraft flying in all kinds of weather. They were a perfect example of the ability of the SAAF to adapt itself, and in the freezing temperatures they ran the aircraft engines frequently throughout the night to prevent radiators from bursting.

On Christmas day 1952, some American Corsair pilots who had mistaken one of our Mustangs for an enemy aircraft and shot it down, killing the pilot, Johnny Moir, came over to our base to pay their respects and offer their condolences which were accepted in good spirit by Johnny's sad and shaken comrades. Our relations with the American forces in general and our 'buddies' in 18 Fighter-Bomber Wing in particular, were excellent, and many long-standing friendships were forged. The Yanks thought we were crazy, for they had been conscripted and we were all volunteers. Chaps like Al Rae, who was on a second tour of operations, were considered 'touched', to say the least.

I flew 28 operational sorties before the war ended, and we all came home to face ordinary life once more. My log book shows that every mission was an exciting adventure, although my comments at the time pretended that they were mere routine. Our main task was fighter-bomber interdiction - attacking bridges, rail communications, ammunition and fuel depots and troop concentrations. Fighter sweeps along the Yalu River tempting the MiG-15s to come up and fight were a routine exercise, but commie pilots seldom seemed keen to accept the challenge. I remember an attack on the P'yongyang radio station, and although there were numerous claims of direct hits and secondary explosions at the de-briefing, the regular propaganda broadcast came on the air that afternoon. Needless to say we were sent back for another attempt to put the station out of action and this time it was silenced for a while.

I have clear memories of dive-bombing attacks; strafing on the way down, watching the altimeter unwinding at an alarming rate, lining the target up in the bombsight for a second or two, releasing the bombs and pulling out low over the mountainous terrain with my G-suit grabbing me tight. On early morning and late afternoon missions anti-aircraft shells were a frightening sight as they spiralled upwards towards our aircraft and each pilot wondered whether his short lifespan was destined to come to an end there and then.

Time has softened the harsher side of memories, although I was fortunate enough to have a fairly easy time. It was an experience that I cherish, and although it all happened 38 years ago, it seems like yesterday that we all set off with such boyish zest.

Some Outstanding Personalities

Frank Richter

Frank was among the first 11 Cheetah pilots to operate in Korea, and he had the honour to be the first South African to complete a tour of 75 sorties. He actually flew 76: one for luck! He was awarded the American DFC.

Very little has been written about how the first pilots of 2 Squadron were selected to serve in the Korean war. My own case is perhaps typical. Volunteers were called for, and most of the 38 pilots chosen were experienced operational veterans who had stayed in the Permanent Force after World War II. Their number included the commanding officer, the second in command, four flight commanders and a sprinkling of sprog pilots.

I was on holiday in Grahamstown at the time with my family visiting my parents, and we were all sitting at dinner listening to the news on the radio when an announcement was made: 'The South African Government has decided to send a SAAF Fighter-Bomber squadron to Korea. The pilots selected are - - -' and my name was read out among those chosen. There was a stony silence, for the family was unaware that I had volunteered.

The squadron assembled at Waterkloof Air Force Station and a condensed, intensive refresher period began. There were inoculations by the dozen, gunnery, dive-bombing instruction and a conversion to Vampires. Personnel embarked on the *Tjisadane* at Maydon Wharf and were given a rousing farewell by a large crowd, with Pearla Gibson, 'the Lady in White', singing on the quayside as the ship pulled away. At Johnson Air Base in Tokyo the CO, Commandant S V Theron, and 11 pilots were selected to form the advance party and gain experience of conditions in Korea. I was one of them.

There were some outstanding personalities among the Americans and South Afs who served in 18 Fighter-Bomber Wing. Captain Trombone was the Wing operations officer who briefed the pilots of the advance party on missions. Invariably he would end the briefing with: 'Remember, those 'Gooks' don't like you, and if they catch you, they are going to cut your big toe off right here.' He would then draw his finger across his throat. Briefings were always thorough and amusing, accentuated by his broad American drawl.

Chappie James was one of the nicest, most capable American pilots I had the pleasure of flying with. His hands were like bunches of bananas; a fine operational pilot who had an uncanny ability to sniff trouble. An incident typical of his unflappability happened during a hectic operational mission, when a plaintive voice called over the radio: 'I've been hit, I've got a hole as big as a mans' heed in my wing!' Chappie replied in a totally calm voice: 'Which wing, boy?' The effect was perfect, and No 6 was gently escorted back to base by No 5.

Jannie Blaauw knew no fear. The story of his valour and loyalty after Vernon Kruger had been shot down is something never to be forgotten in the history of the SAAF. I flew on many sorties with Jannie, and one that I well remember was a marathon flight of six hours while escorting a B-29 photographic mission to Vladivostok.

Jerks McClean, so named because he was strongly antipathetic to physical exercise, hence 'Physical Jerks - Jerks'. It was a custom of the Americans at a debriefing to issue each pilot with a tot of Scotch. During the early morning de-briefings most pilots refused their tot, so there was always an accumulation of whisky at the end of the day. Jerks got wind of this, and nobody could understand why he always volunteered for the dusk sweep. Despite his lack of enthusiasm for exercise he enjoyed his sundowner.

Doempie Cloete, our Padre, was a tower of strength. His presence at take-off on a mission always gave the pilots confidence. He never seemed to rest. What a wonderful man, and what a credit to his church. The Engineering Officers, Stan Brace and Vic Kilburn, were hard working, conscientious and popular members of the squadron. They spent hours supervising the servicing of aircraft under extremely difficult, freezing conditions in makeshift shelters where if a hand touched metal, some skin was lost. 'Foxy' Ruiter, who was shot down and lost in an icy sea, had served with the squadron in North Africa and Italy in the Second World War; he was the neatest pilot I ever saw. 'Dirty' Pottie, as Pottie Potgieter was affectionately called, was the only one of his kind. When the first detachment of the squadron arrived in Korea, apart from heavy flying clothing, no other essential winter clothing had been issued, and pilots wore battledress which was entirely unsuitable in subzero temperatures. A number of our HQ liaison staff based in Tokyo arrived one evening at the mess tent fully clad in magnificent winter clothing. Pottie had to be physically restrained from stripping Colonel Jan 'Grandstand' and taking over his kit. It had the proper effect, and an issue was promptly provided. 'Grandstand' was the name that Pottie had invented for the Colonel because he was one of those who looked on at the war in comfort from the sidelines in Tokyo. But I must take this opportunity to record that the liaison work was indispensable. Colonel Jan and his staff and those who followed did an exemplary job.

I recall a heart-stopping incident during my tour of operations. A flight of 12 aircraft was briefed to dive-bomb a North Korean HQ in P'yongyang. I was No 7 to attack, and when I pulled out of the dive my engine cut out. My heartbeat increased, fear gripped me and sweat started pouring down my brow, but then I realised that I had forgotten to switch over from the gravity fed fuselage fuel tank to the wing tank. My sweaty hands immediately corrected the error, and all was well.

Recollections of an Ops Officer

AQ de Wet

AQ won his spurs as an instructor and operational pilot in the Second World War, and was awarded the DFC and the AFC. He served from 1951 to 1952 as an Operations Officer in Korea.

The voyage from South Africa to Japan in the flagship of the Royal Interocean Line, *SS Boissevain,* was marked by an incident that is always good for a laugh at a party. We were on our way to relieve the first Korean draft, which had completed a year's service, and on arriving at Hong Kong after more than three weeks at sea our men were eager to enjoy the society of the fairer sex once more. The ship anchored in Hong Kong bay late in the afternoon, and almost as soon as it docked the local ladies 'of class' came out to the ship in launches.

Our ground crews were veterans of the Second World War and could organise anything in a hurry. In this case a ladder was urgently needed to enable the girls to climb on board. One was acquired with lightning speed and suspended from a porthole below the lower deck, allowing the frail beauties to shin up the precarious length of wood and rope and wriggle through the porthole. They were then carried off like the top prize in a tombola! After a few visitors had wriggled their torsos through the porthole, 'Shorty', who had organised the ladder, piped up: 'Stand aside, you guys! Give a man a break. This dolly's mine. I did the organising!' and off he went with her.

I shall never forget my luck in acquiring a 'downbag' from an American soldier during the winter in Korea. The weather was unbelievably cold, and I used twelve blankets in bed to keep warm. Some of the American units were issued with 'downbags', which consisted of body-shaped sleeping bags with goosefeather linings. When these were zipped up the occupants could sleep in the open in freezing temperatures. However, the Chinese attacked one of the American units one night when the soldiers were zipped up in their downbags and many of them were bayoneted before they could extricate themselves. Downbags were therefore forbidden in the front line, and I was able to buy one for a bottle of Scotch, which allowed me to discard my twelve blankets!

Soon after we arrived at K-16 near Seoul the telephone in my 'ops tent' rang. At the other end of the line was a member of the New Zealand regiment in the front line north of K-16. 'You fellows have been supplying us with splendid close-support,' said the voice, 'and we'd like to visit you.' I replied that they were welcome, and after a short while two jeep-loads of Kiwis arrived at the ops tent. Luckily I had a case of White Horse in stock and the last wee drappie disappeared three hours later.

Halfway through the party the monsoon struck, and the rain poured down in sheets. The Kiwis four hours' leave of absence had expired by the time they left in open jeeps with the rain still coming down in torrents; a sobering end to their heavy session. I fell into bed and passed out, but my slumber didn't last long. The telephone suddenly rang: 'Take cover; 'Bed Check Charlie' is in the area!'

I must explain here that the Kiwis and I were not the only people to enjoy the party, for I was sharing the tent with several Cheetah pilots from K-10 who were using K-16 as a staging post for operations. I therefore warned them that 'Bed Check Charlie' was up to his tricks again chucking hand grenades over the side of his ancient biplane, but I didn't think he would be foolish enough to operate in such foul weather with the rain flooding down. In any case the slit trenches outside the tent were full of water; so I dived back under the sheets.

Suddenly there was pandemonium as an explosion rocked the area. The pilots scrambled towards the entrance of the tent, but it was tightly laced up to keep out the wind and rain. Desperately someone flung himself at the flap and ripped it open, and as I followed him into the rain two NCO's came running towards me, totally starkers except for tin hats. No doubt they had been sleeping naked because the humidity at that time of the year was very high. The leading NCO sped past me and fell headlong into the slit trench creating an enormous splash.

I then realised that the incessant explosions and accompanying flashes of light were not bombs but a heavy aircraft battery that had taken its position not far from our tent while we were entertaining the Kiwis. I'm sure this gun-crew scared us more than 'Bed Check Charlie' who must have been a very brave character, or quite crazy, to have flown at night in an open cockpit in that filthy weather against a heavily defended airfield. The NCO who led the sprint for the waterhole was sent back to K-10 soon afterwards. Although he was an exemplary man in every other respect, he was highly strung, and his nerves showed signs of failure under severe pressure.

How to Lose 40lbs in 41 Days

George Thom

George was unlucky to be shot down so close to the end of the war after proving his mettle as an operational pilot. When facing a fiery death his escape actions were calmly executed.

I had returned from 'R and R' in Japan after a hectic fortnight of travelling, drinking and socialising. From the age of twelve I had a tendency to be on the heavy side and after living it up for 14 days the scale read 200lbs - life was good.

The race to complete my 100 sorties for a tour of operations ended on 21 July 1953 during my 72nd mission, only seven days before the war ended. The weather that day was bad with low cloud, poor visibility and rain. On the way to the aircraft dispersal area, Al Rae the mission leader, quipped:

'George, I'm going to abort. When you take over the lead and get shot down, please give my regards to Rex Earp-Jones. He's a POW.'

Strangely enough Al did abort, I took over as mission leader and was shot down. We were flying on an armed reconnaissance in the 'Iron Triangle' vicinity. The weather was grim and while attacking some vehicles I felt two thuds behind me and realised my aircraft had been hit by ground fire. Barry Ross and Henry Ludick (known as Black Dick), the other two pilots in the flight, were advised of my predicament.

The forward and aft fire warning lights came on and I throttled back. A fire at the rear end of the tail-pipe was not a serious problem and could be extinguished by throttling back. The forward fire was the real danger, with the warning pick-ups situated round the fuselage tank behind the cockpit. The correct procedure to adopt in this type of emergency was to close the fuel flow by switching off the engine. The time limit was only ten seconds. I cut the engine and by this time Barry Ross was alongside shouting: 'Eject, eject. Your aircraft behind the cockpit is a ball of fire.' I disconnected the 'G' suit, radio leads, oxygen tube and got rid of the canopy. I tucked my arms in, pulled the ejection handle on the seat and Whoooosh - I was tumbling through the air still strapped to the seat! After loosening the harness, and kicking the seat away, I pulled the 'D' ring. Initially nothing happened but suddenly there was a jerk round my crutch which was painful to say the least, the chute opened and I was drifting towards mother earth.

As the ground came closer, bullets began to whistle around me. I landed without a hitch, unbuckled my chute, connected the emergency radio and contacted Barry Ross informing him I was uninjured and on top of a small hill. He repeated my message and then the radio went dead. I checked my revolver and found it to be in poor shape for I had never cleaned or oiled it.

I saw about 15 soldiers approaching - The war was over for me so I hid the revolver, hurled the radio over the edge of the hill and looked for a hiding place - but there was no place to hide and I was captured within five minutes of hitting the ground.

Amongst my captors was a youngster approximately 16 years old who carried an old rifle fitted with an even older bayonet resembling a sharpened rod approximately 2ft long. He seemed intent on running the bayonet into me and the other captors were kept busy controlling him until a Chinese officer arrived and escorted me to a jeep with an American star on the bonnet. At this stage Barry and Henry were flying above obviously trying to find me. Fortunately they didn't spot the 'Gooks' otherwise they might have strafed them and I would have been on the receiving end!

I was taken to a cave/bunker where my arms were dressed. During the ejection they had been badly bruised. At three in the morning the first interrogation commenced. Fortunately I was aware that the 'Gooks' were not a party to the Geneva Convention. It would not have benefitted me to have dug my heels in and provided only my name, rank and number, but any information given had to be devoid of any importance to the UN's war effort. At *Afrikaans Hoër Seunskool* in Pretoria I had written about South African history and only achieved a 20 per cent mark-up, so this was the right type of material for the 'Gooks'. The bunker was close to the front line and I could hear the gunfire but the next day I was moved to a village farther north where the main interrogation centre, Paks Palace, was situated and where the entire interrogation process was repeated at a much higher level of intensity by a Chinese Oxford graduate who spoke English fluently.

After six days of captivity I noticed that UN air activity had ceased and my captors were enjoying a big thrash, in fact most of them were drunk. It suddenly occurred to me that the war must be over, but when seeking confirmation from one of the revellers, all I got was a slap on the face.

In a POW camp near the Yalu River I met up with Chick Fryer who had been shot down by a MiG-15. He had baled out at a low height but the other two pilots in his flight were too busy defending themselves against the attacking MiGs to observe this. He had been posted as missing and it was feared that he had been killed.

It was good to know he was alive and well with only a few scars received from his burns, and sporting a magnificent beard. After amalgamation with an adjacent camp, I met two more bearded South Africans, pipe smoking Chris Lombard and Rex Earp-Jones. My first words to Rex were: 'Al Rae sends his regards.' He gave me an odd look, but the message had been delivered!

A couple of days later we were moved to the Freedom Village and were repatriated after a week. I had been a POW for 41 days and had lost 40 pounds in weight, the most successful diet I've ever undertaken!

POW

Chick Fryer

Chick served with No 1 Squadron SAAF during the Second World War and signed on again for a year to fight against the commies in Korea. He was a promising architectural student before volunteering and when his fellow students heard he was missing, believed killed in action, they promoted a memorial fund, the proceeds to assist a third-year student on an annual basis. On Chick's safe return, some of the funds collected were used on a party to welcome him home and the balance was returned to the donors.

My contribution to 'the Flying Cheetahs' operations in Korea lasted only three weeks for I was shot down on 15 October 1952 when our formation of three Mustangs was bounced by four MiG-15s. I was flying at No 3, and my two fellow pilots saw my aircraft spinning down in flames but were too busy countering another attack from the MiGs to observe me baling out and thought I'd bought it.

As it happened I was lucky not to have been entombed in the Mustang as it spun into the ground, for initially the canopy wouldn't budge. Eventually my desperate attempts to open it succeeded but no further effort was required in extricating myself from the cockpit for I was suddenly shot out like a cork from a champagne bottle, probably because the aircraft was in an inverted spin.

I landed in a tree in mountainous terrain with my face and hands badly burnt and at least 15 minutes elapsed before some North Korean soldiers arrived and led me to their officer. He indicated that I should lie down on a blanket, but from the way he handled his revolver I felt sure my demise was imminent. North Koreans were extremely bitter about the carnage which UN pilots had wreaked on their armies.

I lashed out at the officer, missed and ran for it, but didn't get far before tripping when the soldiers clubbed me senseless with their revolvers. I was then tied to a pole. Fortunately Chinese troops, who had presumably been summoned, arrived and took me to hospital on a stretcher where my burns were treated. The medical care at this hospital was not of a high standard but adequate. At least the food was better than in the camps and now and again a meal of eggs and meat was provided.

In the camps, the food served was mainly rice, potatoes and cabbage with an occasional bowl of 'ditchwater consistency' soup. It was inevitable that we all lost weight. After the armistice the food improved but as one of the POWs remarked, 'the Chinks can't make amends for past treatment in one month.' The clothing issued was blue cotton trousers and thin shirts, and in winter, quilted clothing was provided. A mixture of straw and oak leaves with some feathers thrown in comprised the tobacco ration. At Christmas each prisoner received a packet of cigarettes and when the armistice was signed, parcels of cigarettes were allowed through the Red Cross. During the period when camps were controlled by the North Koreans, prisoners were told that letter writing was a waste of time for their letters would never leave the valley. The Chinese adopted a different attitude and tried to use letters for propaganda purposes. They encouraged prisoners to write home mentioning the wonderful conditions, food and treatment received in the camps but of course little co-operation went their way.

Unlike the German POW camps in the Second World War, the Korean camps housed no more than 100 men in converted schools or community halls scattered round the little villages. There was an assorted bunch of guys at my camp including a Canadian, an Australian, a South African in the RAF but seconded to the RAAF (this really foxed the Chinese), and Americans from all walks of life. They were Marines, airmen and army types whose exploits could fill a book.

Our days were spent playing bridge and volley ball, reading and collecting wood and water. We had many a laugh at the expense of the Chinese for they were imbued with a desire to be dubbed as a peace-loving people. One incident at a medical parade caused much mirth when a well endowed American complained of a rash in a very private area. When dropping his pants, the Chinese doctor's exclamation of 'Holy Smoke' brought the bungalow down!

Meals were prepared for all the surrounding camps in our kitchen and the bread rolls delivered with the food turned out to be an important method of conveying information between camps - news of new arrivals, the peace talks and baseball scores from America.

One of my proudest achievements in the POW camp was the cultivation of my beard which was a magnificent specimen. The same could be said of a fellow Cheetah Squadron POW, Rex Earp-Jones. Our beards were admired by everyone who saw them. Seeing my family again on returning to South Africa after the year of drama, was one of the most nostalgic and emotional moments of my life.

Finale

John Koekemoer

John and his CO, Stan Wells, were the last two pilots of Cheetah Squadron to leave Korea. One of their numerous tasks was to test the Sabres before returning them to the USAF. Stan and John also represented the Squadron when bidding farewell to fellow members of the Commonwealth, taking part in a fly-past in formation with two Meteors from 77 Squadron RAAF. John was awarded the American DFC.

Early in 1953 our Mustangs were flown to Japan, from whence they were returned to the USAF. After that, ground training began with a view to converting to Sabre jets. By mid-March the Cheetahs were ready to do battle with the MiG-15s. My first operational sortie in a Sabre from K-55 was on 22 March as wingman to the CO, Ralph Gerneke, with Ian Gow and David Mather flying as No's 3 and 4. The mission was a patrol along the Yalu River and although we saw four M1Gs they weren't interested in fighting.

On 15 April, while I was flying as wingman to Eddie Pienaar in a patrol between P'yongyang and Kunu-ri, two MiG-15s jumped us, but Eddie turned the tables and scored strikes on one of them. Both aircraft disappeared towards Hamhung. During the latter part of April, bombing missions began and after the bombs were dropped we'd climb up looking for MiGs. A pilot who I appreciated on these occasions was Oupa Stocks, for he had eyes like a hawk and could spot MiGs long before anyone else; and, of course, to see the enemy before they saw you was a good way to stay alive.

Rorke's Inn had been an important part of the Cheetah pilots' lives ever since Mickey Rorke had introduced the pub at K-10, so when the Squadron moved to K-55 another Rorke's Inn was set up. Shag Morris and some of the chaps acquired the materials from an American construction unit, and to reach the pub from our billets, a spruit spanned by a swinging bridge had to be crossed. At the original Rorke's Inn, the patrons had experienced difficulty in crossing the slimy water of Rorke's Drift on a pole, especially after they had consumed one over the eight. The swinging bridge was also precarious, and the only way an inebriated pilot could navigate across it was on his hands and knees!

War is hell in any language, whether Chinese, North Korean or Afrikaans. Pilots are taught to kill and they are prepared to lose their lives, but there were moments of relaxation. After a specified number of operations they were eligible for leave in Japan: R and R (rest and recuperation). Morale was high during May and June, for there were strong rumours that an armistice would soon be signed.

Meanwhile 2 Squadron concentrated on interdiction and close-support missions. On 5 June Ivan Holtzhausen and I had a ball. We were scrambled to attack a train and convoy of trucks north of the front line. Our results were pleasing, but both Sabres were hit by small-arms fire. The airspeed indicator of Ivan's aircraft was put out of action, and he was forced to formate on me while flying back to K-55. On 27 July, every serviceable aircraft and every able pilot was airborne, for this was the last day of the war and the armistice was to be signed at 10h00 at Panmunjom. We patrolled the Yalu River hoping that the MiGs would come up and fight, but these hopes were not realised and the last Cheetah flight of the war returned to K-55 without joy.

The squadron remained in Korea for two more months after the armistice. On 29 September all Sabres of 2 Squadron were grounded, and the task of testing them and handing them back to the Americans was alotted to the CO, Stan Wells, and me, the last two South African pilots to leave Korea. Of the 22 Sabre jets acquired from the USAF in February 1953, 16 were returned, five were written off and one was damaged and transferred to the Chinese Nationalist Air Force. I flew home by Comet three months after the war ended.

Through the Eyes of a Padre

The Rev Charles Scott Shaw

When Charles was asked to contribute to this book, he suggested that exerpts should be summarised from his own book Looking back with Laughter.

At 'Dogpatch' I was suddenly pitchforked into the hive of an operational Fighter-Bomber Wing, nine tenths of which was American. A radical adjustment had to be made. It seemed to me that in the exacting discipline of the Air Force, individual personality counted for very little. The pilots and the aircraft were the gods, to be served at all costs. The Chief Technical Officer was the High Priest, with his lesser brethren, the Flight Sergeants, who, in turn had their mechanics under them. Superimposed upon this was the administration, consisting of the Adjutant, the Padre, the Doctor, the Quartermaster and the Paymaster.

Finding my niche in the squadron would not be easy, at least that was my first depressing thought. As for the pilots, I soon got the hang of their air force ways, discovering that the seemingly callous façade was necessary to keep control of the emotional currents stirred up by combat operations. Each individual, with few exceptions, helped to make up a first class team, each man proud of his work and intensely loyal to the squadron. 'Dogpatch', as K-10 was called, was situated between the mountains, a mere landing strip running parallel to a sea inlet. This base was used by 18 Fighter-Bomber Wing USAF, and it consisted of four squadrons nicknamed 'The Foxy Few', 'Roosters', 'Cobras' and our own 'Cheetahs' which formed an integral part of the whole zoo. It was a tented camp, except for a few wooden hutments housing the Medical Centre, the Chapel, the Administrative Block and four hangars for the aircraft.

A popular figure was the American General Rogers, the officer commanding the wing, who was very fond of us 'South Afs' and often gave us preferential treatment. No wonder he was so popular with us. A peculiarity that hit one at Dogpatch was the stench, for the Koreans used human excreta to fertilise their fields, with the result that the smell seemed to be an integral part of the atmosphere, and there was nothing one could do to get away from it.

One of my first duties on arrival was to conduct a funeral service of one of our pilots at Pusan, which involved a journey of some three hours, allowing me to look at the surrounding countryside and the Korean people for the first time.

The terrain was rugged and mountainous, with many inlets of the sea. The dense population had been increased by refugees from the north, creating conditions of extreme poverty. It was something of a shock to be confronted by the fact that people were literally dying of hunger. Life was so cheap and the oriental fatalism so callous to our western outlook. The hillsides were a patchwork of terraced paddy fields. Every available piece of land was under cultivation, with one exception. There were rounded mounds, millions of them, taking up thousands of hectares of ground. These were the graves of ancestors that could not be disturbed. The dead were seemingly more important than the living. Settling down in the squadron which had been operating for nearly a year, entailed learning a new language or jargon - a mixture of Americanisms and Koreanisms, and to add to the confusion, South Africans had a jargon of our own; but everyone seemed to get along very well with the help of sign language, if all else failed. Afrikaans was taboo in official and operational communications, but those of us from Natal found Zulu useful when we didn't want the Americans or Koreans to know what we were saying about them!

The striking power from the air was a powerful weapon in the hands of the United Nations, and South Africans did more than their share of effective operations. It was, in fact, during this period that the squadron topped the best record in the Fifth Air Force and was awarded the American Presidential Citation - but what a price was paid in human terms. The maintenance teams were magnificent and during the winter weather they became literally blue with cold. I will never forget the times when I would lie in bed gazing at the tent roof and feel a shower of minute icicles falling on my face. The moisture from my breath had frozen and caused this phenomenon. There were other problems created by the cold that we had never experienced back home. All liquids froze, and even beer cans had to be warmed before their contents became drinkable.

There was plenty of excitement each day. The pilots were briefed in the Ops tent, would then warm up their Mustangs in flights of four and taxi them to the airstrip for take-off resembling the magnificent prairie horses they were named after. The ground staff would see the pilots off and wave them goodbye. On their arrival back the number of Mustangs were carefully counted and if all were present we could relax and rejoice. If not, we hurried to the Ops tent to wait with ill-concealed anxiety for news of the missing aircraft. As a single squadron of South Africans we were a closely-knit brotherhood feeling the loss of a friend even more acutely than the average squadron.

Korea in the spring was very beautiful when the winter wheat ripened and turned the valleys into a patchwork of gold and green. It is difficult to single out individual characters among the Cheetah pilots for they were all such a dynamic bunch of fellows, but there were two who made a deep impression on me. Topper van der Spuy was one of those fortunate people who did not believe in bottling up his emotions, and for that reason he was easy to get to know. He was the complete extrovert, a cheerful young man who made music on his guitar and sang sentimental songs with verve and gusto. The other character was our OC who took over command from the popular Dick Clifton. His name was Hendrik Burger, and I shall never forget the bumper farewell party given to him at the end of his tour of operations.

The scene was an animated one, and the flames from a braaivleis lit the upturned faces as Hendrik mounted some ammunition boxes to make his farewell speech. Like so many true leaders of men, deeds came more easily than words to Hendrik. He didn't try to make a formal speech with the usual clichés and insincere compliments. Why should he? He was among his own men and very much one of us. He spoke our language, our slang, and he made no bones about it. We loved him for it and roared our applause which so upset him that he nearly fell off his boxes! He was heard to mutter 'bakgat, bakgat!

And so I completed my tour and returned home. I was once asked to conduct the South African Memorial service held annually at the Memorial on top of Bays Hill near Pretoria. It was a unique experience.

It was on a typical calm, highveld winter's morning. The rolling hills all round were covered with pinkish brown grass stretching as far as the eye could see, from the Magaliesberg mountains in the west to the Bushveld in the east. The Memorial, sublimely simple in its triangular beauty, stands like a sentinel overlooking the surrounding countryside. Within it is a small chapel lighted by its windows with the movement of sun and moon. Round the entrance are Memorial books embossed with a leaping Springbok, the winged badge and the motto: *Per Aspera ad Astra.*

A great crowd had assembled and was seated at a distance along the terraced amphitheatre facing the memorial. Dominee Schalk Burger and I positioned ourselves on the spur of the structure, a natural pulpit, just below the Air Force flag. As the service proceeded the voices of the Air Force choir rolled away into the limitless silent veld. Then the words of my prayers and address were amplified through a microphone and effortlessly spread outwards from the deep emotions that I felt in our tribute to the generations of airmen who had given their lives for our country. Many of those men had been the happy companions of my youth, whose merry laughter we shall not hear again but whose spirit of service will live on in this lovely land of our birth.

270

The service ended. The bugle sounded the Last Post and the flags were lowered in salute. Then followed the most poignant moment of all. As the last sounds of the bugle echoed among the eternal hills, a procession of wreath layers came forward. First the official wreaths were formally laid and then a long procession - the fathers and mothers, the widows and children, the lame and the broken-hearted, all bravely paying their tribute to dear ones lost. I felt a lump in my throat and tears came to my eyes, for the sight moved me more deeply than I have ever been moved in my life.

The Roll of Honour

Captain W J J Badenhorst, AFC	Missing:	2-3-51	Declared dead
Lieutenant G J Baransky	Missing:	20-4-52	Declared dead
Lieutenant F M Bekker	Missing:	23-7-51	Declared dead
Lieutenant N Biden	Missing:	5-9-51	Declared dead
2nd Lieutenant M C Botha	Missing:	28-8-51	Declared dead
Captain J F O Davis DFC & bar	Missing:	10-3-51	Declared dead
Lieutenant G D Doveton	Missing:	15-2-51	Declared dead
Lieutenant R M du Plooy	Missing:	23-7-51	Declared dead
Lieutenant C L de Jongh	Missing:	14-8-51	Declared dead
Lieutenant A G Frisby	Missing:	22-6-51	Declared dead
2nd Lieutenant M O Grunder	Missing:	1-9-51	Declared dead
Captain R A Harburn	Missing:	11-2-52	Declared dead
Lieutenant J O Holtzhausen	Missing:	10-4-52	Declared dead
Captain A Janse van Rensburg	Missing:	29-11-51	Declared dead
2nd Lieutenant H T R Joyce	Missing:	29-10-51	Declared dead
Captain R P G Kotzenberg	Missing:	22-8-52	Declared dead
Lieutenant G H Krohn	Missing:	24-11-51	Declared dead
2nd Lieutenant D R Leah	Killed:	7-2-51	
2nd Lieutenant J N Lellyet	Killed:	29-2-52	
2nd Lieutenant Liebenberg	Killed:	10-6-51	
Lieutenant F A Montanari	Missing:	12-9-51	Declared dead
2nd Lieutenant J Moir	Killed:	25-12-52	
2nd Lieutenant P I Norman-Smith	Killed:	3-12-51	Declared dead
Major L B Pearce	Killed:	9-7-51	
Lieutenant L W Parsonson	Missing:	6-1-52	Declared dead
2nd Lieutenant C J Pappas	Missing:	4-11-51	Declared dead
Lieutenant M H Rorke	Killed:	15-5-51	
Lieutenant D A Ruiter	Killed:	2-3-51	
Lieutenant T C Scott	Missing:	9-8-52	Declared dead

2nd Lieutenant R L Staats	Killed:	17-2-52	
2nd Lieutenant D L Taylor	Missing:	20-3-52	Declared dead
2nd Lieutenant J P Verster	Killed:	1-7-51	
Lieutenant W E St E Wilson	Missing:	2-2-51	Declared dead
2nd Lieutenant K R Whitehead	Killed:	3-12-51	

Prisoners of War

Lieutenant H McDonald	- 1 June	1951
Lieutenant G Thom	- 21 July	1953
Lieutenant T R Fryer	- 12 October	1952
Lieutenant C Lombard	- 7 October	1951
2nd Lieutenant R C Earp-Jones	- 31 January	1952
2nd Lieutenant M I P Halley	- 23 July	1951
2nd Lieutenant D J Earp	- 27 September	1951
2nd Lieutenant R E Casson	- 15 January	1952

Honours and Awards

South Africa: 797 Korean War Medals
America: 2 Silver Stars
                         3 Legions of Merit
                         55 Distinguished Flying Crosses
                         1 Cluster to DFC
                         40 Bronze Stars
                         176 Air Medals
                         104 Clusters to Air Medals
                         1 Soldiers Medal
The Republic of Korea: 1 Ulchi with Silver Star
                         6 Ulchis
                         5 Chungmu with Gold Star
                         4 Chungmu with Silver Star
                         2 Wharang with Gold Star
                         2 Wharang with Silver Star
                         818 Korean War Service Medals
1 Talguk with Gold Star (to the unknown airman)
United Nations: 797 United Nations Service Medals
Commonwealth: 2 MBEs
                         2 Mentioned in Dispatches
Presidential Citations:
No 2 Squadron was also awarded Presidential Citations by the
Presidents of the United States of America and the Republic of Korea.
The United States award was for the period 28 November 1951 to 30
April 1952.

Recipients of the American DFC

(Ranks as at period of initial award)

1. Captain W J J Badenhorst
2. Captain J F O Davis
3. Lieutenant D D Deans
4. Captain S G de la Harpe
5. Lieutenant E N Jones
6. Lieutenant J A Joubert
   (plus cluster)
7. Lieutenant J H Kruger
8. Captain G B Lipawsky
9. Lieutenant G H Marshall
10. Captain H O M Odendaal
11. Lieutenant F B Richter
12. Captain R H J Rogers
13. 2nd Lieutenant R L Staats
14. Captain J W Swanepoel
15. Captain J M Sweeney
16. Commandant S v B Theron
17. Major J G Willers
18. Lieutenant T H Silvertsen
19. Major R F Armstrong
20. Lieutenant J F G Howe
21. Major B A A Wiggett
22. 2nd Lieutenant F Grobler
23. Lieutenant N C van Zyl
24. Captain R V Lyon
25. Lieutenant R W Clark
26. 2nd Lieutenant E M Lance
27. Captain L P T Eager
28. Lieutenant J H Rautenbach
29. 2nd Lieutenant R McClure
30. Captain B J Grové
31. Captain J L van der Merwe
32. Lieutenant J H Naude
33. Lieutenant A C J Bosch
34. Lieutenant A Gardiner-Atkinson
35. Major R Clifton
36. Captain D L Hefer
37. Lieutenant W F Church
38. Lieutenant G C S Dodson
39. 2nd Lieutenant B W Singleton
40. Lieutenant J S S Enslin
41. Major A J P Burger
42. Captain J Z Eloff
43. 2nd Lieutenant R C M Lewer
44. Lieutenant R Turner
45. 2nd Lieutenant E A C Pienaar
46. Captain R A Gerneke
47. 2nd Lieutenant D J Stewart
48. Lieutenant V F de Villiers
49. Captain J F Nortje
50. Captain J S R Wells
51. Lieutenant I Gow
52. Lieutenant J J Koekemoer
53. Lieutenant J R Morris
54. 2nd Lieutenant A S Rae
55. Lieutenant J de Wet

Index

United Nations:
    call for North Korean withdrawal: 13
    commission into Korea: 11
    intervention in Korea: 15
    resolutions: 16
United States Air Force - training programme: 5
United States of America - intervention in Korea: 13, 15, 16
Uys, Captain M J: 2, 106
Uys, Thys: 229
Van den Bos, Willem: 98-9, 110-1, 114-5, 220-2
Van der Merwe, Captain J L (Jan): 136, 152, 276
Van der Spuy, Topper: 140, 209, 214-7, 270
Van Fleet, General J A: 71, 108
Van Heerden, Koos: 35, 54
Van Rensburg, Lieutenant W J: 106
Van Rensburg, Zulu: 105, 144, 217
Van Rooyen, Rodney: 178
Van Vuuren, Dan: 244
Van Wyk, Jan: 232
Van Zyl, Lieutenant N C (Nic): 135, 276
Verster, 2nd Lieutenant, J P (Jessie): 93, 102, 273
Viljoen, Brigadier Bennie: 240
Visser, Andries: 232
Visser, Piet: 184

Von Caues, Captain L: 2
Walker, General: 16, 34
Walter, Captain: 4
War widows: 245-6
Wells, Major J S R (Stan): 169, 173, 174, 175, 177, 178, 179, 184, 187, 191, 194, 195, 200, 267, 276
Weyland, General: 92, 127
'White Horse Hill' - battle for: 162
Whitehead, 2nd Lieutenant K R (Ken): 120, 140, 273
Wiggett, Major B A A (Barry): 108, 111, 122, 234, 236, 276
Willard, W/O: 145
Willers, Major J G: 276
Willmott, Brigadier J: 203
Wilson, Basil: 113
Wilson, Elmer: 25, 45, 64, 66, 239
Wilson, Lieutenant W E St E: 273
Wolfhound: 50
Wonsan: 16, 58, 73, 110, 137
Wright Patterson *firm*: 122
Yalu River: 110, 127, 152, 179, 180, 183, 188, 193, 200, 209, 210, 256, 266
Yangp'yong: 56
Yo-do Island: 137, 169, 234
Yokahama: 4
Yonghong: 66
Yongwonnie: 28
X Corps: 16, 34